EVERY DAY
WITH
JESUS

Treasures from the
GREATEST CHRISTIAN
WRITERS OF ALL TIME

WORTHY

Copyright © 2011 by Worthy Publishing

Published by Worthy Publishing, a division of Worthy Media, Inc., 134 Franklin Road, Suite 200, Brentwood, Tennessee 37027.

HELPING PEOPLE EXPERIENCE THE HEART OF GOD

eBook available at worthypublishing.com

Audio distributed through Oasis Audio; visit www.oasisaudio.com

Library of Congress Control Number: 2011931408

For subsidiary and foreign language rights, contact Riggins International Rights Services, Inc.; www.rigginsrights.com

Hardcover ISBN: 978-1-936034-61-1

Produced with the assistance of The Livingstone Corporation (www.LivingstoneCorp.com). Project staff includes Dave Veerman, Linda Taylor, Linda Washington, Larry Taylor, Tom Shumaker, Joel Bartlett, Ashley Taylor, Andy Culbertson, Lois Jackson, Tom Luke Taylor.

Cover design: Christopher Tobias, Tobias Design

Cover photo: © Lonny Kalfus/Getty Images

Interior design: Larry Taylor and Christopher Tobias

Interior photography: Winter, Summer, Fall: iStockphoto.com; Spring: Cherrymoon2/Photocase

Printed in China

| 11 | 12 | 13 | 14 | 15 | 16 | 17 | RRD | 9 | 8 | 7 | 6 | 5 | 4 | 3 | 2 | 1 |

WELCOME

Even as our technological world continues to advance and books become available in a variety of formats, there will never be a substitute for good writing. We love to read the words of gifted writers—men and women who pen a single sentence and create such a memorable nugget of truth that we simply have to stop for a moment to digest what we've read and what it means to us.

Across the centuries Christians have been expressing God's truth by writing books filled with such wonderful thoughts. That's why we've created *Every Day with Jesus*. We have brought together 365 of those timeless expressions from the greatest Christian writers of all time, along with a devotional thought for each day, a Bible verse to look up and read, and a prayer starter.

The method of delivery may continue to change, but God's truth never changes. The words of these beloved writers challenge us to go ever deeper in our pursuit of God—to daily come before our Lord and learn from fellow travelers how best to live the Christian life. And we need that reminder every day. So relax, open up this book, and spend *Every Day with Jesus*.

—The Publisher

CONTRIBUTORS

Michael Angelo

Nikki Studebaker Barcus

Chandler Birch

Barbara Collier

Cheryl Dunlop

Rick Ezell

Carol Chaffee Fielding

Dennis Hensley

David Jorgensen

Scott Noble

Angie Reedy

Afton Rorvik

Sue Rosenfeld

Meredith Sell

Michael Smith

Anthony Trendl

Caitlin Wilson

JANUARY

OSWALD CHAMBERS

God's Spirit continually reveals what human nature is like apart from His grace.

EVERYTHING OR NOTHING?

Who are we apart from God? We are everything, or we are nothing. Everything (or so we think)—if we tell ourselves we don't need his help and can rely on our own strength and power. Nothing—if we realize our utter dependence on him and our place in the created order. Are you willing to admit that you are nothing so that Jesus can be everything to you? Or are you holding on to areas of your life you think you can handle without him?

Believing in God doesn't always mean we trust him fully. But he is there for us, if we will accept his grace and appreciate how lost we are without him. Don't hold onto your life. Let it go, into the loving arms of the Savior.

Read John 15:5.

LORD JESUS, MAY I BECOME NOTHING SO YOU
CAN BE EVERYTHING IN MY LIFE.

THOMAS MERTON

There is only one unhappiness: not to love God.

ULTIMATE HAPPINESS

At face value, we might disagree that there is only one un-happiness. Why, we can recite a litany of things that make us unhappy! Unhappiness seems to come in significant doses every day of our lives.

But when we look deeper, beyond our outer circumstances and into the inner recesses of our hearts and souls, we have to ask: what do we do with the deep secrets that cannot be solved by any human intervention?

When we do not love God, we have nothing to cling to; we have no hope. That is why *not* loving God is the only true unhappiness. Without him, we have nothing. The converse, however, is that in loving God, we find everything we need for this life and the life to come.

Read Matthew 6:25–34.

GOD, HELP ME THROUGH THIS DAY TO SEEK AND TO
EXPERIENCE MY ULTIMATE HAPPINESS IN LOVING YOU.

BERNARD OF CLAIRVAUX

Dignity is nothing without knowledge, and knowledge can even be a stumbling block without virtue.

HEAD AND HEART

Few people like a know-it-all, but we are happy to have an expert in the IT department fix our computer, an expert plumber fix the leaky pipe, an expert surgeon perform an appendectomy, or an expert accountant handle the books for our business. Their knowledge is invaluable to us.

Yet knowledge can be a stumbling block if it is without virtue. You want experts to fix what you can't, but you also want them to be honest. That experienced but dishonest accountant could siphon funds from your account without you even noticing. Knowledge loses its dignity and becomes an obstacle if it is used for evil rather than for God. Paul wrote that "Knowledge inflates with pride, but love builds up" (1 Corinthians 8:1 HCSB).

Pursue knowledge, but let your knowledge be used for God's glory. Let holiness be your guide.

Read 1 Corinthians 8:1–3.

JESUS, I WANT MY KNOWLEDGE TO BE SEALED BY
VIRTUE AND USED FOR YOUR PURPOSES.

BILLY GRAHAM

Faith is not a blind leap in the dark! It is instead based squarely on what God has done for us in Jesus Christ.

A BLIND LEAP?

Certainly faith involves making an intellectual assent to the truth of God revealed in creation and history. And yet, we can have an intellectual belief in the historical life and death of Jesus, but not have *saving* faith—a faith that promises eternal rescue from sin.

Saving faith comes down to Jesus. What do we believe about Jesus' death on the cross and resurrection from the dead? Do we say with our minds and our hearts, "Yes, I believe in Christ and receive what he has done for me"?

At some point, we all have to answer that question. For some, saying yes may feel like taking a leap, a wild jump, in the dark. But it isn't.

We can trust our souls to God because of what Jesus has done for us.

We can say, "Yes! I believe" without fear.

Read Romans 5:1–2.

THANK YOU, HEAVENLY FATHER, FOR REVEALING YOURSELF TO ME.

DONALD S. WHITNEY

As sleep and rest are needed each day for the body, so silence and solitude are needed each day for the soul.

TOO BUSY?

How often has someone responded to your question, "How are you?" with the answer: "I am so busy," followed by a verbal list of tasks completed that day? Somehow, being busy has become a marker of success in our culture. We have come to believe that *busy* is a synonym for *productive, useful,* and *important.*

What happens, however, when our very busyness not only affects our physical rest but our spiritual rest as well? Are we so focused on our tasks that we miss the soul-strengthening moments within a day—sitting quietly before God in silence, enjoying creation, being thankful?

What if we adopted a new way of living, reflected in a new answer to "How are you?" What if we learned to say (and live out) these words: "I am giving myself permission to slow down and find moments of silence and solitude in each day"?

Might we have healthier hearts? Might we be closer to our Father?

Read Isaiah 30:15.

FATHER, HELP ME MAKE SILENCE AND SOLITUDE A PRIORITY.

HOWARD HENDRICKS

Jesus Christ allowed his men to fail in order to learn.

LESSONS FROM LOSING

Failure. We don't like the word anywhere near us. We don't want it in ourselves, in our children, in our home, in our workplace. We all long for success.

A study of top university athletes revealed that more than 60 percent came from wealthy families. After extensive interviews, researchers discovered that these students became involved in a sport because it provided a venue in which they could succeed *or fail*, and their parents' money would have no influence. They couldn't "buy" a sports record; they had to earn it. Losing and coming back for more led to better focus and greater discipline.

The Bible tells us Peter failed. Thomas failed. John Mark failed. From failure, they gained humility and perspective and, as a result, became heroes of the faith. Have you failed? Don't let that stop you. Ask God to teach you the lesson he has for you in the failure—and then get back into the game!

Read John 20:24–29.

LORD, USE EVEN MY MISTAKES AND FAILURES TO
MAKE ME A BETTER SERVANT OF YOU.

ARCHBISHOP DESMOND TUTU

As I grow older I am pleasantly surprised at how relevant theology has become in my perception.

SEEK AND FIND

We may laugh at the irony, but it's true: the older we get, the smarter our parents become. When we move into our own lives, experience a few knocks, and then have children of our own, suddenly we begin to understand our parents' worries and fears for us. We understand their rules and restrictions, for now we are far too aware of what's "out there," and we want to protect our children from those threats.

Similarly, as we get older, we may discover that theology increases in relevance as well. Our knowledge and understanding of God grows deeper and wider as we willingly engage the greater issues and study the teachings and writings of those who came before. As we advance in years, we must continue to make it a priority to know the Lord more fully, for he will continue to make himself known.

Read Isaiah 46:4.

MAY YOU AND YOUR WORD MEAN MORE TO ME AS I GROW OLDER, LORD.

TERESA OF AVILA

*If you should at times fall, don't become discouraged and stop
striving to advance. For even from this fall God will draw out
good.*

MOVE FORWARD

It is ironic that what seems like failure to us can be turned
into a monumental step forward by God. Bodybuilders
know that muscle must be broken down by stressing it; only
then can it rebuild in a much stronger form. Musicians know
that the minor notes in a symphony can add a mysterious tone
to the concerto that major notes cannot evoke. Bakers know
that when they pinch off a section of dough and let it become
"sour," it can serve as yeast to raise a dozen future batches of
sweet rolls.

The Lord can advance us in similar ways. Peter denied
Christ three times, but this led to all-out devotion. John Mark
was sent home from a mission trip, but he matured and became
invaluable to Paul. If you fail (and you will), know that God
can draw good from the situation. Don't become discouraged.
Move forward. God is with you.

Read 2 Timothy 3:10–17.

---

*LORD, TURN EVEN MY MISTAKES—MY STUMBLING BLOCKS—
INTO STEPPING-STONES FOR YOUR KINGDOM.*

LLOYD JOHN OGILVIE

Whenever the Lord touches a raw nerve in us, it means that He is ready to heal it.

THE CLEANSING PAIN

The very day after a person has surgery, nurses get the patient on his or her feet for a walk. It's agonizingly painful, but it keeps the blood circulating, lessening the chance of clots and hastening the healing process. Similarly, if someone comes to the emergency room because of an accident, that person's wound is first cleansed of all dirt, then is doused in antiseptic. This cleansing process is frightfully painful, but it assists the body in warding off infection.

Often in our Christian lives, we must endure some pain in order to be healed. Saul (soon to be the apostle Paul) was made blind for three days before God restored his sight, thus giving him a lesson in spiritual blindness. Jesus made Peter tell him *three times* that he loved him after Peter had denied Jesus three times, thus helping Peter see that Jesus was fully forgiving him.

The pain is part of the plan. God is there, holding you up. Lean on him.

Read John 21:15–19.

LORD, GIVE ME THE INSIGHT TO SEE MY SUFFERING
AS EVIDENCE OF YOUR LOVE IN MY LIFE.

JOHN OF THE CROSS

This dark night is an inflow of God into the soul that purges it of its habitual ignorances and imperfections, natural and spiritual.

SEEING GOD IN THE DARKNESS

The dark night of the soul is a time when God seems distant, when our soul seems lost. But purpose exists in the darkness. In any worthwhile venture, pain precedes gain, hurt comes before health, cleansing precedes completeness. During these dark seasons, God works in our inner being so we will turn from habits that bring destruction to develop a Christlike character. Like polluted water that flows through a filter, our souls will be purified.

Often when the night is blackest, we feel God has abandoned us. Yet God is working even then. Like the moon hidden by an eclipse, God is present but not visible.

During the dark times, allow God to work. You will see him again. And, better, you will be cleansed, made right, brought whole.

Hang on. Endure the night. Joy comes in the morning.

Read Psalm 30:5.

DO YOUR CLEANSING WORK IN MY HEART, O GOD.

ARCHIBALD ALEXANDER

If Christ be in us there will be communion. . . . And if Christ be formed within us we cannot remain altogether ignorant of his presence.

PRECIOUS COMMUNION

With Christ in us, we have communion with God and with one another. What a wonderful reminder of the oneness we have in Jesus—the answer to his prayer that we would be one, even as he and the Father are one (John 17:11).

How blessed is that communion! The moment we discover that we are fellow believers in Christ, we feel a closeness with complete strangers that we have not felt before. It may be a group gathered at church, students meeting in the local school for a prayer meeting, or even words spoken across the checkout line. The family of God enjoys immediate fellowship within its circle. And where two or three are gathered in Christ's name, he is present.

We cannot remain ignorant of his presence, for it is what draws us together in the first place. No wonder we are at home wherever we find fellow believers.

Read Matthew 18:19–20.

LORD, I THANK YOU THAT MY CHRISTIAN
FAMILY IS EVERYWHERE I TURN.

C. S. LEWIS

*Every step . . . from the Absolute to "Spirit" and from "Spirit"
to "God," had been a step toward the more concrete, the more
imminent, the more compulsive.*

DRAW NEAR TO GOD

We need God; he does not need us. Often we are like
a hapless sailor in a boat who throws a rope at a rock,
hoping it will provide security and stability. When the rock is
lassoed, it's not the sailor pulling the rock to the boat (though it
may appear that way); it is the pulling of the boat to the rock.

The closer we get to God, the more real he becomes. He's
the rock. If you are physically distraught, he is the lifeline that
saves your drowning soul. If you are spiritually famished, he is
the umbilical cord that provides nourishment to your starving
spirit. If you are emotionally depleted, he is the second wind
that enables you to go the distance.

Think of yourself in that boat being pulled to safety by a
loving Father.

Read James 4:8.

I WILL HOLD ON TO YOU TODAY, LORD. YOU'RE MY ROCK.

V. RAYMOND EDMAN

Never doubt in the dark what God told you in the light.

ONLY A GLIMMER

Combat soldiers are disciplined in how to sight an enemy down the barrel of a rifle, gauge the range, and then pull the trigger. But what about at night, when there is no sunshine to make the enemy visible? During the Vietnam War the military developed a special telescope called the Starlight Scope. This amazing piece of technology could amplify the gleam of stars to many times their normal brightness, making it seem like daylight for the soldier looking through it.

As Christians we sometimes feel alone, abandoned, and surrounded in darkness. In those times we are tempted to doubt God's promises, God's faithfulness, God's goodness. After all, we don't seem to be experiencing them.

Do not doubt in the dark what God told you in the light, for his words are always and forever true.

Read Micah 7:8–13.

LORD, I TRUST YOU EVER TO BE THE LIGHT OF MY LIFE.

HANNAH HURNARD

We may know that God is love,
Know his Father's heart. . . . We have seen what hath sufficed
In the face of Jesus Christ.

THE FACE OF JESUS CHRIST

How amazing it is that God wants you to know his heart. He wants you to know how much he loves you. The Creator of the world, the Holy One who is above and beyond anything you can imagine, wants to know *you.*

How do you know the love of God? How do you know the Father's heart? The answer is found in the face of Jesus Christ.

In 2 Corinthians 4, Paul gives a clue to that truth. God has given light in the darkness, and that light shines in our hearts so we can know the glory of God through the face of Jesus. It is Jesus who gives the perfect picture of God. When you know Jesus, you know God.

He wants you to know his heart. He wants you to know how much he loves you. And when you know him, you can't help but return that love to him.

Read 2 Corinthians 4:6.

THANK YOU, FATHER, FOR SHOWING YOUR FACE TO ME IN
JESUS. I DESIRE TO LOVE YOU WITH ALL MY HEART.

MARTIN LUTHER KING JR.

Longevity has its place. But I'm not concerned about that now. I just want to do God's will.

CLIMB THE MOUNTAIN

The picture was sobering. At 6:01 P.M. on April 4, 1968, Dr. Martin Luther King Jr., who had been standing with some friends and colleagues on the balcony of his room at the Lorraine Motel in Memphis, Tennessee, was murdered. A front-page photo in newspapers around the country portrayed the confusion and horror immediately after the event. It was a dark day in American history.

Such is the cost for some who decide to do God's will. Dr. King saw it as a privilege to do God's will, to be invited up the mountain. So did Moses. Because of Jesus, we too have been invited to come close to God in fellowship with him. It is an awesome privilege—and an awesome responsibility.

Read Exodus 19:20.

FATHER GOD, GRANT ME COURAGE TO PRAY, "I
WANT YOUR WILL TO BE DONE IN MY LIFE."

AUGUSTINE OF HIPPO

He is everywhere in His totality; so that in Him the mind lives and moves and has its being, and consequently can remember Him.

THE LIVING WORD

Nurses and doctors report that when aged saints are on their deathbeds and under heavy sedation, they often will revert to their childhood. They begin to recite memory verses learned during vacation Bible school, or they will sing "Jesus Loves Me" or "This Little Light of Mine." Colossians 3:16 (NKJV) says, "Let the word of Christ dwell in you richly."

Such blessings can happen when we have made the Word of God a living, active, vibrant part of our lives, judging every action, every deed, every thought by what the Lord has instilled in our hearts. David said, "Your word have I hid in my heart." The totality of Christ living in us gives Christians a contentment that unbelievers cannot understand. But it is real. It is comforting. It is genuine.

Read Colossians 3:12–17.

JOSH MCDOWELL

We must begin by instilling within our children . . . a healthy fear of God, an acknowledgment of His power and character.

IGNITING THE FLAME OF GOD

Psychologists are continually producing studies that verify that behaviors and character start to form even before a child's first birthday. Meanwhile, Christians have known this for thousands of years. Paul wrote in 2 Timothy 1:5 that he was impressed at what excellent teachers and role models Timothy's mother, Eunice, and his grandmother, Lois, had been. Paul could see that their example and devotion had put the "flame of God" in Timothy.

The world today, with the impact of mass media, is doing its best to woo children to sinful practices. But Proverbs 22:6 (NKJV) says, "Train a child in the way he should go, and when he is old he will not depart from it." This should be all the motivation we need to invest quality time in the spiritual nurturing of our children and grandchildren.

We too need to ignite the flame of God in our children. May it blaze continually bright.

Read 2 Timothy 1:2–7.

LORD, MAKE ME A POSITIVE INFLUENCE ON
MY CHILDREN FOR YOUR SAKE.

W. PHILLIP KELLER

[Joy is] a serene, stable spirit known only to those who enjoy the presence of God's person within their lives.

THE FLAG OF JOY

Don't confuse happiness with joy. Happiness is a buoyant emotion that results from the momentary plateaus of well-being. Joy is bedrock stuff—the confidence that emerges irrespective of our moods or circumstances; the certainty that all is well, regardless of feelings; the hallmark of God's kingdom dwellers.

An old British educator wrote: "Joy is the flag which is flown from the castle of the heart when the King is in residence." Joy supersedes our circumstances, thanks to our relationship with the King of kings. If Jesus is King—sovereign and in control—then what do we have to worry about? If we live in his presence, we have no reason to fret.

Jesus is joy. He brings joy wherever he goes. Get close to him. Live in the glow of his life. Be conscious of his presence. Rest in his strong arms.

Read John 17:13.

JESUS, FILL ME WITH YOUR JOY.

DAVID LIVINGSTONE

He will keep his word; then I can come and humbly present my petition and it will be all right. Doubt is here inadmissible, surely.

JUST TRUST

Our universe contains more than 10 billion trillion stars. That's the numeral 1 followed by 22 zeros. It seems unfathomable. But it's nothing compared to explaining the Trinity—three entities in one, yet one all-powerful being. It doesn't make sense to the human mind, to those of us who are used to finding answers and solving mysteries. We don't like to leave matters unsettled. But some things can't be known this side of eternity. They require unwavering trust in Jesus, without any further explanation. Can we accept that? Do we have a choice?

The Lord knows our desire to seek solutions to life's puzzles. But he is more concerned that we live by faith. If we have the faith of a mustard seed, he said, we can move mountains. He also exhorts us to be still, and know that he is the Almighty.

Read Matthew 17:20.

LORD, HELP ME TO ACCEPT THE THINGS I CANNOT KNOW, AND TO STRIVE TO KNOW YOU BETTER.

FREDERICK BUECHNER

Believing God is . . . less a position than a journey, less a realization than a relationship.

TRUE BELIEF

Nietzsche said God is dead. While Nietzsche, an atheist, wasn't interested in embracing Christian beliefs, his words are a good reminder of what can happen when a society sets God aside. People execute their faith and turn their back on the Savior. They stop pursuing God with resolve and passion. Even those who go to church and claim a religion can quickly veer off course if they stop at "belief" but do not let it affect their lives.

Belief is more than just a position or a realization. We were designed for a relationship with Christ and we find our ultimate purpose and meaning in him. True belief is about the journey through life in relationship with God. True belief is alive and active, affecting your life today and every day.

Read James 2:22.

LET MY BELIEF IN YOU RESONATE IN MY LIFE TODAY, LORD.

G. K. CHESTERTON

By insisting that God transcends man, man has transcended himself.

TRUE TRANSCENDENCE

How do we transcend ourselves? Great thinkers have been trying to answer that question for centuries, often telling us to look within and rely on the resources deep inside ourselves. Indeed, as individuals who possess more than a physical body, we are endowed with inner qualities that go beyond genetics and physiology. We have something intangible about us, something spiritual and eternal that surpasses biological and chemical matter. But it's far from pure or strong; it's sinful and in need of cleansing. Only God, the Creator, can recreate us. He made us and knows our true nature. We are nothing without him. With him, we are capable of leaving our human failings behind.

Our true transformation is initiated and completed by God alone. We transcend ourselves not by looking within, but by looking at the cross and the only Savior who can make us all he created us to be.

Read Isaiah 1:18.

JESUS, HELP ME TO SEE MY DEEP AND ABIDING NEED FOR YOU.

TED ENGSTROM

Godly leadership serves others. God is constantly searching for men with this characteristic.

HUMBLE LEADERSHIP

It is humbling to think God may call upon us to accomplish major achievements for his glory. Joshua wondered how he *ever* could fill Moses' shoes. Gideon was baffled that he, a low-class laborer, could be summoned to serve as a general in God's army. Paul, who identified himself as "the chief of sinners," was forever astounded to think that God would use him to bring the gospel to the Gentiles. But God was able to use something in them that they didn't see; he brought them to a place of humility and willingness to serve.

God does not seek the services of the pompous. He doesn't need leaders who want fame or power—those are a dime a dozen, and they do nothing for his kingdom. God is constantly seeking those who are willing to serve. Such leaders can, through his Son, change the world.

Read John 13:12–15.

I WANT TO SERVE OTHERS AND YOU, LORD,
WHEREVER YOU PLACE ME.

RICHARD FOSTER

Make honesty and integrity the distinguishing characteristics of your speech.

AS GOOD AS YOUR WORD

We have numerous catchphrases that express the idea of a person's word being trustworthy. We'll say, "His word is his bond," or "Her word is as good as gold," or "If he says it, then he'll do it." Interestingly, as Christians, our *word* is the Word of God, which of course is always true, always honest, and always just. Understanding this, our own promises, vows, and agreements should be honorable and dependable—part of our Christian ethic.

Numbers 30:2 teaches us, "When a man makes a vow to the LORD or takes an oath to obligate himself by a pledge, he must not break his word" (NIV). This goes beyond saying our wedding vows or swearing in as a court witness. It applies to our every transaction in life. We are to speak truth and live truth because our Savior identified himself as "the way, the *truth*, the life."

Read Numbers 30:1–9.

FATHER, I WILL SPEAK TRUTH, FOR I AM YOUR WITNESS ON EARTH.

J. I. PACKER

Omniscience governing omnipotence, infinite power being ruled by infinite wisdom is the basic biblical description of the divine character.

GREAT AND UNSEARCHABLE THINGS

Gary Larson's *Far Side* syndicated cartoons were popular for twenty years in America. In one of his sketches, he showed God as a contestant on a TV game show. The score-card in front of God indicated more than a million points, but the other two contestants had no points at all. The game show emcee was announcing, "Yes, that is another correct answer for God, who continues to hold the lead."

His point? No one would stand a chance against God in a contest of knowledge. Jeremiah 33:3 says that the Lord knows "great and wondrous things" (HCSB) that man cannot know. Isaiah 40:13 asks, "Who has understood the mind of the LORD, or instructed him as his counselor?" (NIV). What this means to us is that there is no problem, no question, no challenge that we can bring to our heavenly Father that he is not capable of dealing with. He has infinite wisdom, and it is ours for the asking. We need only seek him in prayer.

Read Job 41:1–11.

RIGHTEOUS AND ALL-KNOWING LORD, I BOW
IN AWE OF YOUR MAGNIFICENCE.

CECIL MURPHEY

I've sensed God's stinging rebuke, and it has hurt deeply, yet I know it was divine faithfulness at work.

GOD'S LOVING DISCIPLINE

Growing up, we all faced reprimands from our parents, teachers, and, later—if we got caught speeding as teenage drivers—even from judges. It's never comfortable, but sometimes it is necessary. The apostle Paul chose not to trust John Mark and travel with him a second time after he had gone home early from a missionary journey. This so changed the young man's attitude and behavior, he was able to earn back Paul's respect, and Paul later sent for him to join him in Rome.

Numerous times in the Bible God himself rebuked individuals because they displeased him. He told Eliphaz the Temanite in Job 42:7, "I am angry with you!" (NLT). Jesus said in Revelation 3:19, "Those whom I love I rebuke and discipline" (NIV). Thus, there may be times in life when the Lord will use physical ailments, financial crises, or career setbacks to chastise us. If so, let us accept such discipline as a sign of divine love.

Read Revelation 3:15–22.

LORD, FORGIVE ME WHEN I STRAY, AND
DISCIPLINE ME WHEN NEEDED.

CATHERINE MARSHALL

In the Prayer of Faith our hand is still in His. . . . The hand of the Father is Jesus' hand!

HAND IN HAND

As the mother and her young child prepare to cross a busy street, the mother grasps her child's hand. A young man bends his knee before the love of his life and puts a ring on her finger. A man and woman with crowns of gray and wrinkled smiles walk hand in hand as they stroll a sandy beach.

Hand in hand we touch, we hold, we love, we protect. Remember the first time you reached out to God and put your hand in his? Perhaps it was a prayer for help, or a prayer for a desperate need, or a prayer of surrender.

Your Father's hand is always there, reaching out to you, holding you, loving you, protecting you. He has not released his grasp. When your prayer of faith touched the heart of God, Jesus took your hand in his with a promise to hold it forever.

If you are in need of a gentle touch today, whisper a prayer asking Jesus to take your hand in his and hold on.

Read Isaiah 41:13.

TAKE MY HAND, LORD, AS I CROSS
THE BUSY STREETS OF LIFE.

JAY KESLER

Kids need elders, male and female . . . not simply to function as a parent functions, but to be, to incarnate, the qualities of God.

FOLLOWING IN OUR FOOTSTEPS

Billy Graham once told of a man who was walking to a bar one winter night during a new snowfall. His seven-year-old son called out, "Take smaller steps, Daddy. I'm walking in your tracks." The man turned around and was horrified to see that his son was following in his footprints. The man hugged his little boy, took him home, and swore off alcohol. Until that moment, he had never understood that his actions were being emulated by his son.

Which young people might be imitating your life? Perhaps children or grandchildren, nieces or nephews, or even the kids in your church or neighborhood. They all need adults who reveal the qualities of God.

You never know how your life will affect the young ones around you. What children are in your circle of influence? Pray that your life shows them a true reflection of Jesus.

Read 1 Corinthians 11:1.

LORD, HELP ME TO MODEL YOU TO
THE CHILDREN IN MY LIFE.

R. C. SPROUL

*It is precisely the presence and help of Christ in times of
suffering that makes it possible for us to stand up under pressure.*

COUNTERMEASURES

Suffering is a universal language. We can't escape pain. Plans
go wrong. Troubles come. Our bodies wear out. We live in
a fallen world, and sometimes the pressure paralyzes us.

Deep ocean waters can crush a submarine made of thick
steel, but little fish with the thinnest layer of skin swim there
without a care in the world. Why aren't they crushed? Those
fish have an internal pressure that perfectly corresponds to the
pressure from the outside. God gives them what they need to
swim in the deep places.

When faced with the pressure of suffering, we don't need
skin made of steel; we need a power inside us that corresponds
to the pressure from outside. That power comes from the
presence of Jesus who lives within us.

Surrounded by pressure? Sense the presence of Jesus. Then
rest secure in him.

Read 1 John 4:4.

LORD, I TRUST YOUR COUNTERMEASURES WITHIN TO
OVERCOME THE MOUNTING PRESSURES WITHOUT.

JOHN BUNYAN

No one knows how many byways and back lanes the heart has in which to slip away from the presence of God.

BYWAYS AND BACK LANES

Where are the byways and back lanes of your heart? What grows along those paths? Too often they are somberly lit, allowing the darkness to hide the actions or thoughts that would be an embarrassment if seen in the light.

Too often, we slip there. A temptation. An angry outburst. A feeling of hopelessness or helplessness. A desire unfulfilled. We justify our actions and walk down the shadowy path. Only too late do we realize that we have slipped away from the presence of God.

In his presence is light. In his presence the pathway is clear and the way is lit by God's Word, as the psalmist wrote, "Your word is a lamp to my feet and a light to my path" (Psalm 119:105 NKJV).

Close off the byways and back lanes. Stay on the path. God has promised that he will show us the way; we merely need to walk in it.

Read Jeremiah 6:16.

LORD, LET ME STAY ON THE CLEAR PATH,
THE ONE MARKED OUT FOR ME.

JONATHAN EDWARDS

There is a difference between having an opinion, that God is holy and gracious, and having a sense of the loveliness and beauty of that holiness and grace.

KNOWING MAKES THE DIFFERENCE

Opinions are a dime a dozen. The person with experience always trumps the person with an unsupported opinion. The experienced person knows; the opinionated person guesses. There's a big difference.

Those who have truly experienced God know the loveliness and beauty of a grace-touched and holy life. Deserving judgment, they are the recipients of a second chance (grace) and a special endowment (holiness).

God's holiness sets apart God's grace. God, who is different from us, stooped to be among us. God, who is awesome in power, came in weakness. God, who sits on the throne of heaven, walked on earth as a servant. He is the One we want to experience and emulate. Knowing him makes all the difference.

Get close to Jesus. His loveliness and beauty will rub off on you in the form of holiness and grace.

Read Titus 2:11.

GOD OF GRACE AND HOLINESS, MAY MY
CHARACTER REFLECT YOURS.

THOMAS MERTON

The secret of my identity is hidden in the love and mercy of God. . . . Therefore I cannot hope to find myself anywhere except in Him.

THE GREATEST GIFT

We take another promotion, seeking status in our work. We build bigger nest eggs, seeking power in our money. We take exotic vacations, seeking adventure in our trips. We relive our past through our children, seeking a lost youth.

We are looking for ourselves as though we were searching for hidden treasure. Yet our gift is the presence of Jesus. Consider his love to us. Despite our faults, he runs to us. Seeing our sin, he forgives us. Knowing we deserve death, he grants us life. Our identity is hidden in the love and mercy of God. In him, our veneers of self-preservation are sanded off; the scaffolding of stuff to hold us up is removed. We are loved by God. What better gift could you find? Receive it as your own.

Read Romans 8:37–39.

THANK YOU, LORD, FOR YOUR GIFT OF LOVE.
IN IT, I FIND MYSELF.

FEBRUARY

BILLY GRAHAM

The Spirit-filled life is not abnormal; it is the normal Christian life. Anything less . . . is less than what God wants and provides for His children.

LIVING IN THE NORMAL

The normal Christian life is life in the Spirit. When we come into relationship with Jesus, the Spirit takes up residence. He fills us. He possesses our mind. He controls our heart. We walk in step with him. We are open to his desires. We think his thoughts.

Our spiritual lives are overcome with God's presence and might, enabling Christ-centered actions. We are under the influence of the Spirit. Instead of doing things only within our own strength and ability, the Spirit empowers us.

This power is greater than our own. It moves us, inspires us, motivates us, encourages us, and anoints all that we say and do, making Christ known.

Be filled with the Spirit.

Read Ephesians 5:18.

LORD, FILL ME WITH YOUR SPIRIT.

BILL HYBELS

No matter how wonderful your character is, it will never be wonderful enough to earn God's approval.

DONE!

From the start we have been taught that we have to earn what we want. No handouts. No free lunches. If you want it, you work for it. So we labor to earn a living, to earn a position in the company, to earn status in the community.

We think such a strategy works to secure God's favor too. It sounds logical. Yet we will never be good enough in God's eyes. In fact, we can't earn his acceptance because he has already done everything for us.

Christianity is not what we do to earn God's favor, but what Jesus has already done for us. Jesus satisfied God's demands. All we have to do is accept his gift.

Because of Jesus we are approved.

Read 1 Thessalonians 5:10.

JESUS, THANK YOU FOR WHAT YOU HAVE DONE FOR ME.

HENRY BLACKABY

Our generation lacks a sense of wonder and reverence toward God. We want to bring God down to our level, to the commonplace. He is God!

FIND THE WONDER

Stop for a few moments and look at creation. Gaze at the tiniest snowflake or the vastness of the sky. Does it make you pause in awe of who God is and what he has done? We should be amazed that he would care enough to create flowers that bloom in vibrant colors, animals of all kinds and shapes, planets seen and yet to be discovered. We should live in wonder that he sent his Son to die for guilty, sinful humanity.

Frequently, however, we bring God down to our level. Movies and books attempt to make him too much like us— with characteristics sometimes bordering on the ridiculous. Yet when we lose our sense of wonder, we lose a sense of the greatness of God.

Rediscover the wonder of who God is and what he has done. It should send you to your knees in gratitude.

Read Psalm 8:1–9.

HELP ME TO REMEMBER THAT YOU ARE A MIGHTY AND JUST GOD.

OSWALD CHAMBERS

Certainty is the mark of common-sense: gracious uncertainty is the mark of the spiritual life.

LIVING BETWEEN THE STEPS

Common sense makes sense. We have confidence and certainty in what we know. Lest life become dull and routine, God challenges even our certainties. Every step for a believer is a step of faith, filled with grace—moving ahead in harmony with God's character.

Gracious uncertainty understands the remarkable gift of today. Mindful that every step is rich with opportunity, we take each one, reflecting God's love. Grace causes us to give more than expected, to serve beyond our time, to help when we are tired, to love when the feelings are gone. Grace upgrades and expands our lives.

Uncertainty forces us to walk by faith—knowing that God walks with us, assured that God directs our steps, confident that we make an impact by the way we love. The unknown becomes an adventure to dispense God's grace.

Step lightly. Walk boldly. Live with gracious uncertainty.

Read 2 Corinthians 9:8.

LORD, SHOW ME THE OPPORTUNITY FOR EXTENDING YOUR GRACE IN EVERY STEP I TAKE.

CLARE OF ASSISI

Look upon Him Who became contemptible for you, and follow Him, making yourself contemptible in the world for Him.

BE CONTEMPTIBLE

Jesus was hated by much of the world, and that hatred still exists today. Then, as now, he was "despised and rejected of men" (Isaiah 53:3 KJV).

In spite of rejection, he died for us.

Being like him means being willing to be viewed with contempt in the eyes of the world. What does that look like today? Others may feel contempt for us when we refuse to bend God's rules, or stand up for what is right, or go against the norm. In spite of that rejection, we are called to rejoice always, to honor Christ in all we do, to never be ashamed of the gospel message, to lift him up everywhere we go, and to extend grace to whomever crosses our path.

Being contemptible in the world's eyes means being like Jesus.

Read 1 Peter 4:12–16.

I WANT TO BE LIKE YOU, LORD, EVEN IF IT MEANS REJECTION.

John White

The more you understand of [Jesus], the more real the companionship will be, and the more likely you are to keep in step with him.

IN HIS STEPS

Who doesn't long for a guide through life—maybe a crystal ball that responds to all of life's questions. Should I take this class? Marry this person? Relocate for this job? Confront this colleague? How easy it would be to wave a hand over the crystal ball and heed its replies.

As humans, we long for such answers. As believers, we need answers that take us the way God wants us to go.

Though we often act like God's will is some mystery that he is trying to keep from us, we don't need magic to figure it out. In reality, God *wants* to show us the way. He wants us to know and follow his will. To do that, we stay close to his Son—we read Scripture, we pray, we do what we already know is right.

The more we understand Jesus, the more likely we are to keep in step with him.

Read 1 Peter 2:17–21.

JESUS, I WANT TO FOLLOW IN YOUR STEPS. SHOW ME THE WAY.

SAINT THÉRÈSE OF LISIEUX

O Eternal Word! O my Saviour! Thou art the Divine Eagle Whom I love—who lurest me.

LOVED DIVINELY

Throughout the ages humanity has been drawn to the image of the eagle. Nobility in particular often used this bird to represent their strength.

God has been portrayed in literature as the Divine Eagle who soars above all, including kings and emperors. And yet surprisingly, this Divine Eagle, so mighty and majestic, longs to draw us to himself. In fact, his love for us is so great that he suffered and died in order to give us an eternal home.

How shall we respond to so great a love? By offering our lifelong love in return.

Open your heart to God. Dwell each day under the wings of the one who gave his very life for you and who longs to teach you to soar with him.

Read Romans 8:35–39.

THANK YOU, DEAR LORD, FOR LOVING ME SO FULLY.

CHARLES SWINDOLL

Waiting is one of God's preferred methods of preparing special people for significant projects.

IN THE WAITING

Patience is a gift. Many say it's one they don't have. Regardless, we wait. Every day. In the store checkout line, as the boss makes a final decision, at the doctor's office, at the busy intersection. Sometimes we must wait in order to wait some more.

Even though it's unavoidable, waiting in the daily details is an unpleasant part of life. And when a mundane job remains mundane, or physical pain clings like a bad shirt, or an anticipated situation refuses to evolve as we dreamed it would, questions arise. What is God doing? Why doesn't he fix it? What's his purpose in allowing the unwanted circumstances to persist?

Your daily routine that seems to never change may last for just one more day. But it could be yours for another month, another year, or even more. What will you do in the waiting? Dear friend, take a new look at this season. Fight your frustrations, and trust that this place of preparation is of great importance.

Read Isaiah 30:18.

LORD, CHANGE MY PERSPECTIVE SO THAT I
CAN SEE SIGNIFICANCE AS I WAIT.

DAVID SEAMANDS

Ask the Holy Spirit to show you what your real problem is and how you need to pray.

HEAVENLY HEALER

A man with pain in his lower right jaw went to the dentist assuming further drilling on his recent root canal was necessary. Once he'd been examined, he was told that the real source of his pain was a wisdom tooth—it badly needed to be pulled. Not until the man was accurately diagnosed by a professional could the actual problem be fixed.

No doubt you recognize certain symptoms in your life. You may not know their source, but they have your attention.

The one who is the expert of your heart knows what's causing those symptoms. He knew the very moment the problem started, and he holds the answers to its resolution. Whether your words and wonderings gush out in a torrent of questions, or the only prayer you can muster is a sigh of desperation, you are not without hope; God knows what you need.

Present your symptoms to him and then wait for him to reveal the diagnosis—and provide the remedy.

Read Romans 8:26–27.

HEAVENLY HEALER, HEAR MY GROANING
AND SHOW ME YOUR SOLUTION.

FRANCIS OF ASSISI

I . . . exhort my brothers in the Lord Jesus Christ that, when they go about the world, they do not quarrel or fight with words.

WORD-WATCHING

Our mouths can get us into all kinds of trouble. James cautioned in the Bible that the tongue, though small, can act like a spark that sets an entire forest on fire.

Not only do we have the ability to do great good or great harm with our words, but as believers, the things we say will either draw people closer to or push them farther from Jesus. If our words don't uphold the message of love that Christ came to bring, then we'll be tearing it down in ways we don't even realize.

Quarreling and fighting don't represent our Lord well. Too often our words short-circuit in our minds and come out before we've thought them through. So take the advice of both James and St. Francis: put a watch on your mouth, and let the words you speak today represent Christ.

Read James 3:3–12.

LORD, GUARD MY MOUTH THAT I MIGHT HONOR YOU TODAY.

C. S. LEWIS

God cannot give us a happiness and peace apart from himself, because it is not there. There is no such thing.

THE INSIDE JOB

I just want to be happy." Plenty of people say those words. People of every age, social standing, vocation, culture, and disposition. Americans have embedded "the pursuit of happiness" into the Constitution. Happiness is a right. Right?

The tragedy is that people look for happiness on the outside—by earning more money, accumulating more stuff, taking more vacations, manufacturing more changes. Once they have fulfilled all their desires, *then* they will be happy.

Wrong!

Happiness is an inside job. No amount of nipping or tucking, investing or traveling will make us permanently content. Happiness is a by-product of the internal filling of God. He cannot give us happiness apart from himself. Why? Because happiness simply does not exist without him.

Read Psalm 68:3.

LORD, FILL ME WITH YOUR HAPPINESS.

MAX LUCADO

I wonder, how many burdens is Jesus carrying for us that we know nothing about? . . . He carries our sin. He carries our shame.

HE CARRIES IT ALL

The famous poem "Footprints" reminds us that in life's most difficult seasons, Jesus does not abandon us; rather, at the times we are unable to go on, he picks us up and carries us.

We are amazed by the picture of a burden-bearing Savior. He took our sin upon himself so that we might have freedom. He takes up our shame so that we are no longer hindered by it. What other burdens have never landed on our shoulders because he would not allow it? What other burdens has he taken upon himself rather than letting them fall to us?

Whatever is loading you down today, you need carry it no longer. Jesus will scoop up the weight in one arm and put his other arm around your tired shoulders. Gently he'll remind you that it is for these very things that he sacrificed his life.

Today, feel him removing the weight of your burden and holding you near.

Read Matthew 11:28–30.

THANK YOU, SAVIOR, FOR CARRYING MY BURDENS.

DIETRICH BONHOEFFER

God's love for us is shown by the fact that God not only gives us God's Word, but also lends us God's ear.

I'M LISTENING

Listening is a mark of love. When you are sure of being heard you can share your thoughts, your hurts, your emotions, your dreams with your beloved. Listening is key to a lasting and healthy relationship.

God is good at listening. He is never too busy for us. He demonstrates his love by speaking through his Word and listening to our voice. He is a two-way communicator. He hears the hurt in our tone. He sees the need in our nuances.

God is a ruler who calms the stormy waves of our lives. God is also a presence who walks the dusty roads with us. He talks with us. And, better still, he listens to our pleas, our tirades, our doubts, and our anguish. He responds as a cherished lover.

What do you need to say to God today? He's listening.

Read 1 John 5:14.

LORD, HEAR MY CRIES.

BERNARD OF CLAIRVAUX

This divine love is true love, for it is the love of one who wants nothing for himself.

GOD'S TRUE LOVE

Divine love. How do we even begin to comprehend it? It is so far beyond what we know as love—our earthly passion for another person.

We may be willing to sacrifice some of our own desires for one we love, but our noble gestures pale in comparison to the ultimate sacrifice our loving heavenly Father made. He sent his Son to give his very life for us. And he did it while we were still sinners, while we were far from being worthy of such a great love.

In our own relationships, how often do we perform a kind deed for our beloved in the hope of receiving a reciprocal response? But God, in his divine love, does not love us in order to get something from us. He simply offers his love as a gift, freely, with no ulterior motive or hope of reciprocity.

The choice is ours.

Read 1 John 4:16–19.

WHAT A GIFT YOUR LOVE IS, FATHER. THANK YOU!

AUGUSTINE OF HIPPO

For Thou madest us for Thyself, and our heart is restless, until it repose in Thee.

RESTLESS HEARTS

Watch any amount of television and you will come away feeling sorry for the people who are seeking fulfillment in a job, a friend, a lover, in a flawless body or a perfect performance. Nothing on this earth—no amount of fame, notoriety, or perceived perfection—can bring rest to our restless hearts. We find peace in God and God alone.

This is how God made us. Humanity is not a random accident. We were created on purpose by God himself, who made us in his image so that we might commune with him, love him, and be loved by him. He made us *for* himself. And only when we find our rest in him will our hearts stop seeking.

When we find him, we find everything we need in this life and in the life to come.

Read Genesis 1:26–31.

JESUS, PLEASE CONTINUE TO BE THE CONSTANT I NEED IN MY LIFE.

JOHN STOTT

There is nothing in the non-Christian religions to compare with this . . . God who loved, and came after, and died for, a world of lost sinners.

THE WAY HOME

Have you ever become separated from your group in an unfamiliar place, longing to find home? Your heart pumps faster. Your palms grow clammy. Your thoughts run wild.

Lostness is not just a physical reality; it is a spiritual fact too. When we are lost, we need someone to show us the way home. Verbal communication is not good enough; personal help is what we long for—someone to take us by the hand to guide us home.

That's the message of Christianity. God dropped everything to seek out and rescue lost humans. It boggles the mind that God would send his own Son so that a lost humanity would find its way to him. Yet that's exactly what God did.

Try to find a parallel story in another religion. Can't do it, can you?

Christianity is God finding us and bringing us home.

Read John 1:1, 14.

LORD, THANK YOU FOR SAVING ME.

MIKE MASON

When joy's heart breaks, it's because joy feels free and safe enough to embrace everything, even the feeling of falling to pieces.

JOY IN HEARTBREAK

Heartbreak and joy don't seem to go together. Joy is parties and balloons and laughter and loved ones. Heartbreak is just the opposite—loneliness, depression, desperation, pain.

We want life to be easy, don't we? We'll take the joy, thank you; hold the sorrow and tears. Some people are even willing to step into sin in order to pursue some elusive sense of joy. But that's the problem. What the world mistakes for joy is really a lesser, more fleeting contentment—happiness. And happiness is tied to events and circumstances. Joy, on the other hand, can be felt even in the midst of heartbreak.

Joy is a gift of the Holy Spirit, with a purity that allows us to face all of life's ups and downs with a steady undercurrent of peace. We may not feel happy—life is full of pain and trouble—but we can be assured that God is in control. And that makes us safe enough to embrace even the sorrow.

Read Psalm 5:11–12.

GOD, GUARD MY HEART AND GIVE ME ENOUGH JOY
TO EMBRACE ANY CIRCUMSTANCE YOU ALLOW.

John R. Rice

Just as a bridegroom wants first place in the love and devotion of his bride . . . God wants the Christian to put Him first.

FIRST IN YOUR HEART

When a bride and groom stand before the altar, they promise love and devotion "till death do us part." How can they make such a promise? How can they *know* that they will always feel this way? It's easy in the beauty of the wedding ceremony; unfortunately, it's not easy when the pressures of life mount in the coming years.

But that's just the thing—the promise is not to *feel* that way forever, the promise is to *live* that way forever. To always live in love and devotion, to act with love and devotion, regardless of how we feel at the moment.

Every one of us longs to be loved—to be first in someone else's thoughts, to sense devotion that overwhelms us with joy. God wants us to put him first in exactly this way. To live with love and devotion, regardless of the doubts, the problems, or the fears. He wants to be first in our lives. He deserves nothing less.

Read Nahum 1:2–6.

LORD, HELP ME TO REMEMBER THAT YOU
MERIT MY TOTAL LOVE AND LOYALTY.

J. I. PACKER

The peace of God is first and foremost peace with God; it is the state of affairs in which God. . .is for us.

WALKING IN PEACE

What would it be like to walk in perfect peace? To do so, we must have peace *with* God before we can have the peace *of* God. In other words, we must know God before we can know peace. And when we are at peace with God, we understand that God is *for* us, not *against* us.

Before we knew God, we were at war. We were the enemy. We were fighting a losing battle. But then, when all seemed lost, Jesus—the Prince of Peace—mediated on our behalf, establishing and guaranteeing eternal peace with God. Once estranged from God, we are now his friends. Once vulnerable, now protected. Once defeated, now victorious. Once downcast, now happy. Once the opposition, now we have joined his forces. We are living on the right side. We live under his watch. We can walk in perfect peace.

Read Philippians 4:7.

LORD, THANK YOU FOR STANDING WITH ME AND FOR ME.

JOHN OF THE CROSS

It is noteworthy, then, that love is the soul's inclination, strength, and power in making its way to God, for love unites it with God.

LET US LOVE LIKE JESUS

What is love? In a word, it's Jesus. He embraced the cross because he loved us. He died so that none of us would perish. He gave the ultimate sacrifice out of godly concern and compassion for us—a people who didn't deserve it. Christ's love looked beyond his needs to the needs of others.

Are we willing to follow his lead, loving as he did with giving, selfless, humble love? While we can't die for someone else's sins, we can set aside our love of work so we can spend more time with our family. Or reconnect with an old friend when it would be easier not to. Or forgive someone who hurt us. Whatever the sacrifice, can we do it for Jesus, uniting our hearts with his? When we do, we are united with God. The power of love does that.

Read John 3:16.

LORD, HELP ME TO LOVE WHEN I DON'T FEEL
LIKE IT, AS A WAY TO HONOR YOU.

TERESA OF AVILA

[The] Lord desires intensely that we . . . seek his company, so much so that from time to time he calls us to draw near him.

COME AWAY

Put down the phone. Push away the keyboard. Turn off the television. God asks you to stop and spend time with him alone.

Like an excited fiancé who wants nothing but to enjoy time with his beloved, God seeks you out to simply be with him. He doesn't need pious prayers. He doesn't ask for lofty commitments or ritualistic practices. He asks for you. *You,* there in the middle of work's madness. *You,* tired and longing for someone to notice. *You,* broken and distant. He wants your company and will not tire in searching you out.

Sometimes God's silence compels us to run and find him. Other times, the glowing sun outside the kitchen window signals us to drop the ordinary and be captivated by him . . . just for a moment.

Bring your open heart today and allow yourself to be drawn near to him.

Read Song of Songs 2:10.

EXTRAORDINARY GOD, I LONG TO SPEND TIME WITH YOU TODAY.

JOHN ORTBERG

Love is why God created us in the first place. . . . God did not make us because he was bored, lonely, or had run out of things to do.

THE REASON IS LOVE

It's a classic story. Gepetto the woodworker carves a boy out of wood and wishes he would become real. His wish is granted, and Pinocchio is transformed into a real boy with a mind of his own.

Pinocchio's boyish ideas land him in the wrong crowd and he runs away from home. This act of rebellion breaks his father's heart, causing Gepetto to experience the ache of separation between himself and the child he has created.

Knowing full well that mankind would make a similar decision to rebel, God created us anyway. He knew our outcome before he formed the dust we were made from, and yet, with love immeasurable, he formed us and shaped us. The human race soon rebelled, but God's love didn't waver.

His love for you doesn't waver either.

Read 1 John 4:7–12.

LOVER OF MY SOUL, TEACH ME TO LOVE AS YOU LOVE.

LLOYD JOHN OGILVIE

Our dissatisfactions show what's driving us. The challenge is to want what our Lord wants for us.

DISSATISFACTIONS

Motivational speakers know the secret to motivating change. First, they explain in great detail why your current situation is unbearable. Even if you weren't unhappy before you began listening, you're likely to suddenly find yourself extremely dissatisfied with your life. After the seed of dissatisfaction has been planted, the desire to change easily sprouts from it.

Dissatisfaction does indeed drive us—we want to make changes. And it can be good—a positive exercise that compels us to look at our lives, see what needs to be changed for the better, and then work to make those changes. The challenge is to want the kinds of change that *God* wants for us, allowing *him* to show us where we need to improve and then letting him guide us into transformation.

Where are you dissatisfied? Take that dissatisfaction to God. He'll show you how to want what he wants for you.

Read Galatians 5:16–25.

LORD, KEEP ME CONNECTED TO YOU, LONGING
FOR WHAT YOU LONG FOR.

J. B. PHILLIPS

It is those who know God to be eternal who most satisfactorily prove that God is their contemporary.

YEARS TO COME

To some folks, God is the great watchmaker in the sky who set time in motion and stepped back to watch from a cosmic distance. Others believe he is intimately involved with specific, daily concerns. A person's picture of God makes all the difference in the depth of relationship he or she will have with the Creator.

Though we cannot grasp the concept of eternity, we can trust that God is eternal. Our lives on earth are governed by time and bookended by conception and death. God, however, is outside of time. He existed before hanging the stars and will continue to exist long past our time on this planet.

When we grasp the significance—the *bigness*—of this fact, only then are we ready to trust him in everything else. When we understand that we can never fully understand, when we trust promises that are beyond our comprehension, then we'll be ready to take God at his word as he walks with us today.

Read John 1:1–5.

GOD OF AGES PAST, BE MY HOPE FOR YEARS TO COME.

JOSEPH BAYLY

I may not long for death, but I surely long for heaven.

THE HOPE OF HEAVEN

Joseph Bayly was well acquainted with death. He and his wife, Mary Lou, buried not just one, but three, of their sons. In 1986, he joined their three boys in heaven.

Many of us, like Joseph and Mary Lou Bayly, have known the great sorrow of losing a beloved *someone* to death—whether a child, a sibling, a parent, or a close friend. Perhaps we were even sitting with that person when he or she took their last breath on this earth and their first breath in eternity.

In such moments, despite our heavy hearts, we catch a glimpse of heaven. We come to understand that heaven is not merely a fictional concept, invented to make the grieving feel better. Rather, it is a real and glorious destination—a place that turns painful death to great joy.

Heaven is indeed a marvelous end for those who love Jesus.

Read 1 Corinthians 15:50–55.

THANK YOU, DEAR FATHER, FOR THE
GLORIOUS HOPE OF HEAVEN.

W. IAN THOMAS

There is nothing quite so nauseating or pathetic as the flesh trying to be holy.

NO POSERS

The *Urban Dictionary* defines *poser* as someone who "tries to fit in but with exaggeration." You've probably encountered such individuals. They desperately want to blend into the group, but it rarely happens because they are so self-conscious in trying to do so.

Posers mingle about in the Christian world, doing and looking good. In public, they tell us life is great and their smiles flow freely—for a few short hours. Eventually, though, they must retreat and reenergize, because relying on self-righteousness runs even the best intentions into the ground.

Are you guilty of posing, of putting on a good face? Stop trying so hard. Become consumed with Christ and who he wants to be in your life. Go forward in the confidence that he is with you, and let his Spirit enable you to find your place.

Read Galatians 5:16.

LORD JESUS, EMPOWER MY STEPS TODAY
THROUGH THE HOLY SPIRIT.

CHARLES HADDON SPURGEON

Truth lies between two extremes, and man, like a pendulum, swings either too much this way or that.

THE TRUTH

Picture truth as a pendulum. Swing too far one way and truth can become a bludgeon with which we hurt those around us—speaking truth that perhaps would be better left unspoken, or speaking it in such a way that we cause hurt, embarrassment, and sometimes irreparable damage.

Swing too far the other way, however, and we skate along truth's edge, nearly falling off into deceit—into that realm where truth is hidden when it should be spoken, when it *needs* to be spoken. At this end of the pendulum, we so fear hurting the other person, even momentarily, that we omit saying what ultimately would help.

How do we find the middle ground? By being so in tune with God that he guides our words, our tone, our timing. By seeking his wisdom for speaking the truth so that he is honored and others are helped.

Listen carefully for his guidance. He will give you the words you need.

Read Ephesians 4:15.

GOD, TEACH ME TO SPEAK AND TO LISTEN
AT THE APPROPRIATE TIMES.

DAVID WILKERSON

Awaken us, O God, from the slumber of ease and riches ere the sword devour us.

THE SLUMBER OF EASE

You may not think you're particularly rich, but most of us live in luxury that millions of our fellow citizens on Planet Earth can only dream of. We sleep in warm houses, flip on electric switches when we want light, open cupboards overflowing with food, have closets filled with clothing, and enjoy hot showers.

There is nothing wrong with any of these things—in fact, we can thank God for every single blessing. Too often, however, these very riches send us into a slumber. We think there's no need to depend on God for the basic necessities of life, and so we take his blessings for granted.

What pleasures and gifts has God given you? What responsibilities have come with those blessings? May you awaken this day to thankfulness and to a sense of urgency about what God would have you do with his riches.

Read James 1:12–17.

FATHER, I APPRECIATE THE ABUNDANCE YOU LAVISH ON ME.

MARCH

FANNY CROSBY

Oh, what a happy child I am, although I cannot see! I am resolved that in this world, contented I will be.

BEAUTY FROM WEAKNESS

We humans are prone to weakness. Our mortal bodies are susceptible to disease and injury, while our emotions and priorities can easily get out of control.

Hymn-writer Fanny Crosby was familiar with frailty. Blind from infancy in an era when blindness could mean an institutionalized existence, no one imagined God had plans for her to become a famous songstress.

Part of the Christian life is the calling God places upon us, and often that calling seems impossible. But God uses our weaknesses to draw us to him. For when he requires something of us beyond our ability, we are forced to depend on him and only him to complete the task. Our emotions and priorities cannot be relied on, nor can our physical bodies.

When we completely surrender, he will use our weaknesses, our blindness—all our frailties—to make us something beautiful for the kingdom of God.

Read Philippians 4:10–13.

USE MY WEAKNESSES TO FURTHER YOUR KINGDOM, FATHER.

HUDSON TAYLOR

The Church is asleep; and armchairs and sofas and English comforts possess more attractions than perishing souls.

WAKE UP, CHURCH!

What happens when the church chooses comfort above seeking and saving the lost? People perish. Without Christ.

In our churches today, how many of us have settled into the security of a loving community where we are known—while choosing a life of earthly comforts that isolates us from others' need? Sadly, the truth may be worse than we care to admit.

God longs for his church—for us—to wake up! Though no one can predict what he will use to wake us up, the remedy is certain: we need a clear sense of God's saving grace in our lives that in turn motivates us to seek out those who are lost.

Will we, as Christ's church, respond? Will we wake up, or will we merely hit the snooze button and keep on sleeping?

Read Revelation 3:1–3.

*OH LORD, GIVE US—YOUR CHURCH—NEW EYES
AND EARS TO RECOGNIZE THE LOST.*

JOSEPH STOWELL

Getting our values straight is a critically important issue in life. And it is particularly strategic for the one seeking to experience Jesus.

"I NEED JESUS AND . . ."

Hopefully we are aware that we need Jesus, but if we're truly honest with ourselves, don't we sometimes think that we need Jesus AND . . . a salary large enough to pay the bills . . . a job that provides a sense of fulfillment . . . a spouse who nurtures and encourages us?

Perhaps we need to remember when we first came to know Jesus—how we eagerly set aside time to meet with him each day, how we found daily joy in being a new creation. Is it possible that we have known Jesus so long that we have begun to take him for granted? Have we shifted our focus instead to the ANDs, such as money, career, and family?

If we want to experience Jesus anew, we must become aware of the ANDs in our lives and come back to him as the priority that matters most.

Read Matthew 6:25–34.

DEAR JESUS, HELP ME TO LET GO OF THE "ANDS" IN MY LIFE.

JOHN MACARTHUR

Jesus Christ is the most incomparable personality of all human history.

THE GREATEST

We think in terms of greatness. Who is the greatest at a particular sport? The greatest president? The greatest musician? The greatest writer? The nominees are nearly endless, depending on who is expressing their opinion. Ask enough people, and the list will only grow.

Two thousand years ago, however, one man singularly became the centerpiece of history. Men devoted themselves to his leadership. A woman poured out a year's wages worth of perfume on his feet. Crowds shouted his praises as he rode a donkey into Jerusalem.

Jesus Christ changed the world more than any other person in history. In his name, people have created awe-inspiring art, initiated wars, and offered up their very lives.

No one can claim to match him in ability to influence or change a life. How about you? How has the incomparable Jesus changed your life?

Read Isaiah 53:2–6.

REVEAL TO ME IN GREATER MEASURE THE
TRANSFORMING POWER OF YOUR NAME.

FRANCOIS FÉNELON

The more one loves God, the more one is content.

MORE

More money, more status, more vacations, more stuff for our kids. There is no end to the "more" society tells us to want.

Our churches also deliver the message that we need more. More Bible knowledge, more ministry programs, more music choices, more activities for our kids.

Though shouts of "More is better! If you get it, you will finally be happy!" echo in our ears, contentment in the things of this earth lies perpetually out of reach. The one pursuit that will truly provide contentment is pursuing more of God himself. More love of him, more passion for his name, more time spent alone in his presence.

More of him is truly more of everything else our heart longs for.

Find contentment even today by lingering in his presence for just a while longer.

Read Ecclesiastes 5:10–15.

GOD, I LONG TO LOVE YOU MORE. SHOW ME THE WAY.

JAMES MONTGOMERY BOICE

We never deserve God's favors. If we think we do, we are in danger of losing them entirely.

UNDESERVED

Are you tempted to give in to the comparison obsession? Do you wonder why God chooses to lavish good gifts on people who don't even care about him, while faithful Christians sometimes go without even the most basic necessities? Maybe you've even wondered why God hasn't distributed gifts to you according to the good things you've done for him!

If it were up to us, the largest share of blessings might go to pastors, missionaries, and others whom we see making huge sacrifices for the sake of God's glory. This way of dividing God's riches seems fair, after all.

But attempting to run God's world in this way overlooks the most important blessing in God's economy: grace. It's the lavish gift of forgiveness that he offers to anyone who simply longs for it. This we could never deserve.

Read Romans 3:21–26.

THANK YOU FOR GIFTING ME WITH UNDESERVED FAVORS.

MALCOLM MUGGERIDGE

In old age faith seems to be the most marvelous possession anyone can have.

NEVER PURPOSELESS

A man spoke at a rural nursing home. His audience was retired, many of them feeling worthless. But instead of reinforcing their feelings of inadequacy, he enlisted them for action. He needed six people to be prayer warriors for a new missions outreach; four people to read books onto CD for the blind; two women to teach a class to Girl Scouts on needlework and crocheting; and two men to judge a historical essay competition for the local high school.

In its opportunities for service, faith gives all of us—young or old, healthy or impaired—a purpose for living. We may not set any world records, star in any films, or record any hit songs, but there is reason to face each new day with optimism. Life never loses its value, because even as our bodies deteriorate, we can still accomplish great things for Christ.

Read Psalm 92:12–15.

OPEN MY EYES, LORD, TO YOUR ALL-ENDURING PURPOSE FOR ME.

RANDY ALCORN

My heart always goes where I put God's money.

IT BELONGS TO GOD

We make a mistake when we look around at our stuff and see it as "ours," when we congratulate ourselves for what we continue to accumulate. We ought to hold this "stuff" loosely, for it is never really ours.

In a very real sense, every penny we earn comes from God. Our ability to work, our job itself, and the salary we earn are all God's gracious gifts to us. What we earn is not *our* money; it's God's money, lent to us. What will you do with what God has entrusted to you? What would please God and honor his kingdom? Remember that Jesus said, "For where your treasure is, there will your heart be also" (Matthew 6:21 KJV).

Everything we have—friendships, skills, cash—comes from and belongs to God. Knowing this, we should seek to honor the Lord in how we use his gifts. Instead of seeing them as things to use for our agendas, we should see them as God's and use them for his purposes and pleasure.

Read Matthew 6:19–21.

Elisabeth Elliot

Whatever dark tunnel we may be called upon to travel through, God has been there.

LIGHT IN DARK TUNNELS

Imagine walking down the stairs into a windowless basement after a storm has knocked out the electricity. You see shadows and hear noises you can't identify—at least until you flip on a flashlight.

We feel much this way when we encounter times of darkness in our lives. Chronic illness, broken relationships, unemployment—everything seems confusing. Is there anything to do but just huddle in the dark, asking God why we are there and begging him to get us out?

Yes. Look to him as your Light. Seek his face and let him guide your steps.

Remember, God knows about each situation in your life. He has promised to be your constant Light, dispelling the shadows and leading you through the frightening places, one step at a time. You can walk confidently through the darkness because he is your trustworthy guide. There's no need to despair, because nothing is too dark for God. He is with you, and he knows the way through.

Read Psalm 18:28–29.

FATHER, REMIND ME THAT YOUR LOVE
BRINGS LIGHT TO MY DARKNESS.

C. S. LEWIS

God whispers to us in our pleasures, speaks in our conscience, but shouts in our pains: it is his megaphone to rouse a deaf world.

A STUBBORN PEOPLE

God speaks, but how seldom do we hear him? We enjoy our pleasures—the very pleasures that come from his hand—and forget to thank him. He loves to bless us, and in those blessings he whispers his love to us. But then bad news comes. The doctor delivers an unexpected diagnosis. The relationship hits a rocky road. The choices that seemed right suddenly look very wrong.

Again God speaks. We search for the meaning and take a sidelong glance at him. Finally, when the full force of adversity hits us, when the pain becomes all too real, only then does God successfully get our attention. *This* is beyond what we can bear. *This* needs extra help. *This* needs God.

We forget that God wants us to hear him all the time. Times of pleasure, times of pain—what is he saying to you today?

Read 1 Kings 19:11–12.

WHETHER IN PAIN OR PLEASURE, HELP ME TO FOCUS ON YOU, GOD.

BILLY GRAHAM

Where is God when we suffer? He is ever-present and all-knowing, with us in all our struggles and trials.

WHERE IS GOD?

When we walk through a storm, where is God? When the floodwaters sweep under the door of our hearts and crash into our lives, where is God? When our hearts hurt until we think they will burst from the pain, where is God?

The deep and abiding truth is that God will never leave us or forsake us . . . no matter what. That does not mean we will not feel the wrench of pain. It *does* mean that God will walk with us through it. He waits for us to invite him to carry the load.

God knows all about our struggles and trials. His Word states that they are the very link to identifying with Jesus. Through struggles we taste the suffering Jesus endured. It is then that his life can be seen in us.

Read Isaiah 41:10.

COME, LORD JESUS, HELP ME TO KNOW YOU
ARE WITH ME . . . NO MATTER WHAT.

CHARLES COLSON

For the first time I felt truly free, even as the fortunes of my life seemed at their lowest ebb.

TRULY FREE

When Charles Colson wrote these words, he was in prison. His father had died, his son had just been arrested, and his fellow Watergate prisoners had recently been released.

And then he received a phone call from a friend. This man and three others had been meeting with Colson weekly, supporting him in his emerging faith. They ended each weekly session together on their knees in prayer.

That day on the phone, Al Quie, a high-ranking politician in Congress and one of the most respected public figures in Washington, said he would petition President Ford to let him serve the rest of Colson's sentence so Colson could be with his family during this difficult time. Within hours the other men made the same offer. That night, overwhelmed with the deep love of Christ expressed through these friends, Charles Colson completely surrendered his life to God and finally felt truly free, despite being in prison.

Have you tasted the freedom that Jesus offers? When the Son sets you free, you are free indeed.

Read 1 John 3:16–18.

FATHER, GIVE ME COURAGE TO LOVE DEEPLY AS YOU DO.

JOHN DONNE

Batter my heart, three-personed God; for You
As yet but knock, breathe, shine, and seek to mend.

HEART SURGERY

When the human heart is full of self and sin, it has no room for God. Only the humble heart has ample space for him.

Do you desire a new heart? How open are you to the Great Physician's recommendations?

To let God perform his work, we must give up our proud self-sufficiency. We never know how he might soften us and change us. Sometimes he uses blessings and answered prayers, overwhelming us with his love. Or he may choose trials, difficulties, and sorrow to polish our faith.

As challenging as the process may be, we can rejoice that God cares enough to heal our hearts—to take them in his hands and restore them to health so that they beat in sync with his heart.

Are you willing to expose your heart to God and let him remake it? Are you willing to let him, piece by piece, day by day, create in you a new heart?

Read Ezekiel 36:26–27.

O HOLY LORD, PERFORM YOUR LOVING SURGERY ON MY HEART.

JOHN PIPER

A prayer-less Christian is like a bus driver trying to push his bus out of the rut because he doesn't know Clark Kent is on board.

ON BOARD

Clark Kent's alter ego, Superman, had a knack for appearing at just the right moment to rescue the helpless from the brink of destruction. Clark would swap his business suit for a superhero's cape at a moment's notice—once all other possibilities for help had been exhausted. It took an emergency—a crisis—to bring out the rescuing hero.

How different God is! He is not the solution of last resort but the source of immediate help. Always. With all power at his fingertips, he stands ready to save any who will appeal to him. In fact, he *wants* to be the one who saves. It's not up to us to save ourselves.

We can call out to him with just a word, asking to be rescued in the moment, or we can spend hours pouring out our deepest concerns. Regardless, he is on board! He saves our souls as surely as he keeps our feet from stumbling on a morning walk.

Read James 5:13–16.

LORD, MAKE IT MY FIRST INSTINCT TO CRY OUT TO YOU FOR HELP.

AUGUSTINE OF HIPPO

Whoever therefore has his own measure, that is, wisdom, is happy.

THE MEASURE OF A SOUL

The word *measure* comes from the same Latin root as our English word *moderate*. When we take our own measure, when we make a modest, honest appraisal of the state of our souls and adapt accordingly, then we walk in wisdom. That wisdom in turn leads to lasting happiness.

What if we made it a discipline to spend time before God once a week, taking the measure of our soul? What if we asked ourselves just two pointed questions—and gave ourselves and God some honest answers?

Are we truly seeking God or seeking to act like our own god?

Have we elevated people or objects above God, making them idols?

Let us resolve to be people who routinely take the measure of our souls and walk in wisdom.

Read James 3:13–18.

HELP ME, FATHER, TO KNOW THE MEASURE OF MY SOUL.

JOHN BUNYAN

Use my afflictions, O God, to demonstrate your love and power and wisdom and faithfulness, even to the praise of your glory.

STANDING FIRM IN THE STORM

In the middle of a storm, the weeping willow sways instead of snapping. As raindrops puddle at the base of its trunk, the tree absorbs the water and stands strong.

At times, the force of the storm threatens to overcome us. When we are diagnosed with cancer, we lose a job, or a friendship ends, we often ask, "Why me?" instead of "Why *not* me?" In those moments, we may not be able to see how we'll ever keep from breaking. After all, the winds and the rain are so strong . . . But God is greater, and he knows. He will be our stronghold.

God wants to work in you and your circumstances today. You may not understand the forces you're up against, but you can trust in his sovereignty. Believe in his omnipotence. Look expectantly for his faithfulness. He is holding you up.

Read Romans 8:26–27.

HELP ME TRUST YOU IN THE STORM, GOD.

SAINT PATRICK

Christ beside me, Christ before me, Christ behind me, Christ within me, Christ beneath me, Christ above me.

SURROUNDED

When we are aware of people's presence, we are careful about what we say and how we act. When the boss is present, we're sure to be seen diligent and not wasting time. We may talk differently with our friends if we know our parents can overhear us. How would we live if we knew that every moment, Christ is beside us, in front of us, behind us, within us, above us, beneath us?

Would knowing that he is within earshot affect what we say? Would knowing that he is in front of us affect our attitude toward the future? Would knowing he is behind us make us less fearful? Would knowing he is above and below us make us stronger in our convictions? Would knowing he is within us make a difference in how we act?

The fact is, Christ is indeed in all of those places. What does that mean for you as you walk into today?

Read Psalm 139:5.

DEAR CHRIST, THANK YOU FOR SURROUNDING
ME WITH YOUR PRESENCE.

WARREN WIERSBE

The paradox of Christian worship: we seek to see the incomprehensible, know the unknowable, comprehend the incomprehensible, and experience the eternal.

THE WORSHIP ENCOUNTER

While worship is the believer's humble response at glimpsing God's incomprehensible, eternal nature, in worship we also can adoringly see, know, comprehend, and experience God. It is, indeed, a paradox.

When Isaiah caught sight of God's holiness and splendor, he fell to his knees in humble contrition, declaring himself sinful and unclean. Yet God not only restored him but sent him out as his representative.

Perhaps the greatest paradox in worship is that when we encounter God, he allows us to live; and though God knows us, he still chooses us.

Catch a glimpse of God. See him as he truly is. Make each part of your day a worship encounter.

Read Isaiah 6:1–8.

MAX LUCADO

Heaven is a perfect place of perfected people with our perfect Lord.

WORTH THE WAIT

Perfect. Now there's an adjective that rarely describes us. And rightly so. This side of the Fall, we are weak, limited, and sinful.

But all is not lost. There is still hope for perfection: heaven. A lot of adjectives could be used to describe it: *beautiful, resplendent, glorious, holy.* But *perfect* describes it best. Life, eternal life, can't get any better than that.

Here on earth we're known for our flawed bodies, faulty reasoning, and clumsy reactions, but in heaven we will be perfected. It's worth the wait.

Read John 14:1–3.

LLOYD JOHN OGILVIE

Mercy is getting inside people's skin, just as God got in ours when He came to live among us.

LOVE IN ACTION

Mercy is far more than nice thoughts, a kind disposition, sympathetic feelings, or a loving demeanor. Mercy realizes that someone is hurting and gets involved.

Just as Jesus took on human flesh and lived among us, experiencing our pain and limitations, mercy gets inside people's skin. The merciful see a need, are moved by that need, and meet that need. Mercy helps the hurting, cares for the sick, brings a cup of cold water to the thirsty, reaches out to the untouchable, forgives the fallen, and is patient with the peculiar.

We are to be merciful because God has shown mercy to us. He has met our needs, eased our ache, and saved our souls—all while sharing our humanness through Jesus. We respond by showing mercy to others. And in that act, we receive even more mercy from God.

Read Luke 6:35–36.

LORD, HELP ME TO FOLLOW YOUR EXAMPLE AND BE MERCIFUL.

CHARLES SWINDOLL

God says, "I know what I'm doing. You can trust Me." And let me assure you. He is a good God.

GOD KNOWS WHAT HE IS DOING

Mourners filled the church. The casket held a young man—a man who had been devoted to God. He knew and lived the goodness of God. He demonstrated that goodness to his family, his church, his neighbors. Wherever he went, God's goodness spilled out to touch others. What was God's purpose in allowing this life to end so soon?

If you are asking God what he is doing and why, know that his Word makes his goodness plain. He has reasons we know nothing of, and a perfect plan that he brings to completion in his time.

Even in what spells tragedy to us, God can be trusted to know what he is doing. For this young man's family—and for us in our own times of trial—the days of grief will be hard, the bumps in the road will hurt, and the holes in our hearts will be vast. But the goodness of God will flow through them if we will trust in him.

Read Romans 8:28.

HELP ME, O GOD, TO TRUST IN YOUR GOODNESS
IN THE DARKEST PLACES IN LIFE.

STUART BRISCOE

Do not long to be someone else, because He made you ideal for His plan.

IDEALLY CREATED

Have you ever felt that you could be more effective for God if only you were more of an extrovert . . . or you had additional financial resources . . . or you had the gift of evangelism?

Here's something to consider: we would do well to spend less time trying to be like other people and more time discovering God's plan for us as individuals.

Who are the people God has placed in your life to whom you can show his light? What talents has God given you, and how might he them to draw others to himself? What resources has God provided that you could invest in his kingdom?

God made you to fit his plan and purpose for *you*. He has given you a unique circle of influence and a unique approach to being his appointed light in this dark world. Ask him to show you how.

Read Matthew 5:16.

THANK YOU, FATHER, THAT YOU CREATED ME JUST AS I AM.

GEORGE HERBERT

Love bade me welcome. Yet my soul drew back
Guilty of dust and sin.

GOD'S GRACIOUS OFFER

We are frail—mere dust. And to dust we will return at the end of our days. When we look deeply into our own hearts, we see that we are weak and prone to sin, inclined to go our own way, not God's way. Knowing these truths about ourselves, we might tend toward despair—except for God's great love.

How do we dare to enter into the presence of such lavish love? A love that does not count our frailty or our sin against us? A love that was willing to die for us on a lonely hill?

We might not even try, were it not for the fact that Love has invited us in already. All we have to do is respond—and come running to him.

As Love beckons you, what will you say?

Read Romans 7:21–8:2.

LORD, YOUR LAVISH LOVE AMAZES ME.

OS GUINNESS

Answering the call of our Creator is "the ultimate why" for living, the highest source of purpose in human existence.

ANSWERING GOD'S CALL

How often, within the first few minutes of meeting someone, have you been asked, "What kind of work do you do?" It's not surprising, really, since in our culture, a person's work is closely tied to their identity.

However, the definition of *vocation* is "a calling"—something well beyond just a job. While God clearly designed us with abilities and interests that help us flourish in certain lines of work, we must not lose sight of the fact that answering his call is far more than finding the right career. Answering God's call means saying yes to his offer of salvation and then investing all that we are, all that we do, and all that we have in living each day for him.

That calling gives purpose and meaning to life. *That* calling answers all the whys of our existence—and even gives us a reason for getting up and going to work each day.

How will you answer God's call today?

Read Hebrews 12:1–2.

DEAR FATHER, HELP ME TO SAY YES TO YOUR CALL EACH DAY.

RUTH BELL GRAHAM

I think it harder, / Lord, to cast / the care of those I love / on You, / than to cast mine.

LET GO

Bringing those we love to God in prayer isn't always an easy task. We see a spouse struggling, a child wandering, a friend hurting—and we want to help. It's our first instinct! Yet sometimes their struggle runs so deep that we can only pray, keenly aware that there is nothing more we can do. The person we are praying for may be blind to God's work. Or uninterested in his answers. Or in too much pain to listen.

It is in those times that we must remind ourselves—minute by minute, if necessary—that God can do far more in a loved one's life through our prayers than we could ever imagine. Just as we trust God to be at work in our own lives, so must we trust him to be at work in the lives of those we love.

Make it a daily habit to hand over your loved ones to the Lord in prayer. He will never let go of them. He promised. See for yourself in his Word.

Read Ephesians 3:20–21.

*HELP ME TRUST YOU, LORD, FOR THOSE I
LOVE WHO ARE WANDERING.*

MARTIN LUTHER

God doesn't test us because he enjoys it. He tests us to find out whether we love him above all things.

POP QUIZ

A car cuts you off and you miss your exit. You will be late for your job interview. You finally arrive and rush up the elevator, only to realize you left your résumé at home.

Someone in your small group gossiped, telling your embarrassing struggle to close friends.

Your in-laws gave you money for your birthday. You buy something special with it, only to find that your check for the water bill has bounced, and the bank fees leave you with nothing for groceries.

Time to sing the blues, or time to trust the Lord? You know the *right answer* is to trust him through it all. God may be using this test to find out whether you love him more than your friends, your job opportunity, or your bottom line.

It is in this moment—during the test—that we find out what's in our hearts.

What's in yours?

Read Galatians 5:19–23.

I AM OVERWHELMED WITH WHAT IS HAPPENING IN MY LIFE, DEAR GOD, BUT I WANT YOU TO KNOW I LOVE YOU.

FRANCIS SCHAEFFER

Love of the creature toward the Creator must include obedience or it is meaningless.

WHAT ABOUT LOVE?

How do you show that you love someone? Plenty of today's most popular songs claim it's all about saying, "I love you." But in the realm of faith, *obedience* is what demonstrates that we love God. Without this one activity, our professions of love lose their meaning. We cheapen those words of devotion when we dismiss God's commands.

Maybe you're doubting his love for you. Remind yourself: *God created me; that's why I am here. He loves me; that's why Jesus died and rose again. He surrounded me with flowers and trees and birds and music and an array of foods, wanting me to have good things.*

Truly, evidence of his care is all around, so you can trust his requests of you. When he asks you to do something, you can respond with confidence rather than fear and trembling.

We all sin and fall short of the glory of God. Grace covers that sin. However, for our love to be meaningful, we must obey.

Do you love God? Obey him.

Read Deuteronomy 11:1–7.

YOU KNOW I SIN, GOD; YOU KNOW I DISOBEY YOU.
I LOVE YOU, AND I REPENT. FORGIVE ME.

E. M. BOUNDS

Our laziness after God is our crying sin. . . . No man gets God who does not follow hard after him.

THE PURSUIT

God says to us, "Seek my kingdom first." It is a command that affects every detail of the day, and those who respond obediently are blessed. But more often than not, we reply, "I'm tired." "Maybe later." "Can't it wait?"

Yet there is hope for us if we will invest ourselves in this most important of pursuits. Seek his kingdom first. How? By unrelentingly pursuing God. Read what he has written in the Scriptures. Doggedly press into each verse and ask, "What is God telling me? How should I respond?" Tenaciously look for God in his creation, in your trials, in the faces of those he would have you love today.

Do you pursue God with all your heart? With all your soul? With all your mind? Following hard after God is the pursuit of a lifetime. Make it your primary one.

Read Matthew 22:37–38.

I GET TIRED, LORD, AND LAZY, BUT I KNOW I NEED YOU. HELP ME FOLLOW HARD AFTER YOU.

PHILIP YANCEY AND PAUL BRAND

The . . . Head of this Body—God Himself in the person of Christ—is not dependent on . . . perceptions gained through the members of His Body.

ANYTHING, ANYONE, ANYTIME

You may be a lover, not a fighter. But chances are you've still resorted to "boxing"—that familiar tendency to put others in a box: *I can't visit that church member in the hospital; that's the pastor's responsibility. Why pick up my mess in the church? The janitor gets paid to do it. I'm not going to serve on the worship team; that's the music minister's job.*

We miss so much when we put limitations on ourselves or other members of the body of Christ. But we especially miss out when we try to limit God himself. God can work through anything or anyone at any time. Remember Balaam's donkey? It spoke words of warning. Remember Moses? God called him from a burning bush. Remember Daniel? God shut the lions' mouths. Remember the earthquake that freed Paul from prison? God did that too.

Fortunately, God will not be put in a box. Trust him to do the impossible, even with you. He may just break you out of your own box even as he is breaking free of the one you've put him in.

Read Exodus 3:1–12.

BREAK ME OUT OF MY BOX, GOD. DO THE IMPOSSIBLE.

EUGENE PETERSON

The faster we move the less we become; our very speed diminishes us.

RESETTING THE TREADMILL

Work, school, family, community. There are some days when an underlying rhythm seems to keep it all together in a smooth flow. On other days, though, all those commitments seem to be cycling on a treadmill that speeds up with each mile we run.

Speed has become the taskmaster in this digital age. We move so fast and handle so many tasks on any given day that we hardly even notice any of our accomplishments. Worse, our connection with God starts to slip. The light of his work in our lives rushes by in an unrecognizable flash.

Still, Jesus is calling. He beckons us to a speed of his design and perfection. He invites us to reset our pace to keep him in our line of vision, just as he did with his Father. As Jesus talked and prayed with God, he was refreshed for ministry and prepared for his Father's pace.

Take some time to refuel, refresh, and regroup today. Hit the "reset" button on your treadmill. Jesus is waiting to help you move in step with him.

Read Mark 1:35.

LORD, HELP ME TO EXPERIENCE FULLNESS IN YOU TODAY.

J. I. PACKER

What higher, more exalted, and more compelling goal can there be than to know God?

A DIVINE HUNGER

It is almost impossible to fathom how a world so full of information can be lacking in understanding. And yet it is true. We are challenged to pursue advanced degrees, prompted to keep up with the newest trends, urged to stay competent in the latest technology. But have such endeavors filled our lives with meaning and hope? No. One problem is that these endeavors—as worthy as they are—aren't big enough to capture our hearts.

A believer has a more exalted, more compelling goal: to know God. Not just to know about God or gather facts concerning God or memorize a creed regarding God, but to have a *relationship* with the living God. The difference is as vast as knowing the recipe for your favorite pie—or actually sinking your teeth into a fresh-out-of-the-oven slice. Formulas cannot do justice to the experience.

Once we know God, once we experience him, we will only hunger for more of him.

Pursue him with all your passion.

Read Philippians 3:8.

DEAR GOD, I WANT TO KNOW YOU MORE AND MORE.

APRIL

HANNAH HURNARD

We can see then, how essential it is that our whole thought life should be brought under the control and reign of the Lord of love.

STREAMS OF THOUGHT

A s soon as the words were out of your mouth, you wished you could take them back. You hadn't meant to *think* those things, let alone *say* those things. But now you've done both!

On some days our thoughts are beautiful and clear, like a mountain stream flowing gently between green valleys. All is well with our world and everyone in it. On other days, though, our thoughts are like raging rapids—full of churning turmoil and unexpected dangers. Interactions with people leave us angry, tense. Circumstances force us to navigate the waters of loneliness or sorrow. Situations tempt us to be reckless and reflect on things that are impure or unlovely.

Amid those rough-water days, how essential it is to take all our thoughts captive. Peace is ours when we submit our thoughts to Christ and resist the enemy. Today, let God calm your thoughts with his truth, his light, his love. He's ready to quiet your mind and your heart.

Read 2 Corinthians 10:4–6.

KEEP MY THOUGHTS IN THE STREAM OF TRUTH, LIGHT, AND LOVE TODAY, GOD.

OSWALD CHAMBERS

The workshop of missionary munitions is the hidden, personal, worshipping life of the saint.

ARMED AND READY

Where do you go to find the ammunition needed for today's battle? With evil spiritual forces rallied against us and an unkind world counteracting us in every way, we would perhaps excuse ourselves for going AWOL (or at least for staying far from the front lines). We feel we do not have the munitions we need; we feel outgunned and outnumbered.

But we are never outdone when we have properly prepared for battle through a life of quiet, personal worship. Only in the hidden times with God—when we stand in awe before him in worship, when we are lost in wonder at his power and grace, when we are captivated by his majesty and holiness and draw close to him—only then are we prepared for the battle.

Read Ephesians 6:10–18.

IN THE QUIET, LORD, I WORSHIP YOU. ARM ME FOR TODAY'S BATTLE.

BILL HYBELS

God . . . is no more intimidated by childish demands for instant gratification than wise parents are.

GOD'S PERFECT TIMING

All good things come to those who wait" is an adage with little charm if you happen to be the one in the middle of waiting. Waiting demands patience, and patience calls for being still and knowing God as all-wise, trusting his perfect timing.

Our culture today demands instant satisfaction. Instant food. Instant solving of problems. Instant relief of pain. Yet wise parents do not succumb to a child's "I want it now" tantrums. God is no different.

Whether you are waiting for the weather to change, the flowers to bloom, the toddler to learn to walk, the pain to cease, the hurt to heal, or for God to answer prayer for a loved one . . . be patient. Trust God's timing and wisdom. He knows the perfect time for all good things to burst forth in bloom.

Read Ecclesiastes 3:11.

LORD, GIVE ME PATIENCE TO WAIT AND TO
TRUST YOUR WISDOM WHILE I WAIT.

CATHERINE OF SIENA

When My Son was lifted up on the wood of the . . . Cross, the Divine nature remain[ed] joined to the lowliness of the earth of your humanity.

DIVINE NATURE

Don't copy the behavior and customs of this world, but let God transform you into a new person" (Romans 12:2 NLT). Try as we may, that change—that transformation—is out of our reach. We vow to defeat the impulse to judge, the flare of anger, the habit that threatens our health. We stand at the door of need . . . a need for a helper. A helper who took on earthly wrappings, but whose divine nature did not die. Jesus' divine nature joined with our humanity to empower us to be transformed into new creations.

Be encouraged if transformation is out of your reach. Invite the Holy Spirit to lead you, to be your Helper. Let Jesus' divine nature live in you.

Read John 16:7.

INDWELL ME, LORD, WITH YOUR HOLY
SPIRIT. FILL ME ANEW EACH DAY.

CALVIN MILLER

The paradox of the cross belonged to Jesus; the cross is at once the greatest picture of love, yet the clearest portrait of hate.

IT DOESN'T MAKE SENSE

Christianity is full of paradoxes: one must die to live, give to have, mourn to be happy, be poor to be rich, surrender to be victorious. But no greater paradox exists than Jesus' cross: love birthed in hate, beauty arising from ugliness, a good man dying so bad men could be saved.

The cross was the Roman Empire's torturous instrument of death. The victim hung suspended between heaven and earth. The crossbeams stood in paradox—the vertical beam jutting upward toward heaven, like a champion thrusting his fist into the air, satisfying the demands of God's holiness; the horizontal beam reaching outward toward the earth like a father's arms, signifying the embrace of God's love.

It doesn't make sense, does it? Paradoxes don't. But that doesn't make it any less true. Delight in the cross.

Read Colossians 2:1–15.

THANK YOU, JESUS, FOR THE CROSS.

E. STANLEY JONES

Death cuts every man down to size except one, and his death enhances him, universalized him, put the symbol of his death, the cross . . . in our hearts.

HOPE BEYOND THE GRAVE

Our life here on earth appears as a vapor and then disappears. Our body is on a funeral march to the grave. It's a difficult reality for us humans to grasp. We avoid death as much as possible—we are all about life and living.

Genesis 3:19 reminds us that we are God's creations, only temporarily on this earth, our bodies eventually returning to the dust from which we were created. It's not great news—and yet God does not leave us there. We have hope through God's mercy and grace.

Because Jesus conquered death, those who belong to him will conquer death also. In the short time we have on earth, we should be enthusiastic and grateful for what Jesus did for us at Calvary. The cross provides the only way to eternal life.

Read Romans 5:17.

*GOD, KEEP ME GROUNDED IN YOUR WORD AS
I LIVE OUT MY DAYS ON THIS PLANET.*

JOHN STOTT

[Jesus] exhibited both the greatest self-esteem and the greatest self-sacrifice.

THANK GOD FOR THE CROSS

We need only read slowly and carefully the familiar accounts of Christ's crucifixion in the four Gospels to be overwhelmed by his sacrifice for us. He was innocent of all crimes, yet false charges were leveled against him and false witnesses lied about him. A lead-tipped whip tore apart his back. A crown of long, sharp thorns was crushed into his scalp. A heavy cross was placed on his shredded back to carry to his own crucifixion. Nails dug into his wrists and feet.

Didn't the Jews know that this was their promised Messiah? Didn't the soldiers recognize that this was no ordinary man? Obviously not. But Jesus, knowing who he was and why he came, willingly submitted to all of the torture. He suffered and died and conquered death so that we too could have the final victory.

Read John 18:4–9.

LORD JESUS, MAY I NEVER FORGET WHAT
YOU DID FOR ME AT CALVARY.

DIETRICH BONHOEFFER

The cross is nobody's private property, but belongs to all; it is intended for all humanity.

THE CROSS

Sharing doesn't come easily. We learn to say, "It's mine," early and then say it all too often. Even the most well-meaning Christians can find their hearts hardened when someone asks for something.

What if Christ had been like that, saying no to his Father's plan for the ages? There would have been no cross—and no salvation. But Jesus was always thinking of others, from making sure guests at the wedding in Cana had enough to drink to ensuring that Peter didn't sink into the Sea of Galilee.

The ultimate example of Christ's selflessness was Calvary, of course. The cross stands as the offer of salvation to all humanity. No one person owns it. It belongs to all.

Read Luke 22:39–44.

GOD, I AM SO GRATEFUL FOR YOUR WILLINGNESS TO SHARE JESUS WITH ME.

AUGUSTINE OF HIPPO

But with the mouth of our heart we also panted for the
supernal streams from your fountain, the fountain of life which
is with you (Ps 35:10).

GETTING DRENCHED

Thirst and hunger are realities of everyday life. Have you ever been so parched that you would do anything, go anywhere, for water? Those thirst pangs reveal the magnitude of our desire and drive. Without water we perish. Without God we die. As the physical body longs for water, our souls long for God.

God's fountain of life bubbles up grace, showers mercy, overflows with love, cascades with forgiveness, and rains down hope. Its perpetual flow and unceasing spray project the rainbow of God's colorful character.

The deer panting for water was an image of the psalmist's soul. The emptiness, the longing, could only be satisfied at God's fountain. From within him comes the living water we need to sustain our spiritual journey. Linger under the downpour of God's fountain. He alone quenches our spiritual thirst.

Read Psalm 42:1–2.

LORD, REFRESH ME AT YOUR FOUNTAIN OF LIFE.

BERNARD OF CLAIRVAUX

There is nothing hidden that is not to be revealed, nothing secret that will not be known.

YOU CAN'T HIDE

X-rays. MRIs. Telescopes. Microscopes. Modern technology reveals the intricacies of the atom and the vastness of the universe. Nothing is too small, nothing too large. It's all visible. There is nowhere to hide our secrets. Scary thought, isn't it?

Yet we think we can hide from God. We've convinced ourselves that somehow activities done under the cover of darkness are not known to the Father of Light. That attitudes held in the inner recesses of our hearts will not be known by the One who knit us in our mother's womb.

The Pharisees—the religious leaders in Jesus' day—thought they were exempt from exposure. Read Matthew 22 for a scathing exposé. The seven churches in Revelation thought that somehow their actions were unknown to the Lord. Read Revelation 2–3, which fully discloses their sins. To each church Jesus says, "I know . . ."

Jesus sees all and knows all. He would prefer an authentic struggler to a religious hypocrite.

Read Revelation 3:1.

LORD, HELP ME BE HONEST WITH YOU. I KNOW YOU KNOW ANYWAY.

A. W. TOZER

[God] meant us to see Him and live with Him and draw our life from His smile.

UNLIMITED ACCESS

In the Old Testament, the curtain in the temple prevented God's people from seeing into the Most Holy Place where his presence dwelt. But the New Testament records that when Jesus died on the cross, the curtain ripped in two, signifying our unlimited access to God through Christ.

You may easily assent to this amazing truth—you may even get it intellectually—but do you act on it? Do you enter God's presence throughout your day? Do you see him, know him, live with him ever in your midst? Or do you hang your own curtain that prevents you from enjoying him?

Perhaps we have allowed our self-focus to become a barrier that keeps us from God. It's possible to even become too self-sufficient to want to be with God—or too full of self-pity.

God wants us to see him and live with him and draw life from his smile. Look up. Because that curtain was torn by Jesus, you can see God smiling.

Read Hebrews 10:19–22.

FORGIVE ME, LORD, FOR THE THINGS THAT
I LET KEEP ME FROM YOU.

JOYCE MEYER

God is calling you and me up higher, to a new level, and on every new level of God's power and blessings we experience new opposition.

A NEW LEVEL

We don't tend to look at difficulties and opposition as opportunities. Instead, we see them as excuses to quit, to give up, to determine that we must have been on the wrong path, misread the signs, didn't understand what we thought was God's guidance.

At times, it's true that the roadblocks are God's way of stopping us. At other times, however, those roadblocks are opposition from our enemy, and our job is to hear God calling us higher, calling us to climb over the roadblocks and continue on his path.

The difficulty, of course, is determining which is true—where is this roadblock from and what should we do about it? Ask God. He will give you the wisdom to discern whether to let the roadblocks guide you onto a new path, or whether to climb right on over them! When you seek God's guidance, he will give you power and blessings for the road ahead.

Read James 1:5.

FATHER, GIVE ME THE FAITH TO FACE OPPOSITION IN YOUR POWER.

THOMAS MERTON

God makes us ask ourselves questions most often when He intends to resolve them.

QUESTIONS AND ANSWERS

The best way to help people who are encountering huge problems is just to be present. There are no quick fixes for the agony of losing a loved one or the shock of being diagnosed with a serious illness. Still, grieving people need to be able to talk to someone, to voice their frustrations, to ask their questions. They need to feel heard. A real friend will be that listening ear.

For each of us, the situations life throws at us produce any number of questions that we will need to direct to God—questions he already knows are coming. And he intends to resolve every one. Perhaps not in our timing or in the manner we would desire, but he *will* resolve them.

Read Psalm 19:14.

LORD, HELP ME LISTEN WELL TO OTHERS—AND TO YOU.

R. C. SPROUL

The death of a loved one involves a loss for those who are left behind. But for the one who passes. . .to heaven it is a gain.

OUT OF THIS WORLD

Imagine a long vacation at a five-star hotel. A valet parks your car. A doorman greets you and welcomes you in. You enter, enjoying out-of-this-world amenities for a time.

Imagine death. Your body is parked in a cemetery—the underground garage. Your spirit approaches the doorway of heaven. It's opened, not by a doorman but by Jesus, the proprietor and architect of this dwelling—the same one who paid the price for you to come and stay. You enter, enjoying out-of-this-world benefits for eternity.

People sometimes say of a bad day, "Yeah, but it beats the alternative." No, it doesn't. For a believer, the alternative is heaven—an out-of-this-world experience that trumps any five-star hotel. Death is the doorway by which we can leave the limitations and pains of this existence and enter into the heavenly realm.

Death is loss, but heaven is the Christian's gain.

Read Isaiah 26:19.

FATHER, I LOOK FORWARD TO HEAVEN'S GAIN.

Max Lucado

We have "put on" Christ. When God looks at us he doesn't see us; he sees Christ. We "wear" him.

DO YOU SEE WHAT GOD SEES?

Look in the mirror. What do you see? Are your sins written all over your face? Pride? Envy? Lack of forgiveness? Prejudice? Judging? Anger? Bitterness?

Look again and see what God sees. Beauty. Loveliness. Perfection. How can this be? Because when God looks at you, he sees his Son. He sees the shed blood of his beloved one given for you. He sees you clothed in righteousness.

A sixteenth-century hymn says it well: "Jesus, Thy blood and righteousness, Thy beauty are, my glorious dress." What God sees is beauty that is not our own. It was bought with a price. The precious blood of Jesus was shed for believers to be right with God . . . to be clothed with Christ.

Be beautiful. Wear Christ.

Read Isaiah 61:10.

JESUS, LET THE MIRROR OF MY LIFE REFLECT YOU.

SAINT THÉRÈSE OF LISIEUX

[God] has always given me what I desired, or rather He has made me desire what He wishes to give.

YOUR HEART'S DESIRE

Sit with an older believer and ask about the workings of God in his life. He will talk about answered prayers and amazing miracles. He may even make the statement, "Well, I thought I wanted this, but then God gave me that, and I found that what God gave me was better than anything I could ever have desired."

That's how God works. As we walk closely with him, our desires become his desires. And when our own desires fall short, God is there, waiting with a gift beyond measure.

God's "other plans" lead to things you never imagined. Suddenly you turn a corner—and find *his* plans satisfying your heart.

He will give you your desires by helping you to desire what he wishes to give. That's how much he loves you.

Read Psalm 37:3–6.

MAKE MY DESIRES YOUR DESIRES, DEAR LORD.

DAVID SEAMANDS

God's love is an action toward us, not a reaction to us. His love depends not on what we are but on what He is.

AN ACTING LOVE

Actions are purposeful maneuvers, the results of desire and longing, by-products of the need to accomplish something. A potter acts by molding clay into a vase. A captain acts by steering his ship out to sea. A construction worker acts by hammering nails into wood. A mother acts by feeding her hungry child.

In 1 John 4, God's love is not only a verb—an action—it is a power with its own will. His will.

His perfect love drives out fear. When God's children accept this powerful, perfected love, they can care for others with the same purposeful intent with which God has reached out to them. His love truly depends on who he is. God himself is love.

Read 1 John 4:16–19.

JOHN OF THE CROSS

For a soul will never grow until it is able to let go of the tight grasp it has on God.

LOOSEN YOUR GRIP

Do you cling to the God you've always known? Maybe he's the God your parents and Sunday school teachers taught you about when you were young. He might be the very same God you trusted for salvation at a tender age. You are comfortable with this God and the ways he speaks.

Being grounded in the knowledge of such a personal God is likely the best blessing you have been given. But if your understanding of God remains the same throughout your life, your growth will be stunted.

God never changes. His attributes remain exactly the same in proportion and number for all eternity. But to a soul open to deeper understanding, God reveals more of himself. Where is he working that broadens your understanding of him? Look, see, and understand that he is much more than you can comprehend. You will never reach the end of knowing him.

Read Matthew 13:10–17.

LOOSEN MY GRIP ON WHO I BELIEVE YOU ARE. REVEAL YOURSELF ANEW.

CATHERINE MARSHALL

God insists that we ask, not because He needs to know our situation, but because we need the spiritual discipline of asking.

WHY PRAY?

God tells us in his Word to pray about everything. Yet he already knows everything. So what is the point of prayer?

Compare it to a child who comes to a parent with a request. When we pray, we are that child—humbling ourselves before our heavenly Father, admitting our limitations, trusting his desire to provide, and acknowledging his resources.

In the process of approaching him, in asking him to take care of us, in making our requests known, *we* mature. We grow both in our understanding of ourselves and of God. And we learn to trust as well.

God commands us to pray, and pray specifically, because he knows it is good for us. Our loving Father wants to help us mature in our faith through the spiritual discipline of prayer. He knows that prayer brings us closer to his heart.

Read Psalm 5:1–3.

DEAR FATHER, THANK YOU FOR CARING
ABOUT ME AS YOUR BELOVED CHILD.

RAVI ZACHARIAS

Prayer is not the means of bringing our wills to pass but the means by which He brings our will into line to gladly receive His will.

NOT MY WILL, BUT GOD'S

Jesus didn't mince words. When facing the horror of the cross, he asked God to take it away. But then came the words that bring us to our knees: he said, "Not my will, but yours be done." Jesus knew his prayer wasn't about getting his way; it was about doing God's will and trusting it.

Conforming who we are to God's will is a process that takes a lifetime. The refining never ends.

Maybe you're in a situation where you're thinking, *I don't want God's will this time!* That hard conversation at home? Deductions at tax time? Choosing to give away money earmarked for a TV?

When those times come, you know it's time to get in God's presence and ask him to realign your priorities—not your will, but his.

Read Luke 22:42.

LORD, YOUR WILL IS, AND WILL ALWAYS BE, THE BEST WAY. CONFORM MY WILL TO YOURS.

JOHN ORTBERG

I have never known someone leading a spiritually transformed life who had not been deeply saturated in Scripture.

GOD'S MASTERPIECE

Masters of foreign language require many semesters of study before they are fluent. Airplane pilots need countless hours of both simulated and actual flight before they can safely soar the skies. Authors and artists alike endure years of creating, re-creating, and being critiqued before realizing their masterpieces. Progressing in our relationship with God—learning his ways and character—takes time and practice too.

Do you want to lead a spiritually transformed life that is worthy of God's kingdom? Then saturate yourself in Scripture—reading it, memorizing it, studying it, meditating on it. Take time to pray, to worship, to be still before your Creator. As you daily immerse yourself in a relationship with the living God and a study of his Word, your life will become his masterpiece.

Read Hebrews 4:12.

GIVE ME A DESIRE TO BE SATURATED IN SCRIPTURE, LORD.

TERESA OF AVILA

How beautiful is the soul after having been immersed in God's grandeur and united closely to Him for but a short time!

IMMERSED IN GOD

We spend a lot of time and money creating beauty for ourselves—whether through our bodies or in our surroundings. We may spend far less energy, however, on beautifying our souls. Yet that is where our beauty—or lack of it—really shines through.

You don't see your soul in the mirror, but it is hinted at there. Look deep behind the eyes; notice the expression of your mouth, the worry lines on your forehead. Those hints reveal what is happening in your soul.

Do you want a beautiful soul? Immerse yourself in the things of God. Stare at the stars. Gaze into the face of a baby. Spend a special day with a friend. Sit quietly and consider God's hand in your life. Journal your prayers. Read his Word just because. Before long, the beauty of God's handiwork within will filter outward and beautify your world.

Read John 15:4–5.

HELP ME, LORD, TO IMMERSE MYSELF IN
PRAYER, AND TO MAKE IT A HABIT.

STEPHEN ARTERBURN

If you are grateful that God has forgiven you through Christ, then you naturally will extend to others what has been extended to you.

ANYTHING BUT EASY

In a child's world, arguments happen all the time over lost or broken toys and even mean looks. Before long, kicking and screaming ensue, and everyone ends up in tears. Usually, though, after a time-out, apologies are made and the incident is forgotten.

If only adult issues were that simple to resolve! In the adult world, differing opinions derail office projects and business partnerships. Marriages turn sour over disagreements. Misunderstandings separate families for generations. Spats divide close friends, turning them into adversaries.

Jesus spoke in Matthew 6 about the importance of forgiveness. Not only does a lack of forgiveness affect others, but it also hinders our own spiritual walk. If Christ willingly forgave us despite our many sins—if he could hang on a cross that *we* nailed him to and ask God to forgive us—surely we can offer that same grace to others. Love and forgiveness do not wait to be earned.

Read Matthew 6:14–15.

JESUS, GIVE ME THE SAME FORGIVING ATTITUDE YOU HAVE.

CHARLES HADDON SPURGEON

Divine love is its own cause and does not follow from anything in us whatsoever. It flows spontaneously from the heart of God.

FOUNTAIN OF LOVE

In Victor Hugo's *Les Miserables*, a priest opens his home to a man named Jean Valjean, giving him food and shelter—only to have Valjean steal a silver plate and cup and run away. When Valjean is caught by the police, they ask the priest to confirm that Valjean stole the items. Instead, in a surprising act of grace, the man of God declares they were a gift and asks Valjean why he forgot to take the candlesticks that go with the set. Valjean, staggered by such kindness, is forever changed. And from that day forward, he vows to lead a life of honesty, generosity, and graciousness.

It took only one act of self-sacrificing love to radically alter the life of that criminal. But for some people, one self-sacrificing act by the Son of God isn't enough. They want more "evidence" before they'll turn from their ways.

What about you? Have you come face-to-face with God's boundless, incomprehensible love? Have you let it change your life?

Read 1 John 4:19.

LORD, I AM NOT WORTHY OF YOUR LIMITLESS
LOVE, BUT I PRAISE YOU FOR IT.

JOHN MAXWELL

Developing an effective prayer life depends on keeping your relationship with God strong and uncluttered by sin and disobedience.

SWEET FORGIVENESS

During the 1970s a management consultant conducted an experiment with results that stunned the companies that hired him. The man would charge into a factory and select a worker at random, then point his finger at the person and yell, "You're fired! And you know why! Get out, now!"

Seven out of ten people he did this to would lower their heads and walk out, red-faced and ashamed. The consultant had no idea what these workers might have done, but it proved his point. Many people are so guilt-ridden about their choices and mistakes that they wilt when they believe they've been "found out."

Likewise, if we know in our hearts that we haven't been honest with God, we are prone to wilt in shame—to avoid coming to him altogether—until we confess. But there is a better way. Let us strive for purity and bring our sins to him instead. There is nothing like the power of his sweet forgiveness to free us from both our sins and our shame.

Read Psalm 38.

KEEP ME CONNECTED TO YOU, LORD, AND
FREE ME OF MY SIN AND ITS SHAME.

ELTON TRUEBLOOD

In this life we are forced to live by faith; in the life to come we shall live, not by faith, but by open vision.

20/20 FAITH

Take a walk down the street on a sunny afternoon, and you'll be squinting in the sun's glare before you know it. Putting on sunglasses enables you to keep going, but your view will still be changed. The scenery becomes dimmer. Details are shadowed. Peripheral vision is narrowed. Yet at least you will no longer be blinded by the sun and hindered from enjoying the day.

Putting on the lens of faith is what enables us to keep traveling on the journey of life. It may be hard to see our destination, blinded as we are by earth's circumstances, but faith allows us enough clarity that we can continue on our way. And then, when we get to heaven, what brilliance we will behold! We'll no longer need the aid of faith; our vision will be clear and complete . . . everything in high-definition!

Persevere on your journey today. Ask God to help you see what you need to see so that you can glimpse a hope and promise for your future.

Read 1 Corinthians 3:12–15.

GOD, HELP ME TO SEE CLEARLY ON MY JOURNEY TODAY.

RAY STEDMAN

The Lord does not simply treat our symptoms and stop there.

THE RIGHT MEDICINE

When we accidentally injure ourselves in the middle of a busy day, sometimes there's barely enough time to slap on a bandage—let alone examine it, clean it, or apply any medicine—on our way to the next task.

Isn't it good to know that the Lord doesn't take that approach with us? As the Great Physician, he cares just as much about the cause of our pain as he does the symptoms.

No matter what your wound or source of pain, call on the Great Physician today. He still makes house calls! Fair warning, though—he'll be thorough. He won't just affix a bandage to the problem. He'll want to evaluate, assess, and examine your life. Then, with skill and precision, he will write the perfect prescription for a comprehensive treatment that will lead to your healing.

What in your life is injured today? The doctor is in, and his appointment book is open.

Read Luke 10:30–35.

LORD, TREAT ALL THAT AILS ME TODAY.

LESSLIE NEWBIGIN

Christian growth means the gradual working out in our own life of what has been given to us.

WHAT'S COOKIN'?

Brisket in the slow cooker. Soup simmering on the stove. Barbecue in the smoker. With time, a few simple ingredients can become a masterful dish that would delight any palate.

Our growth as a Christian is like those savory dishes—and we already have the ingredients. We just need to mix them together and start cooking. The main ingredient, salvation in Christ, is already in the pot. The rest of the ingredients are in the pantry waiting for you. Jars and boxes marked with labels like justice, mercy, love, truth, holiness, faithfulness, goodness, grace, and wisdom fill the shelves.

What's on the menu for your spiritual growth today? God offers all we need for life and godliness. Allow who he is and what he is doing to gradually work itself out in your life today, like the aroma of a delicious, slow-cooked meal.

Read Colossians 1:9–12.

MAKE ME A PLEASING AROMA TODAY, LORD.

JOHN BUNYAN

I cannot form words to express my real spiritual needs, but you can see into my heart—so answer me!

THE DARKEST NIGHT

A young woman lay in her bed. Sleep had eluded her for hours as she tossed and turned. She knew what was keeping her awake: her mind couldn't stop thinking about her problems at work, her shallow relationships, and, even worse, her complete lack of faith that God still cared about her. But then the moonlight shone through the blinds and illuminated her face, reminding her—as silent tears streamed down her cheeks—that the Light of the World still watched over her.

Life is sometimes like the night: with seemingly no end to the darkness, just solitude and loneliness. Problems appear larger than life, and cries to God seem to go unanswered. Paul explained in Romans 8 that at our weakest point, the Holy Spirit will speak for us, communicating what we ourselves do not know we need. After all, who knows our hearts and our needs better than the One who created us?

Read Romans 8:26–27.

THANK YOU FOR YOUR INTERCEDING HOLY SPIRIT, FATHER.

J. I. PACKER

We were made in [God's] image, but we must not think of him as existing in ours.

HOW WE THINK OF GOD

I think of God as a/an _____." Some might fill in that blank with words like *Judge, Father, Artist, Creator, Friend*. But can those titles, drawn from Scripture but interpreted by our finite understanding of human nature, ever adequately describe our great God? Do they even begin to express his character, his omniscience, his omnipresence?

In our considerations about God, we dare not describe him based only on our limited human knowledge. And we must not even imagine him as Michelangelo painted him on the ceiling of the Sistine Chapel. For while such portrayals may evoke a spirit of reverence, they can never show us a complete picture of God.

If we want to know him as he really is, we must devote ourselves to a lifelong study of his Word, an enduring walk with him—and a diligence in getting to know him through his Son.

Read Isaiah 55:8–9.

FATHER, SHOW ME YOURSELF THROUGH
THE PAGES OF YOUR WORD.

MAY

HANNAH WHITALL SMITH

[The will of God] gilds the darkest hours with a divine halo, and sheds brightest sunshine on the gloomiest paths.

LIGHT IN A DARK PLACE

It is no secret that some days are dark. At times, our darkness might be so deep that we cannot see the next step on the path—so we sit on the side of life's road, afraid to take a step because we might fall or trip or walk over the edge of a cliff.

Darkness can be frightening. But our Lord, the Light of the world, understands. In our darkest hours, he shines the brightness of his glory on our gloomy paths. When we look to the Father, he will give us light and show us the way.

When you are lonely, *he is there*. When you are anxious, *he is there*. When you see only darkness, *he is there with the light of life*.

Read John 8:12.

LIGHT MY PATH TODAY, LORD, FOR I NEED THE LIGHT OF LIFE.

MARTIN LUTHER

When you are given a good day, here's what you should do: be happy. In other words, enjoy the present.

DON'T WORRY, BE HAPPY

It has been a long week, but today is Friday. The sun is brightly shining, with a blue sky, light wind, perfect temperature. Could it get any better?

"Could you come into my office?" your boss asks at lunchtime. "You've done great work this month. Take this afternoon off. Here are two tickets to that big show downtown. Fifth row. My treat."

On the way home, you make every green light, even that one at the complicated six-way intersection.

A good day? Believe it! Don't feel guilty. Be happy. Thank God for today (and for next Monday). And remember that he loves you—on the good days as much as on the bad days.

Read Psalm 34:8–10.

YOU ARE THE GOD WHO LOVES ME DURING TOUGH
TIMES AND GOOD TIMES. THANK YOU!

CHARLES SWINDOLL

Some of his choicest deliveries come through the back doors of our lives.

THE PARCEL

We stare at the parcel on the back porch of life, not wanting to pick it up. Its wrapping is ugly, with no return address. The unwelcome package contains a family crisis, financial woes, or a challenge at work—something that will surely keep our thoughts running in circles and leave us numb. We instinctively know that its contents will bring pain and sorrow or anxiety and grief.

Yet God often wraps his choicest deliveries in those unwanted packages. Unexpected provision, deeper faith, more lasting friendships, unfathomed blessings.

Even if you're in survival mode today, stay open. We have a creative God. You may be afraid to check underneath all the wrapping, but he knows exactly what is coming to your back door—and he's got you covered. Hang onto him as you pick up the parcel.

Read 2 Corinthians 9:15.

*FATHER GOD, HELP ME TO LOOK FOR YOUR
GOOD GIFT IN ANY DELIVERY TODAY.*

EVELYN UNDERHILL

Spiritual achievement costs much, though never as much as it is worth.

SPIRITUAL ACHIEVEMENT

When we hear the word *achievement,* we think of objective measures of success, such as a CEO building a company, an athlete winning a race, or a scientist discovering a cure. We don't usually associate *achievement* with the spiritual life. Perhaps that is because we are accustomed to equating achievement with awards, accolades, and acclaim. But spiritual achievement is an inner transformation that is not usually accompanied by outward recognition.

So what is spiritual achievement? It is developing and maturing a life of love and prayer directed to God and serving others in his name. The time and effort we put into our spiritual life will result in inner growth and change, preparing us for an eternity of worshiping God. That is true spiritual achievement. And only God can measure it.

Read Matthew 7:7–8.

DEAR FATHER, HELP ME TO PRIORITIZE MY SPIRITUAL GROWTH.

JOHN WHITE

Unless you can identify and ditch competing goals and loyalties, you will never be a man or woman of faith.

COMPETING GOALS AND LOYALTIES

As men and women of faith, our top priority should be our walk with God. But there are many other things that compete for our attention—family, career, financial obligations, relationships. How do we manage our relationships and responsibilities without letting them distract us so much that we lose sight of God?

It is good to examine our goals and loyalties honestly and determine if we need to eliminate some of them. As you identify your priorities, ask yourself:

Am I focused on achieving something that keeps me from spending time devoted to growing in my faith?

Am I loyal to someone or something that is pulling me away from God?

Sometimes we must say no to the good in order to say yes to the best. Today, be a man or woman of faith. Determine to put God first.

Read Hebrews 12:1.

PHILIP YANCEY

Grace comes free of charge to people who do not deserve it and I am one of those people.

GRACE FIRST

Most of us know that God's grace is free—but do we really believe it? Or do we still carry with us a nagging sense that we need to *do* something to be worthy of God's love and attention, such as have a daily quiet time, serve at church, or overcome a particular sin?

If we are honest with ourselves, performing these deeds makes us feel like we're earning God's favor or even that we deserve God's love. But the simple truth is that no matter what we do or don't do, we cannot earn God's grace.

Grace is a gift.

As we celebrate the gift of God's grace to us, may we also be bearers of that grace to others. And may what we *do* for Jesus simply be the grateful response of our grace-filled hearts.

Read Ephesians 2:8–9.

REMIND ME, LORD, THAT YOUR GRACE IS FREE, AND
I CANNOT DO ANYTHING TO DESERVE IT.

Ajith Fernando

After all that Christ has done for us, we should find it difficult to persist in dishonoring and disregarding Him by continuing in sin.

DON'T CONTINUE IN SIN

Jesus Christ, the King of kings, left his throne in heaven and humbled himself to come to earth, where he was born in poverty, endured suffering, and died on the cross to pay for our sin. How could we dishonor his sacrifice by continuing in the very sin that he died for?

As believers, we should find it difficult to persist in sin. Yet we all struggle with sinful behavior. Like the disciples, we fall asleep instead of laboring in prayer. Like Peter, we deny Christ when we are embarrassed in front of our friends. We give into temptation and wander into sins that lead us far from God. We tire of obedience and whimper at the constant call to submit.

Jesus loved us sacrificially. But when we continue in sin, we are disregarding his sacrifice. Let us refuse to continue in sinful patterns. Let us honor him who gave his life for us.

Read Psalm 51:10–13.

THANK YOU FOR ALL THAT YOU HAVE DONE FOR ME. I GIVE YOU MY LOVE AND OBEDIENCE.

CHARLES STANLEY

God's peace is not a denial of reality. . . . He intends for us to confront reality with our faith and with an abiding peace in our hearts.

REALITY CHECK

How would you describe your life right now—does the word *peace* come to mind? Many believers struggle with experiencing God's peace in the midst of our real, here-and-now difficulties. We think that the only way we'll find peace is by pretending everything is just fine. But God knows the reality you are facing, as well as what is ahead tomorrow and for the rest of your life.

Finding God's peace doesn't mean we have to deny our struggles or pretend that our life is calm and serene. Our Lord never asks us to lie to him, to others, or to ourselves about reality. On the contrary, God wants us to confront our difficulties, knowing that when we approach the cross, we approach an omniscient God who is intimately aware of the difficulties we are facing.

When God offers us his abiding peace, we can trust that he will give it to us, even in the midst of our reality.

Read Hebrews 4:14–16.

THANK YOU FOR UNDERSTANDING MY REAL LIFE.
HELP ME FIND PEACE IN THE MIDST OF IT.

GEORGE WHITEFIELD

Whilst I continue on this side of eternity, I never expect to be free from trials, only to change them.

TIME FOR CHANGE

Choosing to follow Jesus Christ doesn't mean that your life will be free from trials; it means pursuing him no matter what trials you encounter. Our greatest heroes of the faith were men and women who suffered as they served God.

Why do we think Jesus' call to carry our cross daily has changed?

Jesus said that in this world we will have trouble. We can let the struggles of this life cause us to get angry and sulk. Or we can pursue God in the midst of our trials, asking him to help us endure them faithfully.

We might still find this life full of thistles and thorns, but if we are God's servants, the Holy Spirit will bring us through it. He will help us change those trials to become God's tools to do work beyond what we can imagine.

Read Luke 14:25–33.

LORD, TAKE MY LIFE—ALL PARTS OF IT. I GIVE UP
EVERYTHING, COME WHAT MAY; I AM YOUR SERVANT.

TONY EVANS

It should be abnormal for us as Christians not to pray. Prayer should be as normal a part of our daily lives as eating and breathing.

PRAYER LIVING

I 'll pray for you." Have you ever said that to someone, and then forgotten to pray? Or have you closed your eyes at Sunday morning worship only to realize it was the first time you prayed all week?

Chances are, we notice if we haven't eaten in a few hours. It would only take a few seconds to discover we were in trouble if we couldn't breathe. Prayer should be the same— we should be unable to get through a day without prayer. We should notice if a few hours have gone by and we haven't been in touch with our Lord.

Prayer is as important as eating and breathing, for it is our lifeline to the one who guides us and walks with us through each day.

Today, practice the presence of prayer. See what happens!

Read 1 Thessalonians 5:17.

TODAY, LORD, I AM CONNECTED TO YOU. REMIND
ME TO PRAY WITHOUT CEASING.

DONALD MILLER

In exchange for our. . .willingness to accept the charity of God, we are given a kingdom. And a beggar's kingdom is better than a proud man's delusion.

A BEGGAR'S KINGDOM

Everywhere you look, people are busy trying to build their own "kingdoms" of power and influence. They strive and sacrifice to make a name for themselves. Desperate to prove their independence, these men and women exhaust themselves chasing worldly success and self-sufficiency. Yet even seemingly noble intentions reflect insidious pride.

God offers us so much more than the delusion of success—he offers us his kingdom, on his terms. We must come helpless and humble, knowing that we cannot gain his kingdom on our own; we only obtain it when we humbly accept Christ's love and sacrifice on our behalf. We come as beggars, and then we are given an esteemed place in God's kingdom as his adopted children.

Don't be too proud to accept God's charity. Only when we become beggars will we experience the riches of God's grace.

Read Matthew 18:1–5.

FATHER, LET ME REALIZE HOW HELPLESS I AM WITHOUT YOU.

BROTHER LAWRENCE

We must nourish our souls with a lofty idea of God, and in this way we can take great joy in belonging to Him.

NOURISH YOUR SOUL

Can a human body survive on junk food? The answer is, technically, yes; your body can eke existence out of abysmal nourishment, even if all you consume is food with the nutritional value of a paper bag. However, as any dedicated athlete can tell you, feeding solely on cheeseburgers and potato chips will weaken your body and sap your strength. Junk food may taste good for a time, but it inevitably fails to satisfy because it cannot feed your body properly.

Why then do we feast our minds and souls on spiritual junk? We are meant to fill ourselves with holiness, yet we let our minds consume the "empty carbs" of gossip, lies, pornography, blasphemy, slander, and cursing.

Make it a priority to nourish your soul by consuming *good* food for your spirit and mind today, and spend time focusing on our infinitely fulfilling God.

Read Philippians 4:4–9.

GOD, NOURISH MY SOUL WITH YOUR LOVE AND TRUTH.

C. S. LEWIS

"We know not what we shall be"; but we may be sure we shall be more, not less, than we were on earth.

BECOMING MORE

The Grand Canyon is renowned for its majesty and grandeur. Two hundred and seventy-seven miles long, eighteen miles wide, and up to a mile deep . . . few places can make a human feel so small. Yet, if someone has never been to the Grand Canyon, how can we describe it? Mere words aren't enough to capture its breathtaking beauty and magnitude.

Our eternal state is similarly impossible to describe adequately. Some depictions of our eternity in heaven even make it seem boring. But God promises us something far greater: a place of eternal fulfillment. In heaven we will be more, not less, than we are here on earth. What that means, we do not yet know. But one day, we will.

We can trust that God will make our eternity better than we can even imagine.

Read Philippians 3:20–21.

FATHER, I CAN'T WAIT TO BE WITH YOU!

GREG LAURIE

God sees everything. You cannot outwit God. Nor can you mock him—without consequences.

OUR OMNIPOTENT GOD

Popular movies portray God as capricious or even mock him as weak and uncaring. As a result, people often consider God as a distant but doting figure, not really paying much attention to the world or its inhabitants.

But God's Word tells a different story. We serve a God whose voice can melt the earth. His right hand upholds the universe. He speaks, and creation rushes to obey. He knows *everything*. There is nothing we can hide from him. He will not be mocked without consequence. And we cannot outwit, outrun, or outdo him in any way.

Yet this magnificent God—this all-powerful Creator of heaven and earth—stoops to embrace us. He is the unquestionable King of everything . . . but he is also our Father. Knowing this, we approach his throne boldly, secure in our position as coheirs with Christ; but let us never forget that we approach a *throne*.

Read Psalm 46.

HELP ME REALIZE JUST HOW GREAT YOU ARE, LORD.

Henri Nouwen

We cannot speak or even think about the resurrection without entering into the depth of our grief.

OUR GRIEF, OUR JOY

The resurrection of Christ is God's greatest act of redemptive grace. Nothing before or since has demonstrated God's love so grandly. Jesus rising from the grave signified God's triumph over death and the reconnection of humanity to the Father.

Looking back from this side of the cross, it's easy to forget the awful price our sin demanded. Because of our failure, God himself came to save us; because of our selfishness, he died in our place. Too often we fail to reflect on this sobering reality: we are responsible for the murder of our Savior.

We've grown desensitized to the idea that Christ had to die for us to live: how else could we hear sermons about his sacrifice without being overwhelmed with the desire to weep for the death of our Savior?

Yet, even so, our grief contrasts with joy. Though the price was high—higher than we could pay—God has saved us. Praise our Father: we are saved!

Read 1 Peter 2:21–25

FATHER, THANK YOU THAT YOUR SON'S SACRIFICE HAS SAVED ME!

KEN GIRE

With barely a ripple of notice, God stepped into the warm lake of humanity. Without protocol and without pretention.

SECURE IN POWER

There's an odd thing about power: the more powerful you are, the less you need to tell people about it. We all know by experience that the more people need to talk about themselves, the less secure they are.

Imagine for a moment, then, the immense majesty of a God so secure in his power that he is willing to be born to poor parents in a drafty barn; to mingle with dirty, flawed human beings; and, ultimately, to be mocked, scorned, and publicly executed.

We often forget just how much dignity Jesus could have claimed. As the ruler of the universe, the King of kings would have been justified in commanding humanity to afford him *proper* respect.

Yet the Lord of creation humbled himself. Why then do we cling to dignity when our all-powerful God never asked for fanfare?

Read Philippians 2:5–11.

MAKE ME HUMBLE, AS CHRIST WAS.

LLOYD JOHN OGILVIE

Become what you are; live in the status already given. Use the resources already released; claim the gifts already appropriated.

BECOME WHAT YOU ARE

It seems like there's a new smartphone or electronic gadget out every other week. Each incarnation features some fascinating upgrade of computing—only to be outdone in a few months by another version with even more bells and whistles.

We too often think that way about ourselves: we figure we constantly need upgrades. We say that we'll wait to serve until we're "more prepared," we'll get involved in a church "once we find one that we like," and we'll give to missions "when we have more money."

Don't wait. Serve now. Get involved now. Give now. God has already released the resources for the task. He has given you the gifts you need. Use what you have, and God will take care of the rest.

As you are faithful to become what you are, one day you will hear his precious words: "Well done, my good and faithful servant."

Read Matthew 25:14–30.

FATHER, SHOW ME HOW TO USE WHAT
YOU HAVE ENTRUSTED TO ME.

SØREN ·KIERKEGAARD

Oh! Wonderful, wonderful! That the one who has helped to give is the one who says, Come hither!

COME AND SEE!

Once upon a time, people who wanted to cheat others by selling balms and pills that promised much but delivered little, traveled alone and moved from place to place to make a dishonest living. Nowadays, they bark at us from the nearest television or Internet banner advertisement. They clamor for our attention: "Come here! You must see this!" Too often people fall for the flashy ads and spend their hard-earned money on empty promises.

Someone else in our world is calling out to us: "Come hither!" But what God promises delivers more than we can imagine. He calls us to bring our burdens to him so that he can give us rest and peace. He promises to give us life that matters, life that works. He promises to take the bad things and turn them good. He promises to be with us now and forever.

Wonderful, wonderful indeed!

Read Matthew 11:28–30.

THANK YOU FOR YOUR PROMISE OF REST AND FULFILLMENT.

CORRIE TEN BOOM

Worry does not empty tomorrow of its sorrow; it empties today of its strength.

TURNING *WHAT IF?* INTO *WHY NOT?*

So many of us fret about the *what-ifs*. What if this happens, or that? What if it doesn't happen?

God tells us not to worry about the *what-ifs* but rather to pray about everything. So why don't we do it? *We can't possibly bother God with a problem like ours,* we think. Or we believe we can handle it; we can figure out how to solve it if we only worry about it long enough. Yet the more we worry, the more anxious we become.

Instead, we should trust Christ for today's troubles and those coming up. Otherwise, it's hard to be productive or to stay focused on Christ. Philippians 4:6 implores us to tell God what we need, and to thank him for what he will do. Why not give that a try and experience peace, God's way?

Read Philippians 4:4–7.

PLEASE HELP ME NOT TO WORRY AND, INSTEAD,
TO THANK YOU FOR WHAT YOU WILL DO.

RANDY ALCORN

Five minutes after we die, we'll know exactly how we should have lived.

NO REGRETS

Every day we have to make choices: *Should I ask her out? Which college should I attend? Should I tell him about the struggles I'm having at work?* This daily decision making can be tough.

In hindsight, it's often easier to know exactly what should have been done. *That relationship was a bad idea. I should have waited to buy that car. Why did I eat that second cheeseburger?*

Regret is the downside of memory, and it's almost impossible to escape. All people have some sorts of regrets, whether they are minor or life-changing decisions. Regrets are the consequences of being imperfect.

But God has redeemed us from our past, and he's given us a road map in the Bible to a life with no regrets. On our own we would get lost; but, as we seek God and his wisdom, he will show us the way.

Read Psalm 103.

FATHER, I DON'T WANT TO LIVE WITH REGRET. HELP ME TO BE BETTER; PICK ME UP WHEN I FALL.

MIKE MASON

In the Bible joy and rest are intimately linked.

THE JOY OF REST

Superheroes never seem to rest. When does Batman get a personal day? Superman's Fortress of Solitude is always a little cluttered—there's no time for cleaning when the world needs to be saved, after all.

Often, we think we can live like superheroes. We'll spend the whole week running around, and when we reach the weekend, we stay busy with the tasks that need finishing. Soon enough, our days become joyless because even our "rest"— playing video games or watching television—isn't very restful.

Jesus knew the importance of *real* rest: rest found in the Father. After a day spent healing the sick and lame, he would retreat to spend time with God. Today, take a few moments in your own Fortress of Solitude with the God who loves you sincerely. There you will find true joy.

Read Mark 1:31–35.

I AM TIRING MYSELF OUT. LET ME REST IN YOU, O GOD.

JONI EARECKSON TADA

The one who is faithful in tough times catches God's eye.

STAY FAITHFUL

The Bible is filled with the stories of men and women who remained faithful during tough times. Remember the account of Joseph in the Old Testament? From a young age Joseph knew he was special. His dad favored him above all of his brothers, and God favored him by allowing him to dream of the future. Even so, he was thrust into some truly awful circumstances:

His brothers sold him into slavery.

His boss's wife accused him of attempted rape.

He spent years in an Egyptian prison.

Yet Joseph remained faithful to God. With God's blessing, Joseph became second-in-command of all Egypt.

What are you going through today? Tough times take a lot out of us—physically, emotionally, and spiritually. At the time when bad things happen, we might not feel like God even notices. But we can follow the example of Joseph: keep dreaming and be faithful to God, even in the tough times.

Read Genesis 39:20–23.

LORD, HELP ME REMAIN FAITHFUL TO YOU EVEN IN THE TOUGH TIMES, BECAUSE YOU ARE FAITHFUL TO ME.

MADELEINE L'ENGLE

Time to be with God is essential in order that our work may indeed be God's work, not ours.

DEEP ROOTS

Seeds that blow onto rocky soil rarely find a place to put down deep roots. Without solid grounding and nutrition, seedlings wither or stay small.

People need grounding and nourishment too. Perhaps you've set aside a portion of each day to read, learn, pray, and grow more deeply into the rich and nourishing soil of God's Word. This time you spend with him is as important as eating and sleeping. When Jesus was tempted by Satan, he demonstrated that we can overcome the tempter's snares by knowing the Scriptures. The psalmist knew it was important to spend time with God, reminding us that his Word will light our way in a dark world (Psalm 119:105).

Going without nourishment or rest for too long makes you weak. Don't let your spiritual life become weak—keep it strong and healthy by spending time with God.

Read Matthew 4:1–11.

THANK YOU FOR OUR TIME TOGETHER, LORD.

DWIGHT L. MOODY

God never made a promise that was too good to be true.

MEANINGFUL PROMISES

The Bible is filled with thousands of promises from God. The most important promise he makes to us is this: he will save anyone who calls upon the name of Jesus Christ. First John 1:9 tells us that if we confess our sins, he is faithful to cleanse us from all unrighteousness. And he promises us that nothing in this world—not even death—will be able to separate us from his love (Romans 8:35–39).

We know God will keep his promises because the Bible also tells us that God cannot lie (Hebrews 6:18). What a blessing! We have assurance that when God says something, he means it.

God will never make a promise that he cannot keep. His promises are astounding, and they are trustworthy. We can stand firm in our faith knowing it is built upon a solid and unchanging foundation.

Read Hebrews 10:23.

DEAR FATHER, THANK YOU FOR KEEPING YOUR PROMISES!

EUGENE PETERSON

The word busy is the symptom not of commitment but of betrayal. It is not devotion but defection.

DO YOU HAVE THE TIME?

Do you want to spend more time with God? Perhaps you want to read your Bible and pray, but you're just too busy.

An old song by Harry Chapin laments how the busyness of a father keeps him from spending time with his son. When the father is older and regretting lost time, he attempts to make up for it by spending time with his adult son. But his son has no time to give. He's simply too busy.

Our heavenly Father is always there for us whenever we call on him. He's even there watching over us when our lives are so busy we don't have time to think!

Make time for God today and every day. Spend time in prayer, in praise, in person with him. Don't come to the end of your life full of regret that you could have spent more time learning, growing, and sharing God's love.

Read Ephesians 1:18–20.

I WANT TO SPEND MORE TIME WITH YOU, LORD.
HELP ME MAKE THE TIME EACH DAY.

REBECCA MANLEY PIPPERT

The problem stems from our great difficulty in believing that God is glorified in our utter humanity rather than in our spiritually programmed responses.

WEAKNESS OR STRENGTH?

We show up at church every Sunday. We sing the same songs and say prayers from memory. We volunteer and serve and give. We put on a smile and work ourselves into exhaustion for this or that cause.

How much is enough? Is God glorified by our spiritually programmed responses, even if our hearts just aren't in it? We obediently go and give and do, but where is the love, the adoration, the praise?

God's power is made perfect in our weakness. When we try to live the spiritual life in our own power, our weakness is exposed. When we let God take over—when we admit our utter humanity and allow him to lead—he will give us the strength to do what he wants us to do.

The result will deepen our worship, develop our character, and bring glory to his name.

Read 2 Corinthians 12:7–10.

LORD, GLORIFY YOURSELF IN MY WEAKNESS.

TERESA OF AVILA

The soul of the just person is nothing else but a paradise where the Lord says he finds his delight.

GOD'S PARADISE

We think of paradise as a perfect place. A place of refuge. A mighty fortress. We find our paradise in the shadow of the Almighty.

But God? He finds paradise in a soul . . . the soul of a person who is fair, honorable, upright, and filled with his righteousness.

Do you wonder how that can be? Think of your heart as a cup. Take a deep, deep breath and envision God filling your cup—your soul—with himself. Seek his righteous presence. Imagine his delight as he pours goodness, justice, fairness into you.

Imagine his delight when you take that justice into your world!

Read Zephaniah 3:17.

I LONG, O GOD, FOR YOU TO REJOICE OVER ME
AND TO TAKE PLEASURE IN WHO I AM.

AUGUSTINE OF HIPPO

God loves each of us as if there were only one of us.

AN UNDENIABLE TREASURE

We tend to think of ourselves as common, run-of-the-mill, or average. When we look at the extraordinary gifts and talents of other people, we consider ourselves to be ordinary in comparison. But to God, each of us is exceptional, unequaled, beyond measure.

Because we are specially designed by God, we are incomparable, perfect in every way. God has a special love for each of his sons and daughters, as a father loves each of his children. Each of us is an undeniable treasure, in a class by ourselves, one-of-a-kind, and loved uniquely by our heavenly Father. And through the sacrifice of his sinless son, Jesus our Lord, we are a cherished member of God's family, destined to spend eternity with him in heaven.

Jesus Christ died freely for the church, and he loves each of us as if we were the only person on this planet. His shed blood has removed our imperfections. And though we still sin, when God looks at us now, all that's in view is Jesus.

Read 1 Corinthians 15:20–23.

LORD, HELP ME TO NEVER FORGET WHAT
YOU DID FOR ME AT CALVARY.

SAINT THÉRÈSE OF LISIEUX

To soar above all natural sentiment brings the deepest peace, nor is there any joy equal to that which is felt by the truly poor in spirit.

GRACE IN HUMILITY

Living the way Jesus taught is often in direct contrast to the way the world lives. To be poor in spirit means you understand your own helplessness to stand before a holy God. We recognize that we are nothing apart from the grace of Jesus. What a humbling thought!

If we want to experience the joy of living the way God wants us to live, humbling ourselves is a great place to start. This means giving when it's easier to take, assisting when it's easier to be indifferent, loving others when it's easier to ignore. By being poor in spirit you will be blessed beyond measure and experience God's abiding peace. The rewards might come in this life, and then again, they might not. But God promises that the kingdom of heaven will belong to you.

For the deepest peace, humble yourself and follow Jesus.

Read Matthew 5:3–12

JESUS, HELP ME TO HUMBLY FOLLOW YOU.

RUTH BELL GRAHAM

Are you in a crisis of great magnitude? Cry out to God in your pain. Be honest with him about what you are feeling.

CRY OUT TO GOD

Are you experiencing difficulty today? Perhaps you are struggling through a painful situation or bearing the burden for another who is suffering.

The apostle Paul knew hardships firsthand. He was persecuted, beaten, shipwrecked, and imprisoned. He also suffered from a burden so painful that he described it as a "thorn in his flesh." Paul was honest with God, asking him to take the thorn away. But God reminded him that his grace was all Paul needed (2 Corinthians 12:7–10). His faithfulness is tried and proven.

Whatever difficulty you face today, cry out to God. Pour out your heart to him in prayer and lay all of your pain at God's feet. His power is perfected in our weakness and his grace is just as sufficient for us today as it was for the apostle Paul.

Read Psalm 50:15–17.

LORD, I NEED YOU NOW. BRING YOUR GRACE AND
PEACE TO ME IN THE MIDST OF MY PAIN.

JOHN ORTBERG

The most glorious aspect of [God's] being is that he would take our raggedness upon himself before he would give us up.

GREATER THAN GLORY

Our God is too great for us to imagine. His majesty and power surpass our understanding. How can we, as limited as we are, possibly understand the glory of a deity who creates solar systems with nothing but a word?

Yet there is an even deeper aspect to God—a marvelous impossibility that confounds our attempts to explain it. Why would the Creator of the universe shed his glory and be born into squalor? What could possibly drive him to become obedient to death?

It is the same thing that drives a mother to drop everything for the sake of her child, the same strength that compels a man to take a bullet for his friend. Why is God's greatest glory shown in his willingness to save us? Because there is only one thing as great as God's glory: his infinite, all-expansive, uncontainable love.

Read 1 John 4:9–11.

GOD, YOUR LOVE IS TOO GREAT FOR ME TO UNDERSTAND! THANK YOU, FATHER; I LOVE YOU TOO.

JUNE

CHARLES STANLEY

His voice leads us not into timid discipleship but into bold witness.

BOLDNESS FOR THE TIMID

Psychologists tell us that there are four basic personality types: choleric (excitable), sanguine (confident), phlegmatic (calm), and melancholy (persistent). Depending on your temperament the thought of being a bold witness for Christ might ignite a fire in your soul or it might fill you with dread. As Christians we need to remember that being a witness for Christ doesn't depend upon our personality, but on the Spirit of God working in our lives.

Each of us has spiritual gifts bestowed upon us by our Creator. God created our personalities, and he calls us to be bold witnesses for him whether we are assertive or timid by nature. Our hope in Christ doesn't spring from our temperament but from our salvation.

Scripture urges us to always be willing to share the hope that is within us, in the ways God has prepared for us.

Read 2 Timothy 1:6–7.

LORD, HELP ME TO LOVE OTHERS ENOUGH TO BOLDLY SHARE THE HOPE OF YOUR SALVATION.

Max Lucado

Nails didn't hold God to a cross. Love did.

LOVE STORY

The classic love story has a formula: man meets woman and falls in love. Though the woman's heart may be difficult to win, though her suitor may have to overcome many obstacles to gain her love, we always hope that, in the end, their story culminates in a memorable "happily ever after."

How does the man know he's in love? It's not just that his heart races whenever she walks into the room, or that he gets tongue-tied when he tries to speak to her. He also knows he's in love because he would do anything for this woman. He would gladly give his life for hers, knowing that even though he'd be gone, she'd have another chance at life and happiness.

So, too, with Christ and the church. The church is his beloved, his bride. He didn't just *say* he'd do anything for her; he actually sacrificed his life, giving *everything*—all because of love. What a love story that is! And it can be yours.

Christ's deep love for you held him to the cross, where he died so that you might live.

Read Ephesians 5:29–32.

JESUS, THANK YOU FOR YOUR SACRIFICE AND LOVE.

FREEMAN DYSON

You ask: what is the meaning or purpose of life? I can only answer with another question: do you think we are wise enough to read God's mind?

LEAVE THE FUTURE TO GOD

Tarot card readers. Astrologists. Psychics. Fortune-tellers. All claim to foretell the future. And all are frauds!

The Lord warns against these forms of evil. Deuteronomy 18:10–14 admonishes us to avoid such practices and those who practice them. He wants us to trust him for what lies ahead and rely on no one else.

But in case we applaud ourselves for avoiding such evil, 1 Samuel 15:23–26 reminds us that rebellion is as sinful as witchcraft and stubbornness as bad as worshiping idols. We may not be running to palm readers or consulting mediums to see what the future holds. But is our rebellious and stubborn nature keeping us from seeking God's purposes for our lives? What he wants may not be what we had planned. Our job is to love and obey him anyway.

Read Isaiah 44:21–26.

JESUS, HELP ME TRUST YOU ALONE FOR MY FUTURE, AND NOT WORRY ABOUT WHAT LIES AHEAD.

ANNIE DILLARD

God's love is the most threatening of all, for it demands such faith.

A LEAP OF FAITH

Watch children on a playground. One will climb up high on the monkey bars. His daddy will stand beneath him and say, "Jump into my arms." Without hesitation the miniature Tarzan will leap into the air and fly into the secure grasp of his father. Five minutes later the little boy will again be at the top of the monkey bars. A stranger passing by might say, "Jump; I'll catch you." But the little lad will not jump. His father he trusts, for he knows that Daddy will never fail him, but everyone else is under suspicion.

As Christians, we can take a leap that requires faith—risking all yet risking nothing—for we know our heavenly "Daddy" is there to catch us. Deuteronomy 33:27 says, "The eternal God is your refuge, and underneath are the everlasting arms." Are you ready to leap at the chance to serve him?

Read Luke 1:41.

LORD, THANK YOU FOR UNFAILING ARMS TO
CATCH ME WHEN I LEAP IN FAITH.

CATHERINE OF SIENA

For everything you do will be drawn to him [Christ] when he draws your heart and its powers.

DELIGHTING IN GOD

Christians who serve God out of obligation use words like *ought, duty, expected,* and *necessary.* These words aren't necessarily wrong or bad when pertaining to the faith, but those who cite these as primary reasons for following Christ have lost a sense of a loving, personal relationship with their Savior. It is like the lover who knocks on the front door of his love's house on Valentine's Day, and when she answers he holds out a dozen long-stemmed red roses and says in a flat tone, "Here. These are for you. It's my duty." How appealing would those roses be?

When we express our love for Christ out of duty alone, we sound similar: "There. I've read my Bible. It's my spiritual duty." Such obligatory Christianity when absent a delight in Christ can be loveless and stale. But when we truly delight in him, when we are drawn to him in joy, imagine the pleasure that brings to God's heart.

Read Psalm 33.

OH LORD, MAKE MY HEART GLAD IN YOU!

MARY BETH CHAPMAN

It's in the most unlikely times and places of hurt and chaos that God gives us . . . the real light of His hope.

THE REAL LIGHT

The sun sank below the horizon. The clouds blotted out the stars and moon. Darkness swept over like a canopy. The darkness made the hiker wary— of animals, of losing the trail, of stepping in holes—but he'd come prepared. In his backpack he'd placed a flashlight. During the day, as the sun lit up the man's surroundings, the flashlight was unnecessary. More a burden than a help. A useless accessory. It wasn't until the darkness descended that he turned to it for light.

Like the hiker, we often cannot appreciate the Light of the world until we are faced with dark circumstances. In the blackness we need the light more than anything else. We need the light of hope. We need the light that only God can give.

Read Psalm 27:1–6.

LORD, TEACH ME TO SEE YOUR LIGHT IN THE HARD TIMES.

THOMAS À KEMPIS

He rideth easily enough whom the grace of God carrieth.

SAILING IN STORMS

Have you ever had a day when everything fell apart at once? A day when, suddenly, all the careful plans you laid blew up spontaneously?

These days happen to all of us. Everyone who makes plans will, someday, see them fall apart. In our corrupted, imperfect world, nothing is permanent. Something *will* break. At times, it seems Murphy's Law is as reliable as gravity.

In sailing, often the best way to survive an awful storm is to lower the sails and ride it out. The same is true in life. Though it goes against our every instinct, in time of trouble we must lower our sails—whatever we seem to have control over—and ask God to carry us through the storm.

Take heart; God has not left you. He loves you, and he will not let you drown. Remember that when he is at the helm of your life, you can ride along on his grace as he carries you through.

Read Deuteronomy 31:6.

GOD, IT'S HARD TO SURVIVE THESE STORMS; I
NEED YOU TO CARRY ME THROUGH THEM.

GEORGE MUELLER

Be assured, if you walk with Him and look to Him, and expect help from Him, He will never fail you.

STOOPING TO HELP US

A shepherd wandering in darkness and danger to find and rescue one little lamb. A father setting aside his dignity and running to welcome home the son who rejected him and squandered his money. The Son of God reaching out to touch the hand of a leper. Jesus noticing and praising the generosity of a poverty-stricken widow.

So many of the images we have of God, in the parables and in the human face of his Son, show God stooping down to our level.

Christ was willing to humble himself so that he could help those who were in need. And he continues to reach down to us so we might receive his strength when temptation hits. He is eager to help us. Every time we reach the end of our strength and can't find our way out of difficult circumstances, we need to stop and ask him for help. He is never too proud to stoop to our level to give us the help we need—dare we be too proud to ask?

Read Proverbs 10:22–25.

LORD, LET ME HUMBLY LOOK TO YOU FOR
HELP IN MY TIME OF NEED.

DIETRICH BONHOEFFER

*Like ravens, we have gathered around the carcass of cheap grace.
From it we have imbibed the poison which has killed the
following of Jesus among us.*

A RICH FEAST

Do you find yourself settling for scraps, like scavenging birds on the beach? Or have you pursued the deeper delights of intimate relationship with Jesus Christ? The gift of grace remains free and available to all who come, but its price is beyond what anyone could pay.

In the freedom we are given to fail, God's grace also grants us forgiveness. But receiving this gift with a relaxed attitude toward sin demonstrates little appreciation for the price Jesus paid to make reconciliation possible.

While enjoying the gift of grace today, consider the cost of your forgiveness. Allow this understanding to prompt a deeper commitment to following Jesus, who makes grace free.

Read Romans 6:15–18.

*JESUS, MY SALVATION COST YOU EVERYTHING.
PROMPT ME TO GIVE EVERYTHING BACK.*

OSWALD CHAMBERS

If God can accomplish His purposes in this world through a broken heart, then why not thank Him for breaking yours?

BROKEN

Emotional pain so severe it feels as though daggers are actually ripping through muscle. Anguish that seems to have no end. . . These can't possibly be things to embrace. In the suffering of a broken heart, it feels impossible that any good could possibly come from such bad.

But God offers a salve to our wounded world: his sovereignty.

Kicking and screaming, we reject his calming words in search of explanations and immediate relief. Unfazed, the Son leaves his arms around us until, through the slowing tears, we can focus on the hands. The nail-scarred hands that changed the world.

A broken heart is often the first avenue through which the world is changed. Will you dare to find the purpose for yours? Through the broken heart of our heavenly Father and the sacrifice of his Son, the world is free from sin's bondage. Transformation is possible! Restoration can be ours!

Read Matthew 27:45–54.

FATHER, PLEASE REVEAL YOUR PURPOSES FOR MY BROKENNESS.

CHARLES COLSON

The church is the visible presence on earth of the living although invisible Christ.

HIS HANDS AND FEET

Three times in the New Testament the apostle Paul tells believers that we are all a part of the body of Christ. Jesus is not physically walking the earth and preaching today, but through the church, he shares his love and spreads the good news of salvation to the world.

But what if you're not comfortable speaking in front of crowds? Paul makes reference to that in 1 Corinthians 12. Just because you're not a *mouth* doesn't mean you have nothing to offer as a part of the body of Christ. You might be the *hands*, preparing a meal for a sick friend. Maybe you're the *feet* that deliver a meal. Or you might be the *eyes* that are able to recognize those in need.

As a Christian, you are a part of the body of Christ—and together we are the living, breathing representation of Jesus to our world.

Read 1 Corinthians 12:12–27.

HELP ME TO BE A GOOD REPRESENTATION
OF YOU TO THE WORLD, O LORD.

JOYCE MEYER

God's timing is not our timing, because He knows more about the situations than we do.

PATIENCE IN THE JOURNEY

Are we there yet?" It's the question every child asks during a family road trip. Even adults check their GPS to find out "How much longer?" Yet, no matter how much information we have about road conditions, traffic, and construction, the answer is always an estimate.

Aren't we fortunate to have a more reliable source for the timing of our lives than a man-made satellite in the sky—especially when the timing isn't what we expected or hoped for?

Are you waiting on God today for something? Take heart. God never slumbers or sleeps. He is working—even if visibility is poor and you can't see what he's up to. He is trustworthy. Look to him. Talk to him about the challenging road conditions, the heavy traffic, the construction sites that are causing detours in your life. And as you ask him for help, let him guide your doubts and pain into wisdom, strength, and patience for your journey. He knows the way.

Read 1 Timothy 6:13–15.

GOD, HELP ME TO TRUST YOUR TIMING TODAY.

CHARLES HADDON SPURGEON

Let us use texts of Scripture as fuel for our heart's fire . . .; let us attend sermons, but above all, let us be much alone with Jesus.

BE WITH GOD

Do you read your Bible? Excellent. Knowing God's Word is essential to our growth; it is true knowledge. As we study and learn the truth of Scripture, our passion for him will be strong.

Do you attend a good church? Wonderful. Sermons that point us closer to God help deepen our relationship with him, and spending time with other believers strengthens our faith.

There is more to the Christian life, though. Being alone with Jesus, whether in direct prayer or quietly listening— privately, away from the noise and clatter of this world—is essential to the Christian life. In these solitary moments, we praise him, thank him, confess to him, and tell him we love him . . . when no one else is watching.

Close the door, turn off your cell phone, and be alone with our Lord. Hide his Word in your heart, then return it to him with joy.

Read Psalm 119:9–16.

WHEREVER I AM, LORD, I KNOW YOU ARE WITH ME.

BILLY GRAHAM

Being a Christian is more than just an instantaneous conversion—it is a daily process whereby you grow to be more and more like Christ.

LITTLE BY LITTLE

When you repented and accepted Jesus as your Savior, you were given a fresh start. You turned away from your old life of sin and received God's free gift of salvation. You were born again.

Yet conversion is not limited to a one-time experience; it marks the beginning of a new life of growth and maturity in faith. When you accepted Christ, you became a baby Christian. Just as a newborn child needs nourishment to grow physically from infancy to adulthood, a new Christian needs a steady diet of church attendance, prayer, and Bible study to grow up in the faith. Knowing what you believe and why you believe it allows you to share your faith, even defend it.

Is there ever a point at which you are done growing spiritually? Not until Jesus calls you home. So enjoy the growth process, little by little, every day.

Read 2 Peter 3:18.

LORD, GRANT ME THE WISDOM TO DAILY GROW IN MY FAITH.

ANNE GRAHAM LOTZ

Real meaning to your life is found in the glorious dawn of God's story, which breaks into full revelation in the Person of Jesus Christ.

THE MEANING OF LIFE

What joy the Creator must have had in creation, the glorious dawn of God's history with us. Jesus was there with God at the very beginning, and all of history looked forward to the day when he would descend to the earth he created in order to save his people from their sin.

Jesus was fully God and fully man. Because he was willing to wrap his divine glory in human flesh, he truly understands the human condition. During his days on earth, he experienced the fullness of humanity—sorrow, joy, temptation, hunger, thirst, delight, pain, laughter, and so much more. And even though we are totally unworthy, he allowed himself to become the sacrifice to take care of our sins once and for all.

God's story is our story when we choose to accept the gracious gift of Jesus' sacrifice for us. Real meaning in life is found in our Savior.

Read John 1:1–5; 3:16.

THANK YOU, LORD, FOR BRINGING TRUE MEANING TO MY LIFE.

THOMAS MERTON

We have to see history as a book that is sealed and opened by the Passion of Christ.

MOSAIC

The history of mankind is full of hatred, bigotry, wars, and bloodshed. Collectively, our conscience is stained.

Knowing how dark and shameful our history is, it's difficult to think that anyone is in control of it—much less a benevolent, all-powerful God. Yet Scripture tells us that the book of history is in the hand of God. He has a plan greater than what we can see from our limited perspective. We are like ants crawling around on an enormous mosaic, scoffing, "How on earth could a picture be made of this?" Yet God, who stands outside history, has an intended purpose.

Despite all our flaws, we can take comfort in the fact that God has a great plan for us, one more intricate and beautiful than we can imagine. We are—we have always been—his passion.

Read Jeremiah 29:11–14.

FATHER, I CAN'T SEE THE PLAN YOU HAVE FOR
YOUR PEOPLE. HELP ME TO TRUST IN YOU.

JILL BRISCOE

Why do I submit to the Lord? Because he is my life, my breath . . . the foundation of all I believe, and the source of all meaning.

RESTING IN GOD'S BEST

Submission is a four-letter word in our current culture. We resist anything or anyone limiting our personal freedoms, and we equate submission with weakness.

But submitting to God's plan for us and, yes, even to his rules in the Bible, doesn't mean that we are weak. On the contrary, Christians are strong—we stand firm in the faith and defend our beliefs while dressed in the full armor of God. Even the most stout-hearted warriors follow the commands of their leader. The Bible teaches that the most courageous thing we can do as soldiers of the Almighty is to submit to the leadership of our Commander in Chief.

The Lord is the foundation of our faith and the source of all meaning. When we follow in his steps and do things God's way instead of our own way, we receive his blessing and peace.

Above all, our Lord Jesus submitted to his Father's will. Shouldn't we do the same?

Read James 4:7.

HELP ME TO SUBMIT TO YOU, LORD, THAT
I MAY BE HAPPY AND BLESSED.

KARL BARTH

It is always the case that when the Christian looks back, he is looking at the forgiveness of sins.

KEEPING OUR FOCUS FORWARD

Being a true believer can be hard sometimes. God never guaranteed us that life will be easy. Worldly pursuits or pleasures can entice and distract. And trials and suffering can cause us to stumble. At times we get so discouraged by our past sins that we think we simply can't go on.

In these times, we need to keep our eyes on Jesus, who gave up the joys of heaven to experience suffering on earth so we could be free from the punishment of hell. Because of Jesus' sacrifice on the cross, all our sins have been forgiven. If we have accepted his gift of salvation, when we look back over our life's journey, we no longer see a long, winding trail of past sins—only the forgiveness that Jesus provided for us.

We dare not turn back to our sinful ways—but it is helpful to glance back every so often to appreciate just how much we have been forgiven and how faithful God has been.

Read Matthew 16:24–26.

LORD, KEEP ME MOVING FORWARD IN MY
FAITH AS I SEEK TO HONOR YOU.

ELISABETH ELLIOT

God has never promised to solve our problems. He has not promised to answer our questions. . . . He has promised to go with us.

ANCHORED

A flash of lightning and a clap of thunder announce the beginning of a storm. A boat far from shore drops its anchor and waits. Winds howl; waves roar and rise as the storm intensifies. More clouds roll in. The sky grows darker with the sun hidden. The wind and the waves attack the boat, and it rocks back and forth, as if to be torn apart by the elements. But the anchor rests safely beneath the surface, far below the rough waves. It holds the boat in place, stabilizing it in the storm, keeping it secure.

When we face life's storms, however bleak and rocky, we must place our trust in God and make him our anchor. He has not promised a life free from storms or problems or questions. But he has promised us that he will go with us. So in life's storms, let's cling to the anchor of God's abiding presence to stay afloat and remain secure in him.

Read 2 Corinthians 12:1–10.

LORD, MAY I RELY ON YOU AND REMEMBER YOUR PRESENCE.

STEPHEN ARTERBURN

Self-help is not really self-help at all. Self-help that really helps is God help, it is group help, it is expert help.

BOOTSTRAPS

Americans love the idea of self-sufficiency. From the first day at Kindergarten to the last overpriced therapy session, we are told over and over that we are "good enough" and that we can do anything if we just "believe in ourselves." Publishers sell millions of self-help books, all of which encourage us to "pick ourselves up by our bootstraps."

But no matter how good these platitudes may sound, they don't reflect reality. Why? Because self-sufficiency is impossible. As much as we hate to admit it, no one can get through life on his or her own strength. At some point, we all need help, and self-help can't cut it.

God knows we can't get by alone. That's why he didn't leave us to pick ourselves up by our bootstraps; he reaches down to help us up.

Read Psalm 44:6–8.

LORD, I CAN'T PICK MYSELF UP. HELP ME STAND.

JOHN BUNYAN

It is not lip-labor that God regards. It is the heart that God looks at, and it is the sincere heart from which prayer comes.

GOING THROUGH THE MOTIONS

The Pharisees of Jesus' time were very good at giving God lip service. They kept the Hebrew laws, they quoted Scripture, and they stood on street corners and prayed. From all outward appearances, the Pharisees were holy.

But Jesus knew their hearts. He saw the blackness that consumed them through their corruption and pride.

What does God see when he searches your heart? Do the words you speak and the prayers you pray accurately depict the meditations of your heart? Or are you just paying God lip service?

God wants our cheerful obedience. He wants us to show love, not just talk about it. He wants us to give generously, not out of compulsion but from a joyful spirit. He desires constant communication rather than a ten-second prayer before each meal. Our hearts should yearn for him, dwelling in his power, flooded by his grace.

Don't just go through the motions—give God your sincere devotion today and always.

Read Psalm 19:14.

GOD, HELP ME TO MEAN EVERY WORD I PRAY;
BE THE DESIRE OF MY HEART!

TERESA OF AVILA

Thank God for the things I do not own.

MANAGING STUFF

When Jesus stated that it's easier for a camel to go through the eye of a needle than for a rich man to enter into the kingdom of God, he wasn't implying that rich people never go to heaven; he was highlighting the distraction of "stuff" instead.

Is there any doubt about the downside of owning too much? In large quantities, stuff roars up and threatens to take over our thoughts. Even possessions that start off as blessings end up requiring attention.

What is it you find yourself focused on? If the tasks of today include "stuff management," consider taking a break. Let go of the longing for the latest and greatest. Give up the comparisons and remember where true contentment resides.

Read Isaiah 40:6–8.

LORD, CENTER MY THOUGHTS ON YOU
AND NOT ON EARTHLY THINGS.

JONI EARECKSON TADA

Your heart's home is in the heart of God. He has placed within you a yearning for Himself.

HOME AWAY FROM HOME

A popular Christian author wrote a modern-day allegory about the Christian's desire to be close to God. This results in the believer diving into a pool of God's grace and joyfully submerging in God's love, emerging from the water cleansed and renewed. He feels completely at home there, never wanting to leave.

We—the creation—long to be with our Creator. We yearn to be with him in heaven, but for now, we're relegated to this earth.

However, we have the capacity to experience God's presence. He's blessed us with his Word. He's provided family and friends who encourage and love us. We have ministers, Sunday school teachers, and small group leaders who help us grow. We can listen and sing along to countless melodies that praise his name. He hasn't left us to fend for ourselves!

God's presence is in our hearts here, even as we long to be at home with him.

Read 2 Corinthians 5:1–8.

LORD, THANK YOU FOR YOUR PRESENCE IN MY
LIFE, DRAWING ME CLOSER TO YOU.

CHARLES SWINDOLL

Distance from God is a frightening thing. God will never adjust His agenda to fit ours.

GOD'S AGENDA

King David was a man after God's own heart. He loved God and followed his commandments . . . until David's agenda changed. Instead of going to battle with his troops, King David stayed home, allowed his eyes to wander, and gave into temptation. His sin affected many, but when David repented, God forgave and restored. David readjusted his priorities back to God's agenda.

There's no question that we're selfish, and we want to do things our way. But our way isn't always God's way. When we realize the path we have chosen has put distance between us and our Creator, we have a choice: repent and be restored, or keep doing things our way. The distance that our pride and sin generates between us and God is not liberating—it is frightening.

Make God's way your way. Adjust your agenda to fit his.

Read Psalm 51:1–8.

KEEP ME CLOSE TO YOU, GOD.

CHARLES STANLEY

God's voice is still and quiet and easily buried under an avalanche of clamor.

THE VOICE OF GOD

When we pray, we should be quiet in order to hear the voice of God speaking to us. But how often is God's voice drowned out by the chaos of our busy lives?

God is the most powerful being in the universe. When he spoke, our solar system and everything on planet Earth came into being. He breathed and Adam lived. With that much power, imagine what might happen if he were to sing or shout! But the Bible says he speaks to us in a still, small voice.

Maybe the reason we don't hear God's voice when we pray is that we are surrounded by too much noise. Like the music at a concert when we can't hear ourselves think, the cacophony of everyday life can overshadow God's voice—no matter the volume.

It's time to remove the distractions and dial down the chaos. Listen for God's voice beyond the clamor. It will be a welcome sound indeed.

Read 1 Kings 19:11–12.

I NEED TO HEAR YOU, LORD. HELP ME TO
REALLY LISTEN FOR YOUR VOICE.

C. S. LEWIS

If only the will to walk is really there He is pleased even with their stumbles.

BRUISED CHRISTIANS

Like a toddler just learning to walk, we Christians some-times stumble as we make our way along the narrow path. Some days we get by without a scratch; still other days we barely limp through, bruised and bleeding.

The amazing reality about our Christian journey is that we don't take it alone. We have other Christians before us, behind us, and beside us to pick us up when we fall. Better still, we have our Savior who wipes away the tears, cleans our wounds, and applies the healing salve of forgiveness.

When we stumble, we learn from our mistakes. Having come through the rough times we have the wisdom to help others in similar situations. God knows we don't like to stumble, but he makes sure that everything works together for good—our good and the good of his kingdom.

Step forward boldly, knowing he walks with you.

Read 1 Kings 8:23.

I'M SO GLAD I'M NOT ALONE ON MY JOURNEY, LORD. THANK YOU FOR WALKING WITH ME.

DWIGHT L. MOODY

A good example is far better than a good precept.

MAKING OUR "FOR INSTANCES" FOR REAL

D o what I say, not what I do" may work for earthly fathers, but it won't fly with the heavenly Father. With him, our words must always be congruent with our behavior. Otherwise, they are just useless chatter.

But when our advice matches our actions, then we honor God and show respect to others. We set a good example for fellow believers and also keep nonbelievers from discrediting our faith and denouncing us as hypocritical. Not living out our biblical principles is a huge strike against us in their eyes—and is an affront to Jesus, who set the ultimate example of putting beliefs into action. He wants us to trust him to live his life in us, encouraging us to make our "for instances" for real.

Read Matthew 12:33–37.

LORD, HELP MY WORDS TO BE GODLY AND ALIGN WITH MY BEHAVIOR.

PHILIP YANCEY

It would be easier. . . if God had given us a set of ideas to mull over. . . . He did not. He gave us himself in the form of a person.

MAKE YOUR CHOICE

We love to sit around with cups of steaming coffee and talk about ideas. How would we solve the budget problems in our country, or what's the best way to grill a steak? We express our opinions and walk away changed or unchanged, ready to act or not. It doesn't really matter—we were just discussing ideas.

Many people treat God as if he were just an idea we could discuss and then walk away unchanged. That is precisely why God did not leave us with just a set of ideas; he gave us a person, himself. He gave us some*one* to follow rather than an idea to discuss.

Because God gave us a person, that leaves us with a choice. We have to *do* something about this person. We have to decide whether to believe what God said about himself or not. We have to choose.

And that choice makes all the difference.

Read Joshua 24:15.

FATHER, I CHOOSE YOU—TODAY AND EVERY DAY.

HANNAH WHITALL SMITH

Nothing else is needed to quiet all your fears, but just this, that God is.

GOD IS

God *is*. Meditate on this for a moment. His existence is without question. As we accept the reality of a God who is eternally present, our doubts are washed away.

If we examine our fear and break into its core, we will see that every fear is rooted in doubting God's existence—thus, doubting that anyone is out there who can help us. When we know that God *is*, however, we can be assured that his promises are true. Knowing this, we can live fearlessly.

Because God *is*, he will be who he is eternally. He will keep his promises—to stay close, to walk with us through the trials, to turn evil to good, and to raise us again at the last day.

Be still and know that God is. And think about what that means to you today.

Read 1 Corinthians 15:54–58.

QUIET MY FEARS, GOD, BECAUSE OF WHO YOU ARE.

LLOYD JOHN OGILVIE

We come to God with our desires, and He answers according to our needs.

HEAVEN'S ANSWERS

Have you ever thought God wouldn't want to hear about a deep longing of your heart? Have you spent your quiet time talking with God about what you *think* he wants you to pray, rather than what was really on your mind?

Prayer is one area where we need not hesitate or fear. We can run to God and tell him honestly about the desires of our heart—the need for a job, concerns for a spouse, the desire to conceive a child, handling health issues, facing financial struggles.

God longs to hear whatever is troubling us, whatever is occupying our thoughts. And as we come to him with our problems, requests, and desires, he asks only that we lay them at his feet and trust his answers to come in his time, his way.

He knows us far better than we know ourselves. He knows the beginning from the end. So when you pray, be open to his answers, for he will respond according to your true needs.

How can we know this for certain? Because he knows and loves us best.

Read Matthew 6:5–8.

DEAR LORD, HONEST PRAYER IS A GIFT, AND I AM GRATEFUL FOR IT.

JULY

JOHN ORTBERG

Having faith does not mean never having doubts or questions. It does mean remaining obedient.

REMAINING OBEDIENT

Quoting a hymn of praise from the early church, Paul speaks of Christ's obedience to God the Father in obtaining our redemption. He wrote, "[Jesus] humbled himself by becoming obedient to the point of death, even death on a cross" (Philippians 2:8 ESV).

We would expect the Son of God to obey even in crucifixion. What we might be less apt to recall are Jesus' doubts in going to the cross. He prayed, "My Father, if it be possible, let this cup [of suffering] pass from me; nevertheless, not as I will but as you will" (Matthew 26:39 ESV). That's our pattern for faith. The night before his crucifixion, Jesus had doubts and questions, even fears, but he trusted in the will of God the Father ahead of his own. He got up from praying, left the garden in chains, and obediently died on a cross.

Faith takes our doubts and fears and yields them to God's will by doing the next right thing we know to do: obedience.

Read Philippians 2:1–18.

GOD, GRANT ME THE COURAGE IN THE FACE OF MY
DOUBTS AND FEARS TO REMAIN OBEDIENT TO YOU.

AMBROSE

The whole human race could rest under the shadow of the cross's outstretched limbs, guarded from the pestilent heat of the world's pleasures.

THE SHADE OF THE CROSS

What a delight it is on a blistering hot day to sink beneath the spreading limbs of a tree and partake of its shade. Under the shadow of the tree's branches, we are physically refreshed by the cooler temperature and protection from the sun's hot rays.

We can also find spiritual relief beneath the spreading limbs of another tree. This tree is the cross—the ultimate heat blocker. The shade of the cross guards us from the scorching winds of the world and its false pleasures that lure us off God's chosen path and beckon us toward the destructive fire of judgment.

Just before his crucifixion, Jesus reminded his disciples that his death on the cross would draw people to him. Through his death, Jesus promised that he would supply the ultimate rest for our souls—the power to overcome temptation.

Are you feeling the heat today? Come into the shade of the cross and be eternally refreshed in his presence.

Read John 12:32–36.

FATHER GOD, GUARD MY HEART AND MIND AND GRANT ME REST THIS DAY.

J. I. PACKER

The prayer of a Christian is not an attempt to force God's hand, but a humble acknowledgment of helplessness and dependence.

GENTLE PERSISTENCE

Have you ever tried to force open a door that is stuck? You push and push until something gives way—either a pulled muscle or a splintered door frame. This is a perfect example of impatience running ahead of wisdom, with disastrous results.

Sometimes we approach prayer the same way we tackle a stubborn door. In our hurry to get through our prayer time, we push and shove. We know exactly what should be done, why it should be done, and how it should be done. And we're not shy about letting our opinions and feelings about the matter be heard!

Effective prayer acknowledges our need for the Master Craftsman instead of trying to force the key in the lock. God wants us to spend time with him, getting to know him and being shaped by him. As you talk to him today, let your words and attitude be characterized not by demanding insistence, but by gentle, humble persistence. We aren't forcing God's hand in our prayers; we are merely acknowledging that we need him.

And that is exactly the way he wants it.

Read Psalm 17:1–9.

HEAR MY CRY, LORD. I NEED YOUR HELP TODAY.

JEROME

Offer to God that which no enemy can carry off and no tyrant can take from you.

YOUR OFFERING

When it's time to collect items to give away or to sell at a garage sale, we think about the things we don't need: that extra coffeemaker someone gave us, that picture frame gathering dust, those books we never read. But we keep a vise grip on the things we think we need the most—the items of most value to us. Ironically, some of those things end up at the next garage sale.

Jesus advised his disciples to let go of the things on this earth and to transfer their grip to the things that aren't of this world. The possessions of heaven can't be lost or stolen here on earth. Offering ourselves and our belongings to God is a way of storing up treasure in heaven. It also helps us to hold things loosely in this life. We came into this world with nothing and we can take nothing we have in this world into the next.

What will you offer God?

Read Matthew 6:19–21.

O LORD, I OFFER YOU MY LIFE AND ALL THAT
I HAVE. USE THEM AS YOU SEE FIT.

FRANCIS CHAN

It's pride, plain and simple, that keeps me from giving God all the glory and keep[s] some of it for myself.

I DID IT

The lame man could walk. The leper was healed. The shriveled hand was restored. All were miracles accomplished by the power of God. But what if each individual had taken the credit instead?

The lame man bragged, "I used to be crippled, but I did a lot of physical training and over time I strengthened my legs so they could move on their own."

"I used to be a leper," another said, "but I cleaned myself constantly and eventually the spots went away."

The man who had a shriveled hand said, "I used to have a deformed hand, but I stretched it and put lotion on it every day for years and it healed."

Sounds ludicrous, doesn't it? Yet so often we take credit for blessings that come to us from God. Pride tells others that we accomplished the miracles in our lives—whether a healing, a renewed relationship, or some other success—on our own, when the credit belongs to God.

Read 1 Samuel 2:1–11.

MAY I ALWAYS CREDIT YOU FOR THE GOOD IN MY LIFE, GOD.

BERNARD OF CLAIRVAUX

When the soul deserts such a Bridegroom and pursues such lovers [Hosea 2:7], it is not surprising that it cannot grasp the glory that is prepared for it.

A CHEAP INHERITANCE

In the 1960s James Coburn starred in a movie titled *Dead Heat on a Merry-Go-Round*. Coburn played a con man who was always seeking to swindle people out of their money. As part of one of his schemes, he wooed a woman, making her think he would marry her—when in reality, he was hoping to steal the money from her bank account. Ultimately, he was successful, cheating her out of fifty thousand dollars. Ironically, though, two days after the woman discovered she'd been swindled, she was notified that a relative had died and left her millions. Had the con man only been faithful, he could have shared in an utter fortune.

Like Coburn's con man, anyone who lives in falsehood—whether it's telling lies and cheating others or devoting oneself to pagan rituals, witchcraft, or other false religions—will one day discover that he or she has forfeited a glorious inheritance of eternal life in heaven. What a truly poor trade-off that is.

Read Matthew 19:28–30.

LORD, THANK YOU FOR MAKING ME AN HEIR TO YOUR KINGDOM.

HELEN KELLER

We could never learn to be brave and patient, if there were only joy in the world.

CHANGED BY TRAGEDY

In 2007, a tragic car accident took the life of a high school senior, Chris, the Thursday before Easter. A girl who barely knew him was shaken. A young Christian, she'd distanced herself from God. As her shock from Chris's death changed into fear and tears, she returned, weeping, to God's arms. She took comfort in his Word, explored it more, and clung to its truth. She rested in God's strength, found peace in knowing he was in control, and drew closer to him than she ever had been before. The direction of her life changed. Without Chris's death, she might have remained distant from God for much longer. Her love for God and others would have grown more stagnant. The tragedy served as a reminder to her of what was really important.

Although most of us want a life filled only with joy and blessings, God knows that sometimes we must endure difficult circumstances and tragedies in order for him to build the strength of character he wants in us. Unexpected tragedies reveal what is most important in our lives—and they often lead us to the arms of the One who is the source of life.

Read Psalm 22:1–11.

GOD, HELP ME TO GROW THROUGH THE PAIN.

CYPRIAN

Considering His love and mercy, we shouldn't be bitter, cruel, or inhuman toward believers.

CONSIDER HIS MERCY

The honey locust thorn tree is a great provider of shade. Yet it has one drawback: long, sharp thorns. Botanists have determined that the thorn is the tree's means of self-defense. A prick from the thorn can cause a very painful wound that can lead to swelling and infection.

Sometimes we use prickly words as our self-defense against hurt. Yet a careless word is like the thorn of the honey locust thorn tree—it can cause a deep wound that can lead to the "infection" of bitterness setting in and causing even more problems. That's why believers should stop and consider the love and mercy of God before allowing thorny words to hurt others.

This is especially true when it comes to our interactions with other believers. When we consider how much God has forgiven us, we should be eager to extend forgiveness toward our brothers and sisters in Christ. As our hearts are filled with God's love, we should honor him by choosing words that express mercy and kindness.

Our words can be honeyed, rather than barbed. The choice is always ours.

Read Ephesians 4:25–32.

MERCIFUL LORD, I NEED YOUR HELP TO REFLECT
YOUR MERCY AND YOUR GRACE.

J. OSWALD SANDERS

It is as we apply the cross to our lives and die to the self-dominated life that the Spirit can make our lives fruitful.

APPLYING THE CROSS

The notion of leaving a splinter in your finger seems silly. If the splinter is ignored, your finger turns red, and if left long enough it becomes infected. It is as if your body screams, "Get it out of me!" How much more absurd is the notion of embracing a cross. It represents a cruel form of physical torture that causes loss of blood and suffocates you. It is as if your body and soul scream, "Get me down from here!"

The cross that God calls us to bear adds nothing to Christ's cross and sacrifice for our sin. But in their various forms—a cross of depression, a cross of a terminal disease, a cross of job loss, or a cross from weariness at life's daily grind—they crucify the self-dominated life. As we apply the cross to our lives and die to ourselves, we begin to live instead to the Spirit, who brings forth the fruit of his character in us.

Read Mark 8:34–38.

LORD JESUS CHRIST, I WANT TO BE RAISED TO
FRUITFUL LIVING OF YOUR SPIRIT.

JONATHAN MORRIS

Our longing for more love than what humans can give and receive can lead the honest soul to love the Perfect Lover.

THE PERFECT LOVER

To love people is risky. The greater the love, the greater is the risk. We long to be loved completely by someone who will never disappoint us or hurt us. But we soon discover that mere humans—no matter how well-intentioned—simply aren't capable of loving perfectly. After we experience the heartache of receiving a "Dear John" or "Dear Jane" letter we might feel that it's not worth the pain to give our heart away in love to another, only to have it broken again.

We can never completely insulate our hearts from the pain in loving others. Nor should we. As humans, we are all imperfect, so we are not able to love perfectly. We can, however, let our heartache lead us to the One whose perfect love casts out fear. When our hearts know his love we no longer try to find from humans the love that we can only receive from God, our Perfect Lover.

Read 1 John 4:7–21.

BOOKER T. WASHINGTON

I will permit no man to narrow and degrade my soul by making me hate him.

WHAT WOULD HE DO?

In the 1990s, the question "What would Jesus do?" spread across America as youth groups studied Charles Sheldon's 1896 novel *In His Steps* and wore bracelets with the letters WWJD. This question called believers to ask themselves whether or not they were living as Christ would have them live. It encouraged them to model their lives after Christ's and to become walking testimonies of the Savior.

The Lord has called us to be more like him, to show his love to the unlovable and to reach out to the unreachable. Jesus loved Judas, who betrayed him, and Pilate, who sent him to the cross. And he taught his followers to follow his example by loving their enemies and praying for those who persecuted them.

If we truly are to do what Jesus would do, then we will respond to others in love, not hate. We will love others as Jesus himself loves them.

Read Luke 6:27–36.

LORD JESUS, HELP ME LOVE LIKE YOU.

MIKE MASON

Who wouldn't be overjoyed with a God who "has given us everything we need for life and godliness" (2 Peter 1:3)?

OUR JOY SOURCE

It's no secret that many people suffer from depression. While some people endure clinical depression, many of us just find ourselves under a cloud of gloom once in a while, and we wonder why. As Christians we are not immune to depression, so how can we find joy?

Our joy comes from God. Second Peter 1:3 says that God "has given us everything," which tells us that God began giving in the past and continues giving right into today. God never stops giving. As our source, though, he gives what "we need for life and godliness" and not everything we want—not always what is easy, luxurious, and successful. Yet God gives his children what we need so we are more satisfied in him, not less satisfied in him. Our joy source is God, who can fill us so we are overjoyed on our saddest and happiest days.

Read 2 Peter 1:3–11.

HOLY SPIRIT, FILL ME TO OVERFLOWING WITH YOUR JOY!

A. W. TOZER

Our concepts of measurement embrace mountains and men, atoms and stars, gravity, energy, numbers, speed, but never God.

THE MEASURE OF GOD

Miles and meters. Light-years and leagues. Newtons and knots. From the tiniest particle to the tallest mountain, all of creation is considered and calculated by scientists and mathematicians. From the far reaches of our galaxy to the physical bodies we inhabit, everything is reduced to a number or a measurement and recorded for academic study.

Infinite and omnipotent. Everlasting and eternal. Almighty and I AM. While many of the details of creation can be captured in a book or on a computer screen, the Creator himself cannot be measured. His very name defies description. He is without measure, without end, without boundaries or limitations. The God who is the beginning and the end is not bound by the restraints of time. The omnipotent God is not hampered by the unknown. The Creator who is the first and the last holds all of creation in his hands.

Nothing is too difficult for our God or beyond his capabilities. Great is the Lord and worthy of praise!

Read Psalm 145:1–9.

GOD, I THANK YOU THAT NO PROBLEM, TRIAL, OR PAIN IS BEYOND THE REACH OF YOUR HAND.

CHARLES HADDON SPURGEON

By perseverance the snail reached the ark.

HE KEPT GOING

Chris Gardner had a stack of parking tickets he couldn't pay. After a short stay in jail for failure to pay the tickets, he landed an internship by his character, not his clothes.

Gardner had no job, no car, and no place to live, only a thousand dollar a month stipend from his internship and a young son to take care of. He worked at his internship like a madman, arriving early and leaving late. He did what he could to keep his son safe and their homelessness private, even sleeping in the locked bathroom of a transit station.

In time Gardner's perseverance paid off: he became a full-time stockbroker. Had he given up at any point, *The Pursuit of Happyness*, the movie from his memoir of the same title, would never have been made.

Are you far from your own happily ever after today? Take courage in this: God knows the end of your story. Look to him as you persevere day after day.

Read Hebrews 11:30–40.

LORD, STRENGTHEN ME TO PERSEVERE WHEN I WANT TO GIVE UP.

JOHN STOTT

God is making human beings more human by making them more like Jesus.

HEROIC HUMILITY

Most children have a hero, a man or woman they look up to as someone they want to be like. Adults often have heroes too. More than just admiration for their accomplishments and skills, we are inspired by such heroes to try harder, to live braver, to go farther than we would have without their examples. By imitating their lives we hope to accomplish more, to be more than we could on our own. Yet all earthly heroes have their blemishes, some more glaring than others.

Then upon the human stage enters Jesus. Being both fully man and fully God at the same time, he alone is our true hero, elevating the human heart to true heights of greatness. By imitating his life of humility and service, we become more human—the way God intended humanity to be.

Our hero, Jesus Christ, humbled himself and became obedient to death on a cross on our behalf. Through his sacrifice we gain our glorification so that for eternity we may live fully like Jesus.

Read Philippians 2:1–11.

LORD JESUS, MAY I HAVE YOUR ATTITUDE OF HUMILITY IN SERVING ALL THOSE I MEET TODAY.

J. Edwin Orr

The one who forgives is the one who suffers.

COSTLY FORGIVENESS

The film *The Passion of the Christ* gives viewers a vivid emotional understanding of Christ's suffering for our forgiveness. In the movie, the events of Christ's crucifixion are portrayed in sights and sounds that are almost beyond what a person can bear to watch!

Attempt to imagine what it was like for the heavenly Father to put his Son on the cross to suffer and die. "Stop it!" we might scream from the perspective of our human justice. "Jesus does not deserve to suffer!" Yet for God the Father, that is the point of Calvary. As a sinless man Jesus did not deserve to die, but he willingly took on our sin. He suffered for our forgiveness.

As beneficiaries of his suffering, should we offer anything less to others? Though we will never suffer as Christ did for us, we must accept in our forgiving others that sometimes we too must bear suffering for the sake of love.

Read Colossians 3:12–15.

AS YOU SUFFERED FOR MY FORGIVENESS, GRANT ME A
WILLINGNESS TO SUFFER IN FORGIVING OTHERS.

JOHN OF THE CROSS

God dwells secretly in all souls and is hidden in their substance, for otherwise they would not last.

FINGERPRINTS OF GOD

The fingerprints of God are upon all souls. In the Garden of Eden, God scooped up dirt from the ground to form the first man, Adam. Into the man God breathed life and proclaimed it was very good. Every person since has value as God's crowning achievement.

What makes us prized by God ahead of the eagle with its grandeur, the ant with her diligence, the lion with his majesty, and all his other creatures? The distinction lies with God who said, "Let us make mankind in our image, in our likeness" (Genesis 1:26). As humans, we have the distinction of the only beings in all of creation who were made in the image of God.

As ennobling as it is to bear God's likeness, far nobler is having the very Spirit of God dwelling in us. On this side of heaven we are jars of clay dusted with the fingerprints of God as his chosen vessels in Christ, redeemed to display his glory!

Read Genesis 1:26–31.

MAY YOUR FINGERPRINTS BE ALL OVER MY SOUL, GOD,
AS YOU SHAPE ME INTO THE LIKENESS OF CHRIST.

JOHN PIPER

Jesus himself—and all that God is for us in him—is our great reward, nothing less.

JESUS, OUR GREAT REWARD!

Winnie the Pooh, written by A. A. Milne in 1926, is a classic children's story with many lasting lessons. In it we discover a delightful troupe of characters with their own unique personalities: Christopher Robin's kindness, Rabbit's nervousness, Tigger's playfulness, Pooh's curiosity, and Eeyore's sadness. In his perpetual gloom, a gray cloud follows Eeyore, raining down wherever he goes as he sighs, "Woe is me."

Many Christians have an Eeyore-like outlook on life. What's with the long faces on so many of God's children? Jesus said, "I came that [you] may have life and have it abundantly" (John 10:10 ESV)! If that is Jesus' intent, then as his followers, we need to enter the joy of the Lord more faithfully and earnestly.

Jesus himself is our great reward! What else could we possibly want? Let's wipe off our frowns and choose to live in the joy of the Lord today.

Read 1 Corinthians 2:6–13.

JESUS, I BELIEVE THAT YOU ARE MY GREAT REWARD;
HELP ME TO RECEIVE IT EVEN MORE.

BILLY GRAHAM

It is not the body's posture, but the heart's attitude that counts when we pray.

HEART ATTITUDE

When you pray, what is the attitude of your heart toward God? Are you assuming the posture of prayer and giving God lip service while your heart is secretly resisting his call to obedience and submission?

In the tiny Old Testament book of Obadiah, God's followers are warned about having a bad attitude. When we harbor anger, bitterness, or resentment, it affects not only those around us but also our attitude toward God. We should be showing gratitude, but are we?

The only way to overcome bad attitudes of the heart is to allow God to shine and reveal all the darkness that is there. But we also need to be willing to repent. Daily prayer and Bible study are essential for this to happen. We need to bow before God in our heart and show true thankfulness for his enduring grace.

Read Hebrews 4:12

LORD, HELP ME TO BE HUMBLE IN MY HEART AND TRULY THANKFUL

MARTYN LLOYD-JONES

The very essence of the Christian life . . . is that it is a mighty power that enters into us; it is a life . . . that is pulsating in us.

A MIGHTY POWER

Imagine what it would have been like to be a follower of Jesus while he was on earth. He might have come to you and said, "Stop what you are doing; come, follow me. I am going to make you a fisher of men." You would have been there when he gave sight to the blind, strength to the lame, and food to more than five thousand people from just five small loaves and two fish. You would have watched in awe as evil spirits and raging waters obeyed his every command.

Then you learn that he is leaving and returning to his Father in heaven. Doubts flood your mind and fear grips your heart as you ask yourself, "How can I go on? Without Jesus here with me, I can't!"

On Pentecost, the Holy Spirit, the power of God from on high, descended into that first band of timid disciples and empowered them to carry out God's mission. For every Christ follower since, the same Holy Spirit enters our hearts and pulsates the power of God into us day by day.

Read John 16:5–15.

HOLY SPIRIT, I WANT YOUR MIGHTY POWER TO PULSATE WITHIN ME THROUGH THIS DAY.

G. K. CHESTERTON

Perhaps God is strong enough to exult in monotony. . . . God makes every daisy separately, but has never got tired of making them.

ONE IN A BILLION

We fight against monotony. We may feel like we are just one speck on a massive planet filled with billions of other tiny dots. How can we possibly matter to God?

Our God, however, must exult in a certain amount of monotony. While we exclaim at the wide variety of flowers all over the globe, we should also stand in sheer wonder of a field decorated with millions of daisies. Just one flower, duplicated a million times, yet each daisy is created separately and put into its own special place.

Similarly, we are much like all other humans. We exhibit the same general size, shape, and functions. Yet each of us is created by God, different from the next person and lovingly put into the place that God has specially planned for us.

No one on the planet is just like you. You were uniquely designed in your mother's womb. God knows you intimately and intricately.

Monotonous? Boring? Not on your life. You're one in a billion!

Read Psalm 139:13–16

*HELP ME TO UNDERSTAND AND APPRECIATE
YOUR INTIMATE LOVE FOR ME.*

MAX LUCADO

We need a shepherd. We don't need a cowboy to herd us; we need a shepherd to care for us and to guide us.

THE TENDER SHEPHERD

The job of a shepherd involves much more than sitting on a hillside keeping an eye on his flock. A good shepherd knows where to lead his sheep for nourishing food and fresh water. He moves his flock from one place to another along the safest route possible. When one of his flock is missing, he leaves the others in a safe place and doesn't rest until the lost one is found. He protects his helpless lambs from danger.

In Psalm 23 we affirm, "The Lord is my shepherd." What a wonderful image! Christians know that Jesus Christ is our shepherd. He cares for each of us. No matter what comes our way, our shepherd will always be present to protect our hearts and minds from danger. When we hurt, he comforts us. When we don't know which way to turn, he guides us. When we lose our way, he leads us home.

Look to your shepherd today.

Read Psalm 23.

THANK YOU, LORD, FOR BEING MY SHEPHERD.

CHARLES SWINDOLL

God specializes in things we think are totally impossible.

THE SPECIALIST

After hours of work and effort, you finally accomplished a seemingly impossible task. With a sigh of relief, you energetically moved on to your next task. However, when your plan hits a crater-sized pothole and you end up on the side of the road waiting for a tow truck, quite the opposite happens. Instead of relief and energy, you feel frustration and disappointment.

Are you dreaming for something today that seems out of reach? Do your needs seem impossible for you to meet on your own? Are you facing a challenge that seems unsolvable? Take courage in the fact that God specializes in impossible situations.

When your circumstances seem impossible, don't look down in despair—look up to God and his goodness, graciousness, and mercy as you eagerly wait for his answers and provision. Redemption in Christ is just the beginning of what God has in store for you. Believe God for the impossibilities in life. He is able to handle anything that comes your way.

Read Mark 9:20–29.

GOD, I GIVE MY IMPOSSIBLE SITUATION TO YOU TO HANDLE.

C. S. LEWIS

I need to believe in Christianity as I believe that the sun has risen: not only because I see it, but because by it I see everything else.

SEEING THINGS CLEARLY

Colors didn't seem as bright to Reginald. Street signs were getting harder to read. For a long time he didn't notice, and then he shrugged it off as a normal consequence of getting older. But the doctor told him cataracts were causing his problems. If he had them removed, he could again have clear eyesight. Now that he has had the surgery he can see again, even without glasses. Proper focus has helped Reginald enjoy his daily walks again—and to drive more safely too.

How about you? Do you need a vision check? Is Jesus out of focus on the edges of your life? Spend some time with the eye doctor of your soul, and ask him to remove any obstructions so you can see clearly again. Doing so is a way to honor Jesus and put your faith in the proper perspective.

Read Ecclesiastes 2:13–14.

HELP ME TO EXAMINE MY OWN LIFE FOR SIN, AND TO SEEK FORGIVENESS.

HENRY BLACKABY

To understand and believe that in fact God did know you and choose you from eternity will give you an enormous sense of purpose in life.

GOD'S ETERNAL PLAN

Every human heart yearns for a sense of purpose in life. Just below the surface of our consciousness lie such questions as: "Is what I am doing significant?" "Who cares about what I do?" "What really matters in life?"

It might surprise you to learn that Solomon, a man who had achieved astounding success as king of Israel, also struggled with his own significance. Despite all his earthly achievements, he mused, "Vanity of vanities . . . all is vanity" (Ecclesiastes 12:8 ESV). If a man as wise and wealthy as King Solomon struggled to find purpose in life, where does that leave the rest of us who will never attain such a lavish, royal existence?

We can trust in God's Word, which says that we do have a purpose. According to God's eternal plan, he predestined us for adoption as his sons and daughters through Jesus Christ. He designed each of us with a unique purpose—to love him and serve him.

Read Ephesians 1:3–14.

GOD, HELP ME SEE YOUR ETERNAL DESIGN IN
THE DETAILS OF MY DAILY PLANS.

Thomas à Kempis

If you carry the cross willingly, it will carry and lead you to the desired goal where indeed there shall be no more suffering.

TAKING A BACKSEAT WILLINGLY

An elderly mother is in need of care and supervision. But her children are too busy with their own lives. They argue over who should take care of her: "It's your job—you're the oldest." "You live closer to her." "But you have more time." And on and on it goes. The mother goes without the care she needs, and the siblings only get cross with each other.

Another elderly mother is also in need of care. But her children willingly come to her aid and provide what she needs. They are grateful for the chance to care for their mom, even though it may be inconvenient. And the family grows closer together as they express love for one another.

There's quite a difference between those who carry their crosses willingly, and those who do not, or who do so begrudgingly.

Maybe we all need a reminder about the first being last and the last being first in God's kingdom. Each of us has burdens to bear. No one is immune from suffering. And while we will find an end to our troubles in heaven, we should strive to finish strong here, honoring our Savior and loving others.

Read Matthew 20:20–28.

LORD, MOVE ME TO SERVE YOU WILLINGLY.

MADELEINE L'ENGLE

As Christians we are not meant to be less human than other people, but more human, just as Jesus of Nazareth was more human.

MORE HUMAN

This side of heaven, Christians do not live perfectly. Yet all Christians do have a perfect standing before God, having received "the righteousness of God through faith in Jesus Christ" (Romans 3:22 ESV).

Our position in Christ, however, does not always match our process of living like Christ. We are still very much human with all our foibles, fears, and sinful desires. When a saved saint acts less than saintly, those outside the church cry, "The church is a bunch of hypocrites!" Certainly, more often than should happen, Christians fail to live up to their name.

We never deny that we are still human and as such can sin like all the rest of humanity. What makes us different is that we have the presence of One in us who transforms us desire by desire, attitude by attitude, and action by action. Through him we become more human as we become more like Christ in our thoughts, actions, and lives.

Read John 14:15–31.

JESUS, MAY THE WORDS OF MY MOUTH AND ATTITUDES OF MY HEART REFLECT YOUR PRESENCE IN ME.

DIETRICH BONHOEFFER

To deny oneself is to be aware only of Christ . . . to see only Him who goes before and no more the road which is too hard for us.

RUNNING THE RACE

In the face of shin splints, overwhelming thirst, exhausted muscles, and suffocating heat, it's amazing that any marathoner ever finishes those 26.2 miles. Even more remarkable is the winning attitude these runners have, for it would be easy to quit halfway through when the finish line seems a continent away. Half of the battle in running, experts say, is mental.

Life itself is a marathon, with a finish line seemingly nowhere in sight much of the time. Mundane tasks like answering the phone, cleaning, or cooking supper make each day drag on. Even more tiring are the times when emergencies happen, when all hope appears lost, when we want to quit in hopes of escaping unwanted situations. The key to perseverance when the road gets too hard is to keep our eyes focused on Jesus, who is cheering us on at the finish line.

Read Philippians 3:12–14.

HELP ME TO STAY FOCUSED ON YOU, JESUS.

AUGUSTINE OF HIPPO

This, therefore, is the complete satisfaction of souls, that is, the happy life: to know precisely and perfectly Him through whom you are led into the truth.

A SATISFIED SOUL

When you're thirsty, cotton-mouth parched, water is what you want and need. Scientists have told us that we can survive for only a matter of days without water. Being thirsty reminds us that we need to drink; therefore, our thirst helps keep us alive.

Another thirst is crucial in keeping us spiritually alive. That is the thirst of our souls. This soul-thirst recognizes when we have let our lives become arid deserts, wandering far from the fountain of life. With only sand around us, we look for the oasis, the soul-quenching satisfaction that only God can give. Jesus invited soul-thirsty people to come to him, "If anyone thirsts, let him come to Me and drink" (John 7:37 NKJV).

Only in him will our souls find complete satisfaction. Only through his Spirit can we know precisely and perfectly the One who is the eternal source for a fully satisfied soul.

Read John 7:37–39.

HOLY SPIRIT, I WANT YOU TO QUENCH MY THIRST TODAY WITH RIVERS OF LIVING WATER!

DWIGHT L. MOODY

There are many of us that are willing to do great things for the Lord, but few of us are willing to do little things.

DOING LITTLE THINGS

Have you ever heard someone say, "I want to be second place"? How about, "I'd like to get straight Bs on my report card," or "I plan to own a string of second-rate restaurants"? Sounds silly, doesn't it?

No matter how small or seemingly insignificant the task God is asking you to do, it is something he designed you to do for the body of Christ. Maybe God hasn't designed you to be a world-renowned preacher or famous missionary. Maybe inviting your neighbors to dinner, working on the assembly line, or serving in the church nursery are the very things God wants you to do. Are you willing to accept doing those little things, and nothing more, if that is God's will?

Even a little cricket's chirping can be heard from a great distance. Be faithful to do the little things cheerfully and God will be glorified.

Read Luke 16:10.

HELP ME TO BE SATISFIED IN DOING THE LITTLE THINGS FOR YOU, LORD.

JONI EARECKSON TADA

This is the God I love. The Center, the Peacemaker, the Passport to adventure, the Joyride, and the Answer to all our deepest longings.

A JOYRIDE WITH GOD

God's attributes draw us to him. This unique list of what can make a heart swell with love for God gives us the opportunity to look at our loving Father in new and exciting ways.

He is the Center, the point around which everything else in life revolves. No spinning out of control when God is your Center. He is the Peacemaker, bringing peace to your worried heart, to broken families, to a dying world. He is the Passport to adventure. When you become a citizen of heaven, that passport grants you entry to places unknown, places of adventure God has prepared for you. He is a Joyride, taking you through life with your hands in the air and the wind in your hair. Above all, he is the Answer to any and all longings, whatever yours may be.

With God, your life is an adventure—a veritable joyride! Where is God taking you today?

Read John 14:6.

TAKE ME ON THE RIDE OF MY LIFE, LORD!

AUGUST

BRENT CURTIS AND JOHN ELDREDGE

The desire God has placed within us is wild in its longing to pursue the One who is unknown.

OUR WILD LONGING

What is the deepest longing of your heart? We often pursue that for which we long. C. S. Lewis, author of the children's series the Chronicles of Narnia, is well known for his use of the German word *sehnsucht,* which means "longing" or "intensely missing." This deep longing moves us when we see a beautiful sunset, hear a masterful symphony, or feel a baby's small hand wrap around our finger. God placed this longing within us, and this desire can be satisfied by nothing and no one besides him. No matter how intensely we pursue other people, places, and things, we "intensely miss" the author of all: God.

The wild longing we all experience will be finally fulfilled when we reach heaven. The most beautiful sunset or symphony is only a shadow of the glory that is to come and the One with whom we will spend eternity.

Filled with longing? Turn to the One who desires to take his place on the throne of your life.

Read Ephesians 2:14–18.

I LONG FOR YOU, LORD.

CHRYSOSTOM

How can we have victory over the enemy? By running to God for shelter the way Christ taught us.

GOD OUR SHELTER

When you were a child, what was the first place you ran when you were scared or overwhelmed? More than likely a parent's arms offered the perfect place of safety. Your fears about the monster lurking in the closet or the bad storm outside gave way in the presence of a parent's strong and steadfast love.

When we get older, problems and temptations become like monsters in our closet that don't go away, no matter who hugs us. Victory eludes us as long as we focus on our faltering ability to fight. So where can we turn?

If you're in the midst of the fray today, become like a child again. Seek shelter in the loving arms of your heavenly Father. Jesus taught us to run to God in prayer whenever we feel afraid or overwhelmed by the struggles in this world.

Need shelter? Your heavenly Father eagerly waits with outstretched arms to comfort and protect you.

Read Matthew 6:9–13.

I'M GRATEFUL THAT I CAN COME TO YOU AND BE SAFE, LORD.

T. D. JAKES

If He told you He was going to bless you, then ignore the mess and believe the God who cannot lie.

IGNORE THE MESS

Ever wish you could find a restart button to push when life gets messy? That frustrating job. That complicated friendship. That circumstance that seems to get more and more untidy the more you try to fix it. Sometimes our difficult situations can feel like a skein of yarn that keeps getting more and more tangled as you work through the knots.

In the midst of the mess, it's easy to forget that God promises to bless his people with victory and peace. He invites us to take our messes to his cross and leave them there, instead of making them our focus. The cross is a restart button. Even when our difficult situation wildly beckons us and ignites our worry, we can choose to believe that God is still in control and he can bless our messes.

Choose to take him at his word. Give him your doubts and your fears. Accept his hope.

Read Psalm 29:10–11.

HELP ME STAND STRONG AND FIRM ON YOUR PROMISES.

MARTIN LUTHER

Pray, and let God worry.

WHO ME, WORRY?

When we face difficult circumstances, it's much easier to be anxious than to hand our worries over to God. Instead of letting go of our troubles, we desperately want to hold on to them—ignoring the amazing offer from the Creator of the universe to take our burdens, if we would only release them to him. But we seem hardwired to rely on ourselves first and God second—or in some cases, not to lean on him at all.

In times of difficulty and uncertainty, we should pray and let God do the worrying. This means the next time we are tempted to fret about our finances or relationships, our health or loved ones' safety, our job or anything else, we should let the Lord handle it—and step out of the way. It won't be easy at first. Old habits die hard. But if we are to truly live out our faith and experience other-worldly peace, we must give our worries to God and trust him to work out all things for our good and for his glory.

Read Philippians 4:6–9.

GOD, HELP ME TO PRAY AND LEAVE THE WORRYING TO YOU.

EUGENE PETERSON

The joy comes because God knows how to wipe away tears,
and, in his resurrection work, create the smile of a new life.

THE RIGHT TOUCH

Sorrow. Hardship. Affliction. Few of us escape these painful circumstances in our lifetime. When others don't notice the tears bottled up behind our eyelids, trickling down our cheeks, or flowing freely over our chin, God notices. And he cares.

With just the right touch God tenderly wipes away our tears. He might use a friend's hug, a phone call, or a Bible verse he brings to mind to demonstrate his love and comfort us. Or he may simply provide an awareness of his presence as we walk through the pain.

What resurrection work does God need to do in your life today? Reassurance? Comfort? Hope? Let God breathe new life into your soul as you depend on him for joy. Let the smile on your tear-stained face come because of who God is—even if the circumstances seem hopeless.

Do you need a tissue today? God's supply is stocked. Ask him to wipe away your tears and to create the joy that comes from your new life.

Read Revelation 21:1–5.

WIPE MY TEARS AWAY TODAY, GOD, AND GIVE ME YOUR JOY.

JEROME

We don't reach perfection because of our will or because we run towards it, but because God pities us and helps us to reach the goal.

CHASING PERFECTION

At the Montreal Olympics in 1976, Romanian gymnast Nadia Comaneci became the first gymnast to be awarded the score of a perfect ten. The whole world watched, breathless, as her routine on the uneven bars earned her a place in history. At the tender age of fourteen, Nadia set the bar high for those who strived for a perfect score.

Countless gymnasts and other athletes who make perfection their goal toil endlessly hour after hour, day after day, year after year. And chasing after perfection isn't limited to athletes. Believers who become ensnared in the chase begin to see only the goal instead of the God behind it. And thus is legalism born.

God gives us rest from the chase with the promise that someday we will reach perfection by his grace. For now, he helps us in our imperfection. He forgives us when we give in to temptation and fall far short of the mark. He takes pity on us and helps us in our weaknesses.

Chasing perfection? Pursue the perfect God.

Read Hebrews 2:14–18.

GOD, MAY MY CHASE FOR PERFECTION LEAD TO YOU.

BRENNAN MANNING

On the last day, Jesus will look us over not for medals, diplomas, or honors, but for scars.

RISKY BUSINESS

What do we seek most in life? Most of us want to do well—and there's certainly nothing wrong with education and honorable service and quality work and receiving kudos for those things. Few of us, however, are out trying to get scars.

This is not a call to jump into any number of extreme sports sure to give us physical scars. But it *is* a call to do something risky. It's a call to do the things that will bring glory to God, regardless of how much they might hurt.

Far too often, safety sits at the top of our priority list and hides God's agenda for our lives. God is looking for people who are willing to live dangerously and be risk takers for the honor and glory of his name.

In the end, he'll be looking for scars that show we have taken the risk to sacrifice ourselves in service to him. What will he see on you?

Read 2 Corinthians 4:7–15.

*FATHER, I AM WILLING TO RECEIVE SCARS
IF THEY BRING YOU GLORY.*

A. W. TOZER

What peace it brings to the Christian's heart to realize that our Heavenly Father never differs from Himself.

UNCHANGING

Life is filled with times of transition and change. The celebration of a wedding is followed by the adjustment into a new home, a new family, and a new name. The joy a mother experiences as she watches her young child proudly head off to kindergarten is mixed with the bittersweet feelings of change.

It is possible to have peace amid all the transitions of life because our heavenly Father never varies. While situations and people change around us, God never changes.

Our heavenly Father is unshakable and unchangeable. Scripture assures us that God is immutable—he is the same yesterday, today, and tomorrow. He is the solid rock we can rest against. And when we reflect on his unchanging nature, we can find stability. As we lean on him, the tension in our shoulders dissipates. Our muscles relax. We find peace.

Whatever changes you're facing today, lean on your unchanging God. Peace is waiting.

Read Hebrews 13:8.

THANK YOU, FATHER, FOR YOUR PEACE.

MIKE MASON

What we lack as Christians isn't just the will to believe the gospel, but the will to be happy about what we believe. Indeed, our lack of joy is a sign of unbelief.

A STATE OF GENUINE JOY

Katelyn struggled with the mistakes of her past. Over and over, she mentally replayed the memories of the nights she'd snuck out of the house, the secrets she'd kept from her parents, the lies she'd told. Guilt dominated her life, filled her thoughts, controlled her actions, and contorted her expressions. Plagued by the thoughts and emotions of her past sins, she was never truly happy.

After accepting Christ in her life, Katelyn confessed her sins to God and repented. She told her parents about her deceptions, and her parents forgave her. Still, for Katelyn, the feelings of guilt remained. God and her parents had forgiven her, but she couldn't accept their forgiveness. Unable to comprehend the depth of their love, Katelyn couldn't fathom the idea of total forgiveness for all the wrongs she'd done.

The gospel—that God sent his Son to save us from sin, that God forgives us completely—is the greatest reason for us to be joyful. Let's show our faith through our words, our thoughts, our actions, and our smiles. We *are* forgiven.

Read Psalm 96.

I AM THANKFUL FOR YOUR FORGIVENESS, LORD. LET ME BE JOYFUL IN YOU TODAY AND FOREVER.

HARRIET BEECHER STOWE

Many a humble soul will be amazed to find that the seed it sowed in weakness, in the dust of daily life, has blossomed into immortal flowers.

GOD IN OUR WEAKNESS

Sometimes it feels like we're not strong in Christ at all. We falter. We trip. We try and fail. We serve to the point of exhaustion. How can we possibly be of any value to God and his kingdom?

Oddly enough, it is in our weaknesses that God works in us the most. His strength gives us power even when we don't realize it. The weaker we feel, the more of God we bring to the situation. This is when we make the strongest impressions on others. We fade into the background as God's presence and glory are revealed through our weaknesses. We become the strongest of examples for him when we least know it.

In those weak moments, we sow seeds of faith. Under God's watchful eyes, those little seeds, sown in the dust of our daily lives, will blossom into immortal flowers of eternal life.

Keep planting. God will tend the garden and produce the growth.

Read 2 Corinthians 12:9–10.

WORK ESPECIALLY IN MY WEAKNESS, LORD.

STEVE BROWN

In order to understand God's lack of anger, you have to understand how much you deserve the anger of God.

LOVE DESPITE

In the movie *Marley & Me*, John Grogan and his wife adopt a hyperactive, out-of-control Labrador puppy they name Marley. Through the course of the book, Marley eats drywall, takes the dog-sitter for an all-out sprint around town, almost escapes a moving car by climbing out its window, and jumps into the pool of a house that's being shown to prospective buyers. He makes life for the Grogans complicated and sometimes miserable. They are constantly cleaning up Marley's messes and making up for the damage he's caused. They have every reason to be angry with Marley for his misdeeds. But despite all of this, they still love him and keep him in their home.

We constantly mess things up, return to our sin, and do wrong against God and others. He has every reason to be angry with us. Yet, as much as we don't deserve it, God chooses to love us—and continues loving us—despite our shortcomings. It's inexplicable, but true.

Read Romans 5:1–11.

LORD, THANK YOU FOR LOVING ME WHEN I DESERVE IT LEAST.

JOHN OF DAMASCUS

One can easily see that God provides, and provides excellently. For God alone is good and wise by nature. Since He is good, then, He provides.

GOOD ALWAYS

How would you define the word *good*? Based on your definition, is there someone or something you would consider good *all of the time?* Fifty percent of the time? Perhaps you have a friend who is a good friend most of the time, but sometimes he or she frustrates you or makes you mad. Or perhaps you read a book you thought was good once, but now you can't stand it.

God alone is good 100 percent of the time. But at times, our view of God's goodness can change, especially when we are going through difficult circumstances. Sometimes our definition of *good* is like shifting sands—changing based on feelings. But the Bible assures us that God is good all of the time, regardless of our circumstances or feelings. And because he is good, he cares about our needs.

Believe that God is good and that he delights to make his goodness known by providing for us.

Read Matthew 6:25–34.

LORD, YOU ARE SO GOOD TO ME.

MOTHER TERESA

Today it is fashionable to talk about the poor. Unfortunately, it is not fashionable to talk with them.

IN THEIR DEFENSE

Many celebrities are known by their causes. They host benefits for those who suffer with AIDS, rock concerts to help the victims of earthquakes or floods, and telethons to raise money and awareness of diseases. Raising money for the plight of the helpless is in vogue today.

Jesus had a soft spot for the poor and needy too. But he did much more than host a benefit concert or raise money. He got eyeball-to-eyeball with them and their suffering. He touched the leper, healed the blind, and spoke with the widow, the adulterous woman, and the Samaritan at the well. His approach was unpopular. It was scandalous. It was radical.

Jesus calls his followers to follow his example to help the poor and defend the defenseless. Will you adopt an orphan or befriend a homeless individual? Will you clean up after disasters or volunteer in a soup kitchen, food pantry, or shelter? Raising money helps fund causes for the poor, but it is only when we get personal, when we look into their eyes and touch them, that we love the poor the way Jesus loves them. And that's radical.

Read Psalm 82:2–4.

SHOW ME TODAY HOW TO GET PERSONAL IN HELPING THE POOR AND DEFENDING THE DEFENSELESS.

HENRY CLOUD AND JOHN TOWNSEND

The ultimate answer, then, to the problem of pain is a person. It's God himself.

THE PROBLEM OF PAIN

People seek pain relief in many forms today: aspirin, ibuprofen, prescription muscle relaxers. And those are just for physical pain. To alleviate emotional pain, some try to medicate themselves in other ways: alcohol, legal and illegal drugs, work, relationships, hours spent trolling the Internet. Still the pain lingers like an unwanted guest. But pain is usually the symptom of an underlying problem. Unless the problem is dealt with, the symptom of pain will remain.

Jesus assured his disciples that they would face the pain of persecution and suffering—symptoms of living in a fallen world. But he also gave them some good news: Jesus never met a problem he couldn't overcome. Yes, his followers would go through deep waters. But they would not be alone and defenseless. Jesus would be with them.

None of us will pass through this life pain free. But the ultimate pain reliever still is, and always will be, Jesus.

Read John 16:25–33.

JESUS, I OFFER YOU THE PAIN I FEEL AND ACCEPT THE PEACE OF YOUR PRESENCE.

HERMAS

Trust God that you will obtain from Him everything that you ask.

TOSS THAT MOUNTAIN

Mountains can be a beautiful sight when they're stretching over the horizon in all of their purple or snowcapped majesty. But when the only mountain you see is a problem you can't solve, words like *impossible* come to mind, instead of *beautiful*. In the face of such a seemingly insurmountable situation, you consult your resources—only to find that they are dwarfed in comparison. What will you do?

If you're facing a mountain-sized problem, Jesus invites you to give that mountain a toss. Impossible, you say? Not for God. Moving mountains is his specialty. All he requires from us is trust. Trust in God is the great mountain mover. When we believe that he has our best interests at heart and delights to hear from his children, we can pray with confidence that God will answer and provide everything we need.

Why not exchange your doubt for the rest that trusting God provides?

Read Mark 11:22–25.

I WANT TO TRUST YOU, LORD. HERE ARE MY
DOUBTS; PLEASE PROVIDE WHAT I NEED.

DALLAS WILLARD

To present [Christ's] lordship as an option leaves it squarely in the category of the white-wall tires and stereo equipment for the new car.

NO OPTION

If you want to follow Christ, making Jesus Lord of your life isn't optional. He doesn't wait on the sidelines of our lives, tossing in a little grace here and there while we run back and forth considering the decision of total devotion to him. As disciples of Jesus Christ, we are already on his team. We are committed, and that commitment means accepting his lordship over our lives as well.

Lordship means that Jesus is the center of our lives— not an extra addition thrown in, mixed with all of our other priorities and focuses and desires. As the King of kings and Lord of lords, Christ is over all and in all and through all. He is the very reason for our existence.

Lordship means that our lives revolve around him in every decision, every word, and every step.

Lordship means that we walk with him every step of the way.

Lordship means we are his and he is ours—totally and completely.

Read Isaiah 50:4–5.

JESUS, BE LORD OVER EVERY PART OF MY LIFE.

HANS CHRISTIAN ANDERSON

Every man's life is a fairy tale written by God's fingers.

THE FAIRY-TALE LIFE

As children, we were delighted to read fairy tales and dreamed that once upon a time we, too, would fall in love with a princess or Prince Charming and live happily ever after. But as we grew older, we realized that real life seldom has a fairy-tale ending.

We only need to scan the headlines to realize all the disappointments, from failed celebrity relationships to scandals that cause millionaires to lose their castles. But those who let the Lord write their story find that he composes one that is redemptive and eternal.

Each person is unique and valuable to God. If you honor him for what you've been given, whether it's much or very little, you may still experience troubles in this world. But if you've trusted Christ as Savior, your tale is guaranteed to end well—if not in this life, then in the next, where everything is perfect forever.

Read Psalm 139:13–18.

JESUS, I TRUST YOU WITH THE STORY OF MY LIFE AND LOOK
FORWARD TO MY HAPPILY EVER AFTER WITH YOU!

FREDERICK BUECHNER

The tortured's love for the torturer. This is God's love. It conquers the world.

I LOVE YOU

A Jew enduring torture during the Holocaust looks up at her torturer and says, "I love you." A POW in Vietnam raises his bleeding head and tells his tormentor, "I love you." A person walking through the wrong neighborhood says, "I love you" to the gangster whose gun is against his head.

"I love you." These are not words usually spoken to try to change an adversary's mind. These are words of honesty and truth, used to express what is in a loving person's heart. But these three words of immense meaning gain even more profundity when uttered in perilous situations toward one's enemies.

How is it possible to love someone who causes so much pain? How could we possibly love our enemies? Ask God, because that's the way he loves us. While we were still God's enemies, he loved us enough to send his Son to die on the cross in our place. And he continues to demonstrate his love for us yet today.

Read Luke 23:27–38.

I HOPE I NEVER STOP WONDERING AT YOUR LOVE FOR ME, PRECIOUS GOD.

DENNIS F. KINLAW

Christ died to do more for us than get us past the judgment. He died to give us . . . freedom . . . and he now waits for us to accept it.

BECOMING MORE LIKE CHRIST

Most of us can remember the day or even the hour we accepted Christ as Savior. Regardless of the details surrounding our conversion, it was a wonderful experience when our sins were forgiven and our eternal home was determined.

But Christ's death and resurrection did more for us than just spare us from eternal damnation; his saving power is also alive and at work in our daily lives. While we were yet dead in our sins, we could not experience the freedom that life in Christ provides. This freedom gives us victory over our sin and the ability—through the Holy Spirit—to daily live in communion with our heavenly Father.

This freedom also prepares us for an ever deeper relationship with Jesus, a relationship that daily draws us closer to him and changes our desires and objectives to align with his.

Never lose sight of the journey of freedom and faith that follows salvation.

Read Romans 8:1–4.

DAILY DRAW ME CLOSER TO YOU AND MAKE MY DESIRES YOURS.

CHARLES STANLEY

He wants you all to Himself to put His loving, divine arms around you.

THE WINGS OF GOD

If you were raised on a farm, you have likely witnessed the resolute protection of a mother hen. Whenever a hen senses that her chicks are in danger, she spreads her wings over them and pulls them close. This act of care places her in harm's way, but provides safety for her chicks. No matter the risk, she's willing to sacrifice herself for them.

The psalmist compares God to a mother hen. God loves us so much that he opens his arms wide and gathers us in. His loving embrace draws us close, letting us know that we are cherished and protected. He shields us under his wings, and he will gently guide us in the direction he has set out for each of us.

Ultimately, Jesus spread his arms wide and allowed himself to be sacrificed in order to save us. There is no gesture of love greater than that.

Read Psalm 91:1–4.

SAVIOR, DRAW ME CLOSE TO YOU, INTO YOUR EMBRACE.

ERWIN LUTZER

No other religion lays claim to an exclusive creator God who becomes a man in order to redeem us. . . . Christianity is exclusively original.

IT'S THE REAL THING

*O*riginal. When that word is strategically placed on a product's packaging, a restaurant's menu, or a designer suit's label, it increases the value. We willingly pay more for something that is original. We hold it in higher regard.

In Christianity, we see an exclusive creator God working out his exclusively original plan to save humanity. Some religions may try to imitate aspects of Christianity. Others might offer a "new and improved" package that includes customizable options. Still others may suggest what they think is a better alternative to the way of salvation outlined in the Bible.

But Christianity transcends them all. Christianity alone stays true to God's original plan of a perfect God-man who died in our place and rose again so that we might have eternal life.

Hang onto that truth today. No matter what others may say or do, Christianity is still exclusively original. It alone offers God's saving hope.

It's the real thing.

Read John 14:1–6.

GOD, I AM BLESSED TO KNOW I CAN TRUST
YOUR ORIGINAL PLAN OF REDEMPTION.

ELISABETH ELLIOT

To be a follower of the Crucified means, sooner or later, a personal encounter with the Cross.

OUR ASSIGNED CROSS

Jesus told his followers to take up their cross daily and follow him. Then he explained, "For whoever would save his life will lose it, but whoever loses his life for my sake will save it" (Luke 9:23–24 ESV). For the Christian, taking up our cross means loss.

The Bible assures us that we have been saved by grace; it is not our actions or our circumstances that bring us salvation. But a personal encounter with the Crucified does mean carrying our assigned cross and walking our own path of suffering for Christ in this life. For some, that may mean enduring criticism from friends or loved ones. For others, that may even include persecution or martyrdom.

When God allows us the high calling of carrying our cross, will we be as eager to follow the Crucified as when we follow him as the Rescuer, Strong Tower, and Healer? For all who follow the Crucified, there is no other way home.

Read Luke 9:23–27.

WHETHER MY CROSS IS LIGHT OR HEAVY, GRANT ME TODAY THE NEEDED COURAGE AND STRENGTH TO BEAR IT.

ISAAC NEWTON

Trials are medicines which our gracious and wise Physician prescribes; . . . he proportions the frequency and weight of them to what the case requires.

WELCOMING GOD'S TRIALS

When we are sick, the doctor often prescribes medication to treat the illness—but the medicine can taste terrible and have negative side effects. And even without adverse effects, our daily dose of medicine is a daily reminder we are sick. This is sort of like trials from God. Who wants them? But trials are necessary to strengthen our faith and improve our spiritual health.

Trials don't usually appear to be helpful, but cruel, unfair, and unloving. Why would a good God send trials into our lives? But sometimes the Great Physician sends trials into our lives as a form of spiritual medicine. God's discipline isn't much fun at the time, Hebrews 12:11 tells us, but it bears the fruit of righteousness and peace. The Lord loves those he tests. God's discipline shows that we are truly his sons and daughters.

So the next time we want to complain about the pain, or worse yet, consider abandoning our faith, it's time to ask the Lord for strength to endure our trials—realizing that, like medicine, our trials are for our good, as much as we might not want to take it.

Read Hebrews 12:1–14.

LORD, HELP ME TAKE MY "MEDICINE" FROM YOU, AND ACCEPT IT.

RICK WARREN

Trusting God completely means having faith that He knows what is best for your life. You expect Him to keep His promises . . . and do the impossible when necessary.

HE CAN DO THE IMPOSSIBLE

Sometimes we think that we know what's best for our lives. We make plans and do our best to prepare ourselves for the outcome we want to attain. Yet when our plans go awry, we realize that we don't know what's best for us. Only God does. And sometimes his plans take us through the territory of the impossible.

More than likely the Old Testament patriarch Abraham didn't imagine that he would be changing diapers at the ripe old age of one hundred. But God knew what was best for them. Sarah's response of laughter when she learned of God's decision to give them a child in their old age showed that she doubted God could do the impossible. But he could—and he did.

Do you trust God to not only know what's best for you but also to do the impossible? Are you willing to journey with him even if he changes your plans and takes you to a place you once thought impossible?

Read Genesis 18:9–15.

I TRUST YOU TO DO THE IMPOSSIBLE.

GREGORY OF NYSSA

God isn't pain, but He is pleasure. He isn't cowardice, but boldness. He isn't fear, anger, or any other emotion that sways the unguided soul.

WHAT GOD IS LIKE

In a time when the people of Israel misunderstood God the most, God gave Moses a rare gift: the proclamation of his name. He placed Moses in a safe place and then allowed his presence to pass before Moses, helping Moses understand just what he was like: gracious, merciful, slow to anger. God's decision to show his goodness to Moses came as a result of Moses' request to see God's glory (Exodus 33:18–23). While Moses went to talk with God on Mount Sinai, the people assumed that God and Moses had abandoned them. But they were wrong.

How many times have we explained or viewed God through the lens of our human limitations? He is the God without limits. We grieve God when we believe he won't continue to forgive because *we* can't fathom forgiving someone the ninetieth time for the same offense. As God helped Moses see, he never changes. He is always gracious. He is always merciful. And he is always slow to anger.

Read Exodus 34:5–9.

FORGIVE ME, LORD, FOR ASSIGNING LIMITS TO YOU. HELP ME TO ACCEPT THE TRUTH.

C. S. Lewis

Joy is the serious business of heaven.

SERIOUS ABOUT HEAVENLY JOY

What motivated Jesus to die for us? Was it love? The Bible says, "Greater love has no one than this, than to lay down one's life for his friends" (John 15:13 NKJV). Was it obedience to God? Scripture tells us, "[Jesus] humbled himself by becoming obedient to death—even death on a cross" (Philippians 2:8). Was it to satisfy God's wrath against sin and evil? "God set [Christ] forth as a propitiation by His blood" (Romans 3:25 NKJV).

These verses all help answer the question: why was Jesus crucified on our behalf? Yet the Bible also tells us another reason that Jesus stayed on the cross, though he could have called many angels to his aid—*joy*. "Jesus . . . for the joy that was set before Him endured the cross, despising the shame" (Hebrews 12:2 NKJV).

If joy is the business of heaven, should it not also be the serious business of earth?

Read Psalm 66.

KEEP ME FROM GLIB LIVING AND GUIDE ME INTO
THE SERIOUS JOY OF YOUR STEADFAST LOVE!

BILLY GRAHAM

My prayer for you today is that you will feel the loving arms of God wrapped around you.

HIS LOVING ARMS

Think back to a time when you promised someone that you'd always be there for them. Maybe it was a pinky-swear when you were just a child, or perhaps you wrote something to that effect in a best friend's senior yearbook. Where is that relationship now? How long has it been since you saw that person . . . or even thought about him or her?

God said that he will never leave us and never forsake us. We must understand that he made that promise to last forever, through all generations. No matter what circumstances we may face, God will always be right beside us, guiding, protecting, and loving us.

You can believe God's promise that he will always be with you. And when you feel the loving arms of our ever-present God, your life will be transformed.

Read Deuteronomy 31:6.

FATHER, THANK YOU THAT YOU REMEMBER
YOUR PROMISES—AND KEEP THEM.

MAX LUCADO

We learn brevity from Jesus. His greatest sermon can be read in eight minutes (Matthew 5–7).

IMPORTANT WORDS

One of the most important lessons that students learn in a writing class is to choose words carefully. They're taught to use plain, familiar, active words. They're taught to keep paragraphs short and to remove unnecessary details or descriptions. Every word must help communicate the point, and the point must be worthwhile. People today are too busy to read something meaningless. If a point isn't made by the end of the first paragraph, many people will stop reading.

When listening to a testimony, people want to hear the events that brought a person to Christ. When listening to music, the audience wants every note to lead fluidly to the next one. When listening to a speaker, a class wants to learn a memorable point. Once a person's attention is caught, it must be held. No word can be empty or meaningless.

Each word must be important, and that is especially true when we represent the Word made flesh. Instead of trying to impress people with our many words, let's follow Christ's example of communicating clearly and effectively, so that others may hear and follow him.

Read Matthew 7:24–27.

PLEASE MAKE MY WORDS IMPORTANT FOR OTHERS TO HEAR, LORD.

LLOYD JOHN OGILVIE

The future is a friend. The Lord can help me overcome the past and not repeat its mistakes.

DON'T TOUCH THAT!

A child can be obstinate. She wants to touch the pan on the stove, but you tell her no because it's hot and it will burn her hands. As soon as you turn away, she walks back to the stove and reaches for the pan again. You remove her from the danger and discipline her, explaining that it's for her own safety and urging her to obey.

We adults aren't that different from children. We make the same mistakes over again, and we sin today in the exact way we swore we wouldn't sin yesterday. Because God knows what's best for us, he sometimes has to warn us; he sometimes has to do something forceful to get our attention. In the moment, his correction might seem "mean" to our wayward minds, but take a step back—get away from the emotion of that instant—and you'll see he was really protecting you.

Our futures are at stake, and God wants us to overcome our temptations, our failures, our straying wills so that we may wholeheartedly embrace all that he has waiting for us ahead.

Read Romans 8:28–29.

GOD, HELP ME TO LEARN FROM MY PAST MISTAKES.

OSWALD CHAMBERS

Never try to make your experience a principle for others, but allow God to be as creative and original with others as He is with you.

INDIVIDUAL PREFERENCES

Ask college students how they ended up attending their school, and you'll receive a variety of responses. Some students will say their parents graduated from there. Some will say they followed siblings or sweethearts. Others will talk about scholarships or desired fields of study.

Similarly, Christians have a variety of preferences for forms of worship and ministry. Some people like the worship style of their parents' congregation, while others prefer more modern music. Some serve God in simple, everyday acts of service, while others serve God in more visible, exciting ways. Trying to force our modes of worship and preferences of ministry on others will only backfire. Traditional hymns may be used to worship God, and Christian rock may stir others to worship God as well. Private devotional time may be one person's favorite time of the day, whereas another may look forward to preaching or leading a group Bible study.

As long as God is the focus for worship that is in spirit and truth, that's all that counts.

Read Hebrews 11:1–16.

LORD, HELP ME TO NEVER PLACE YOUR CREATIVITY IN A BOX.

AUGUSTINE OF HIPPO

Those things which are to be enjoyed make us blessed.

THE BLESSED LIFE

The movie *Chariots of Fire* tells the story of Eric Liddell, a Scottish Christian born to missionary parents in China who competes for God's glory on the track in the 1924 Olympics.

After Eric misses a prayer meeting, his sister—who disapproves of his athletic pursuits—questions just how much his running really honors God. "I believe that God made me for a purpose," Eric responds. "But he also made me fast, and when I run, I feel his pleasure."

The activities we enjoy are blessings from God. Liddell eventually returned to China and, upon his death, all of Scotland mourned. His was indeed a blessed life.

Find those pursuits where you feel God's pleasure—and you, too, will be blessed.

Read Psalm 37:4.

LORD, HELP ME TO FEEL YOUR PLEASURE.

SEPTEMBER

DIETRICH BONHOEFFER

The test of whether we have truly found the peace of God will be in how we face the sufferings which befall us.

THE FIRM PEACE OF GOD

Suffering can make the world feel like an unstable place. In the midst of suffering, what we thought was a solid foundation beneath us turns to sand. During those dark times, our faith may be tested. In those dark times, we discover if the peace of God is truly in our hearts, for that peace will show itself even in the midst of dire suffering.

We have a choice about how we will undergo these trials. When we are filled with God's peace, we can view our suffering with a calm and understanding spirit. We still suffer, but the peace of God that "surpasses all understanding" (Philippians 4:7 NKJV) will help to restore our sense of stability. When we turn to God in times of great suffering, his peace will be our comfort.

In our suffering, we find God's peace. Without him we would be lost; with him we are forever found.

Read Philippians 4:4–7.

THANK YOU FOR CALLING ME, GOD, SO I MIGHT NOW TRUST IN YOU.

JONI EARECKSON TADA

[Contentment is] an internal quietness of heart, supernaturally given, that gladly submits to God in all circumstances.

THE DESTINATION

Using a road map or following the directions on a GPS helps us go from point A to point B with relative ease. But when we set off on our own trying to locate a destination using only our sense of direction, we often end up going in circles, backtracking, and generally stressed out.

Submission to God is a lot like using a road map. He knows the path we should travel and he's ready to be our guide. We shouldn't try to make the journey on our own—we are not wise enough to get ourselves out of the pitfalls and dead ends that show up as we travel. We need his help!

As we submit to God in all circumstances, we not only reach our destination but we experience contentment and joy in the journey. And through submission, we will one day reach our ultimate destination—kneeling before the throne of God, where true contentment will be ours forever.

Read Jeremiah 29:11.

I WANT TO FOLLOW YOU, LORD, IN PERFECT SUBMISSION TO YOUR WILL.

PHILIP YANCEY

By instinct I feel I must do something in order to be accepted. Grace sounds a startling note of contradiction, of liberation.

A TREASURED POSSESSION

The Bible describes the Israelites as a stiff-necked people. Often prideful and stubborn, they chose to go their own way time after time. They were a small nation, yet God made them mighty. They were foolish, yet God trusted them with his very Word. They were unfaithful, yet God continually drew them back, rescuing them when they called out to him for help.

A human father might tire of the antics of such a rebellious child, but the Lord refused to break his covenant with his children. The Israelites couldn't earn his love after their failures, because they had not earned it in the beginning. They were a holy people only because God made them holy. He treasured them, and it was because of his grace that he remained faithful toward them despite their wayward spirits. He chose them, bought them, and because of his great love, he refused to abandon them.

He feels the same way about us today.

Read Deuteronomy 7:6–9.

HELP ME STOP STRIVING, LORD, AND REST SECURE IN YOUR LOVE.

CLEMENT OF ROME

Let us hurry with all energy and readiness of mind to perform every good work. For the Creator and Lord of all Himself rejoices in His works.

A PARADIGM SHIFT

What do you hurry to do each day? Sometimes we rush through the activities of our day to get to what we think is the best part: quitting time, mealtimes, bedtime. We don't have to be forced to do the tasks we *really want to* do: play a sport we love, spend time with our family, read a good book. We give to the tasks we love our best energy and purpose.

Does the performance of "every good work" stir the same energy and readiness of mind? If we're honest, we'll probably say, "Not always." Sometimes we approach our service to the Lord with reluctance, knowing the limitations of our strength or desire. But it's time to make a paradigm shift. We can readily "perform every good work" when we know that the God of peace equips us. Relying on his limitless strength instead of our flagging energy or desire enables us to rejoice in the tasks to which he has called us.

Ready to rejoice? Rely on God.

Read Hebrews 13:20–21.

STIR ME, LORD, TO THE GOOD WORKS YOU WOULD HAVE ME DO.

STEVE BROWN

The reason the church will never die . . . is because the church is the resident place for the God of the universe.

UNITY IN THE BODY

A tornado ripped through an Oklahoma town in the fall of 2010 and left nothing standing. Debris covered the ground, power lines were down, and buildings lay flattened. One of the most unrecognizable buildings was the community chapel. The residents were devastated by the damage done to their beloved house of worship. Its beautiful stained-glass windows were shattered, and the pews where they had sat, cried, and prayed fervently were now reduced to splinters.

Too often we think of the church as a building, and we confine God to that structure. But the church is more than drywall, carpet, and electrical wires. The church is the body of Christ, and we are all members of it. We are the church, and come what may—wars, famine, even tornadoes—God will reside in us.

Read Romans 12:4–8.

ATHANASIUS

What then is our duty, my brethren, for the sake of these things, but to praise and give thanks to God, the King of all?

DUTY CALLS

What do you think of when you think of your "duty" to God? Some equate *duty* with a long, religious to-do list that gives them little joy. This to-do list mentality hinders their relationship with Christ and wearies them with marching orders that contain words like *should* and *ought. I should love others. I ought to praise God.*

Yet a fuller realization of God's goodness and mercy will automatically bring praise and thanks to your lips. It takes the burden out of ministry and sees every act of service as a love offering to our gracious God. In the way that a sparkle in the eyes and a smile on the lips are signs of being in love, our joyful praise of our Savior demonstrates our love for him.

Have you fully accepted the fact that you are beloved of God? Drink deeply at the well of his presence and you will hear the words of praise and thanks fill up your heart and overflow into your life of service to God.

Read Psalm 100.

LORD, MAY I ALWAYS PRAISE YOU, HEART AND SOUL.

JOHN MACARTHUR

When you pray, you set God in His rightful place, and everything else flows from there. All prayer is to begin with the character of God.

SETTING THE TABLE

As a child, learning to set the table can be a daunting task. The piles of glasses, plates, and utensils in the middle of the table can be confusing. Where does everything go? Regardless of how you learned to set the table—from a family member, a sample place setting, or a diagrammed placemat—the plate is key to the proper arrangement. Once the plate is in its rightful place, the center, everything begins to make sense.

In prayer, God's character is the plate we start with. When we focus on who God is first and foremost, our confidence in him grows. As his attributes form the foundation of our prayer, our needs are put in perspective. His priorities become our priorities. All prayer begins with the character of God.

Set the plate of God's character first today in your prayers. And answered prayer? Put it right in the center of the plate for all to see!

Read Matthew 6:25–34.

GOD, REMIND ME OF YOUR CHARACTER TODAY.

LACTANTIUS

So then, what does God require from us? Pure and holy worship of our minds.

WHAT DOES GOD WANT?

Most families, schools, places of employment, and neighborhoods have rules or expectations of behavior. The wise person learns what is required of him or her in order to be a successful participant. When a group's rules are unspoken, however, frustration can quickly set in as those new to the group try to meet expectations they can only guess at.

Have you ever asked yourself what God wants from us? Some believers fear that God has unspoken requirements they can't meet. They consult self-help books or the advice of other believers, all the while fearing God's anger if they get his requirements "wrong."

But God doesn't leave us to wonder what his expectations are; he tells us clearly in his Word. So what does God require? Sincere gratitude and worship. You can never go wrong when you praise God with a thankful heart. You don't need special skills to tell God thanks. Just be willing to spend time with the Father who loves you!

Read Micah 6:6–8.

PLEASE ACCEPT MY THANKS AND PRAISE TODAY.

THOMAS MERTON

*True solitude is a participation in the solitariness of God—
Who is in all things.*

RELYING ONLY ON GOD

Finding peace is increasingly difficult in our technological and informational world. No matter where we go, it's difficult to completely escape mobile phones, the Internet, television, or a hundred other things that vie for our attention. Yet maybe that's the reason we need to seek solitude today more than ever.

We read of Christians many centuries ago who went out to the desert for long periods of time to be alone with God. We also hear about modern-day Christians who take retreats of solitude—for a day, a weekend, or a week—to seek God and his will for their lives.

No matter the length of time, it's important for us to limit the world's hold on us and to increase the hold God has on us. There is hardly a better way than to spend time alone—without any distractions—with the Creator of all things.

When we escape from the noise of the world to spend solitary time with God, we will emerge refreshed, rejuvenated, and closer to God.

Read Mark 1:32–35.

TEACH ME TO SPEND TIME ALONE WITH YOU. PLEASE, GOD.

ORIGEN

The Savior not only said, "Knock, and it shall be opened to you; and seek, and ye shall find," but also, "Ask, and it shall be given unto you."

GO AHEAD AND ASK

We may think we've hit the prayer lottery when we consider the words of Jesus, saying, "Ask, and it will be given to you" (Matthew 7:7 NKJV). Like a kid in a candy store, we might eagerly ask for this, this, this, and some of this. After all, we have a green light, thanks to the Savior and the knowledge that God delights in his children's prayers.

Yet God reserves the right to answer prayer however he pleases. He does not always say yes to our requests. He's best pleased when his people persist in prayer, rather than insist on a certain answer.

Prayer is an open door to God's ear and heart. Neither is ever closed to his child's softest plea or grimace of pain. No need is considered too great or too insignificant. So, go ahead and ask and keep on asking. According to God's purpose and time frame, he will answer.

Read Matthew 7:7–11.

LORD GOD, THANK YOU FOR GIVING ME THE FREEDOM
TO ALWAYS COME BEFORE YOU IN PRAYER.

DONALD MILLER

The more I climb outside my pat answers, the more invigorating the view, the more my heart enters into worship.

RICHER AND DEEPER

One of the hardest parts of reading is diving deeper into the text. Literature classes are difficult for most students because they're prone to simply skim over the material. That's why professors push their classes to evaluate every word, sentence, and paragraph—it's the only way to find the symbolism and discern the author's intent.

Though God is richer and deeper than any text will ever be, we are too often content with complacency in our relationship with him. God, the Creator of the universe and the Lover of our souls, is yearning for us to shed our ambivalence—to give up the obligatory gestures and *enter in*! To enter into an intimate relationship with him. From that vantage point, we will be so invigorated that we won't be able to keep ourselves from worshiping him.

Read Psalm 76:4–9.

FREE ME FROM COMPLACENCY. LORD, I WANT SOMETHING DEEPER.

CHRYSOSTOM

Beloved, let us draw near to faith, since its powers are so great.

THE POWER OF FAITH

Ever wish you knew a real-life superhero—one who could leap tall buildings at a single bound like Superman? Wouldn't you keep that superhero's phone number at the top of your cell phone contacts list when life's problems loom larger than tall buildings? Yet the power of an imaginary superhero doesn't come close to the power of our very real God, accessed through the power of faith.

Perhaps you have days when your faith seems powerless. Even now you might long for the kind of faith embodied by the biblical heroes described in Hebrews 11. Yet a tiny bit of faith in a big God is all you need. A tiny bit of faith is all that many of the people in the Bible had. But our God can do a lot with just a little bit.

The power of faith is the power of God. It invites you to draw nearer to God, who is the only superhero you will ever need.

Read Hebrews 11:1–6.

MY FAITH RESTS IN YOU, O GOD.

PAUL LITTLE

*The best and clearest answer to how we know there is a God is
that he has visited us.*

HE HAS VISITED US

It's easier for us to believe something if we can see it, touch
it, smell it, or hear it. Something about our human perspective requires tangible evidence in order to believe something
with absolute certainty.

Yet as Christians living two thousand years after Christ
walked the earth, we don't have the luxury of ministering
alongside him on his journeys. We can't walk with him on the
road to Jerusalem or see him heal the sick or hear him teach
the crowd on the mountainside.

Don't be discouraged! We know that Christ lived among
us and died on the cross to forgive us of our sins. Scripture
is not the only reference we have for this. Secular historical
accounts also record Jesus' life and ministry—and he also
appeared to hundreds of people after he rose from the dead.

Because of Christ, we can be assured that God is real—
and he is as real and alive today as he was two thousand years
ago.

Read Matthew 16:14–21.

JESUS, HELP ME NEVER TO LOSE SIGHT OF HOW REAL
YOU ARE—YESTERDAY AS WELL AS TODAY.

CHARLES HADDON SPURGEON

The prayers of God's people are but God's promises breathed out of living hearts.

PRAYING GOD'S HEART

Have you ever noticed an elderly couple who bear an uncanny resemblance to each other? They may mirror each other's expressions and mannerisms. It is said that the more time two people spend together, the more they look alike.

The same is true with God. The more time we spend in his Word, the more his words echo from our tongues. The more we invest in prayer, the more his thoughts reverberate within our hearts. If we want to look like him, we will hang out with him.

We know that God can be trusted to keep his promises, so we enter boldly into his presence in prayer. We present our requests, not like slaves or servants trembling before a harsh ruler but as dearly loved children approaching a gracious Father. We trust that God knows what we need. We believe that when our hearts seek his will, he will answer. We know that he is good and faithful to guide our prayers until they become his very promises breathed out through us.

Read Hebrews 10:19–23.

GOD, LET MY THOUGHTS BE YOURS, MY
PRAYERS ALIGNED WITH YOUR WILL.

AUGUSTINE OF HIPPO

Let me know you, for you are the God who knows me; let me recognize you as you have recognized me.

KNOWING YOU

It can be intimidating to realize that someone knows a lot about us, at least until we understand the person's motives and how much he or she cares for us. But when it comes to God the Father, we can take comfort in the fact that he knows all about us. We can rest comfortably in his sovereign knowledge because he knit us together in the womb according to his own unique design. We need not fear God's intimate knowledge of us, for we know his motives and his love for us.

Nevertheless, God doesn't want this to be a one-way relationship. He offers us the chance to get to know him too. We can never know him as well as he knows us, but he longs to enter into a deep and intimate relationship with each of us. He wants us to know him so well that we easily recognize his heart and his will.

Knowing God, understanding his love for others, and contemplating his desire for justice are things we can experience by deepening our relationship with the Father.

Read Psalm 42:1–2.

HELP ME TO KNOW YOU AND LOVE YOU MORE, DEAR LORD.

BERNARD OF CLAIRVAUX

For God is sought, not by the movement of the feet, but by the desires of the heart.

SLOW DOWN AND YOU WILL FIND HIM

We all know people who seem to be always in motion, always working on something, always in the midst of some new project or endeavor. Most of us consider those people to be successful. After all, our society admires and esteems busy people.

Yet in our spiritual lives, we are given a completely different model. God's model for success is not so much focused on movement as it is on attitude. The movement of obedience will come later, but first we must make sure our attitudes—our hearts—are in the right place.

If we want to draw closer to God and his will for our lives, we must pause what we are doing to make time for him and determine his heart for us. We cannot do this while we are constantly in motion; we can only do this by slowing down through prayer, meditation, Scripture reading, and an earnest desire to become more like him.

Read Luke 12:22–34.

LORD, CREATE IN ME A DESIRE TO LEARN AND KNOW YOUR HEART.

JOHN ORTBERG

Here is a key task for spiritual vitality: we must arrange life so that sin no longer looks good to us.

LESSENING SIN'S APPEAL

Have you ever wished God would simply put us on autopilot or cruise control to heaven? Picture it: never missing a day in your Bible reading plan, heartfelt worship every Sunday at church, a consistent prayer life, making the most of every witnessing opportunity, and most of all a deepening love for God and the things of God each day.

An automatic, struggle-free Christian walk sounds appealing. But in that kind of an experience, sanctification would no longer be part of our Christian life. Faith in God to save us would not be faith to grow us. We would miss out on opportunities to grow stronger in our faith and to learn how to resist the temptation of sin along the way.

Instead of autopilot Christianity, we choose to arrange our days so that the kingdom of God has first place in our desires and our daily planners. Then our passion for God grows and the appeal of sin atrophies in our hearts. God's ways never looked so good!

Read Psalm 1.

GOD, HELP ME ARRANGE MY DAY SO SIN NO LONGER
LOOKS GOOD TO ME, BUT YOUR WAYS DO.

JOHN OF THE CROSS

Reveal your presence, / And may the vision of your beauty be my death; / For the sickness of love / Is not cured / Except by your very presence and image.

A LONG COMMITMENT

Life is so temporal and fleeting. Throughout the history of humankind, we see that our lives are but a mere speck. Many spend their allotted years chasing after physical pleasures and accomplishments that neither satisfy nor leave a lasting mark.

Yet those who have faith in Christ are blessed, for we are promised eternal life. More than that, we are also promised that we will experience the very presence of Christ in our daily lives. As we continue to seek him, he will reveal more and more of himself to us. And if we commit ourselves to him and his work, he will ensure that our labor on this earth will not be in vain.

So let us throw off whatever sins, habits, or other earthly barriers constrain us, and attach ourselves completely to Christ's presence. Let us seek his vision for our life, filled with love for our neighbors, service to our fellow man, and allegiance to whatever Christ lays on our hearts.

May his presence be the sole focus of the remaining days we walk the earth.

Read 1 Peter 4:12–19.

*LORD, FILL ME WITH A COMMITMENT TO
SERVE YOU WITH ALL I HAVE.*

LLOYD JOHN OGILVIE

Failure will bring us to either self-condemnation or repentance. Which one will determine our character?

A HEART FOR GOD

Failure can be very painful. Even the most highly trained professionals, skilled in competitions of winning and losing, cannot hide the agony of failure on their faces. The higher the hopes—Super Bowl, World Series, or Stanley Cup—the greater is the portrait of loss. When the camera pans the losing team with their blank stares, we see their hearts: "We've lost. It's over. We've failed." Then we observe the winning team with bright smiles on their faces, and we grasp their hearts: "We've won. It's ours. We've succeeded!"

As much as in winning, in losing we can see the true heart of a champion. This is especially true when it comes to our moral failure—when we stumble and sin, we discover our true character. Instead of wallowing in the pain of self-condemnation, the next step for a Christian is to turn back to God in repentance. The heart of a moral champion is a heart that longs for God's.

Read 1 John 1:8–2:3.

WHEN I SIN, MAY I TRUST CHRIST'S FORGIVENESS
TO RESTORE FULLY MY HEART FOR GOD.

BILLY GRAHAM

The gift of new or divine life to the regenerated person comes to the soul from Christ through the Holy Spirit.

A GIFT

A friend holds a package out to you. The paper covering it is stained and crumbled, but your friend assures you what's inside is beautiful and life-changing. What would you do? Do you trust your friend and open the gift despite its package, or do you turn away in disgust and exclaim, "I don't care what you say; I'm not opening that ugly gift"?

It amazes us as believers that God would give us—the undeserving—new life through the torment of his Son on the cross. The fact that he would take something as ugly as crucifixion and make it beautiful causes us to wonder.

And even more wondrous, God does the same with us. He takes our ugly, sin-stained lives and regenerates them with the purity of his Holy Spirit. He offers us a life-changing package that could be wrapped only one way: the blood of Christ. Only by opening this gift will we receive new life from Christ.

Read Ephesians 2:1–10.

LORD, THANK YOU FOR YOUR GIFT OF NEW LIFE IN YOUR SON.

A. W. TOZER

How completely satisfying to turn from our limitations to a God who has none.

ENDLESS POSSIBILITIES

Who then can be saved?" the disciples once asked Jesus. In response, Jesus reminded them of the truth that still stands today: "With men this is impossible, but with God all things are possible" (Matthew 19:25–26 NKJV).

No matter how hard we try, we cannot save ourselves. Left to our own devices, we will fail every time. God tells us to have faith, but we doubt. God says to believe, yet we question. God commands us to trust, but still we hesitate. God understands our limitations, so he grants us the faith. He supplies the belief. He earns our trust.

How amazing that not only does God tell us the qualities he wants us to possess, but then he places the seeds of those traits within our hearts and waters them. He knows our weaknesses and gives us everything we lack. We need not do anything on our own. We are fully supplied for every decision, every journey, and every task by the One who has no limits.

Read Mark 10:23–27.

THANK YOU, GOD, FOR EQUIPPING ME TODAY.

C. S. LEWIS

To know God is to know that our obedience is due to Him. In His nature His sovereignty de jure is revealed.

HE RULES THE WORLD

In this modern age, we sometimes forget how dependent we are on life's basics and necessities. No matter how advanced our technology or how cutting-edge our modern scientific breakthroughs, we still need air to breathe. We still need sufficient water and food to survive. And we still depend completely on our planet, which is perfectly situated within our galaxy in order to sustain life. Without any one of these, we would be doomed.

When we realize that God is completely in control of all of the details of creation, it should make us even more astounded at who he is. As we realize the limitlessness of his power and sovereignty, it should cause us daily to fall on our knees and worship him.

As we contemplate who God is and all that he has in his power, we should respond to him in unrestrained devotion and obedience. We serve an incredible, powerful, and majestic God!

Read Romans 1:18–20.

FATHER, HELP ME NEVER TO FORGET JUST HOW WONDERFUL AND POWERFUL YOU ARE.

CHARLES SWINDOLL

Don't worry if evil seems to be getting the upper hand as you humble yourself and obey God. He is Lord above all, including evil.

LORD ABOVE ALL

When we obey God, we sometimes feel strong enough to take on any opposition. However, how do we feel when we humbly obey, only to see evil continue to get the upper hand? What happens when, even with all of our obedience, things don't quite turn out as planned? Did we mess up? Did we misread God? We might even be tempted to doubt if obedience was worth it.

We must never forget that we are in a spiritual battle. Our obedience naturally stirs up the world of evil, with our enemy seeking to discourage us and make us doubt our God. Instead of doubting, remember that in obedience is strength. When we obey God, when we put our faith and trust in him, he imbues us with such power that evil has no hope of ruling over us. Our strength may falter and fail at times, but the strength of the Lord is everlasting. He is Lord above all, including evil.

Read Psalm 34:11–16.

GOD, LET MY OBEDIENCE SPUR THE GIFT
OF YOUR MIGHT IN MY LIFE.

R. C. SPROUL

The gospel of love may not be sugarcoated with saccharin grace.

UNMERITED GRACE

Grace is a magnificent concept that is particularly meaningful to those who follow Christ. Because of grace, our fallen nature and sinful behavior no longer form a barrier between us and God. He bestows his grace upon us without merit—meaning we don't deserve it and can't do anything to attain it.

Yet God's grace is offered to us free of charge. All we have to do is ask for it. His grace is available to us when we are not yet believers in Christ but ask earnestly for him to enter our hearts, and it's available to us each time we fail but honestly seek his forgiveness. And God's grace never runs out. We can never approach God for grace and hear him answer, "Sorry, but you have used up your allotment of grace." He continually offers us his abundant, overflowing, undeserved, amazing grace.

Let's live in light of the freeing power of God's unmerited grace in our lives.

Read John 1:15–17.

*DEAR GOD, MAY I UNDERSTAND YOUR GRACE AND LIVE
PURPOSELY, KNOWING ITS POWER IN MY LIFE.*

JOHN NEWTON

I am not what I ought to be. . . . But blessed be God, I am not what I used to be, and by the grace of God I am what I am.

WHO AM I NOW?

It's interesting to look back on our lives and review certain decisions and behaviors from the viewpoint of being a more mature adult. As we grow older, we gain insights and experiences that help us make better decisions.

The same applies to the Christian life—only more so. We all remember the person we were when we were new in Christ: the struggles we had, the sins we wrestled with, the truths we tried to apply to our lives. Yet as we grow in our faith, we notice that we are less like the person we used to be and more like the person we want to become. We're not quite there yet, but we can thank God for bringing us this far.

God didn't give up on us when we were lost in our sin, he didn't become frustrated with us when as new believers our growth was slow, and he still doesn't walk away from us when as more mature believers we still struggle. We can thank God for his presence through it all.

Read 1 Thessalonians 5:23–24.

THANK YOU FOR MAKING ME WHO I AM TODAY, HEAVENLY FATHER, AND FOR WORKING TO MAKE ME MORE LIKE YOUR SON DAY AFTER DAY.

James L. Snyder

The true follower of Christ will...say, "This is truth. God help me to walk in it, let come what may!"

TRUSTING IN THE CONSEQUENCES

How many times have we decided to follow through with a request from someone after he or she said, "Just trust me. Everything will be fine"? In doing so, we put our trust in a fallible human being. And those times don't always end favorably for us.

The person making the request may be a friend, a coworker, a relative, or some other trusted person. Nevertheless, we are putting our faith in a person who has motives that are less than perfect and intentions we often know little about. And as humans, their trustworthiness is limited by imperfect knowledge and reasoning ability.

But for the Christian, what joy and security we have when Christ calls us to trust him and the truth of his Word. We can completely rest in the fact that regardless of the direction, Christ leads us with perfect knowledge and motives. He will take care of us and give us the strength we need in any situation.

As long as Christ leads us, we have nothing to fear.

Read Psalm 4.

LORD, EQUIP ME TO TRUST WHERE YOU LEAD,
REGARDLESS OF THE CONSEQUENCES.

HENRI NOUWEN

God is not someone who was or will be, but the One who is, and who is for me in the present moment.

LIVING IN THE PRESENT

When we read the Bible, we sometimes get caught up in the historical facts presented in God's Word. The Old Testament is filled with dramatic events that happened thousands of years ago. Likewise, the New Testament recounts many details about the ministry of Jesus and the formation of the early church, events that occurred in history two thousand years ago.

Yet God is not the God of the past or the God of a certain historical period. He is the God of the past, present, and future. His power, guidance, and redemptive plan are current and ongoing.

In the Old Testament, God told Moses to tell the Israelites that "I AM" sent Moses to them. In the New Testament, Jesus told those gathered around him "before Abraham was born, I am!"

God does not exist in some past historical context, but he exists eternally, eager to interact with us and to be present with us in our lives.

Read John 8:57–58.

ENABLE ME TO SEE YOU AS THE GOD OF THE HERE AND NOW.

ELEANOR POWELL

What we are is God's gift to us. What we become is our gift to God.

KNOWING OUR POTENTIAL

We accomplish countless goals in our lives. Whether we sing, write, paint, play a sport, work with numbers, teach, or play a musical instrument, we should thank God daily for the abilities he has given us, for we realize that who we are is God's gift to us.

What we do with these gifts from God is, in turn, our gift back to him. Will we use our abilities selfishly, seeking to enrich ourselves or to take advantage of others? Or will we humbly use our gifts to bring glory not to ourselves, but to our God?

When God formed each of us, he created us with a purpose in mind. We can trust that God knew our potential, even before the moment of our conception, so we can use what we are to give him glory. There is no greater gift we can give to God than becoming what he always meant for us to be.

Read 1 Corinthians 10:31–33.

MY GIFTS ARE YOURS, LORD. USE ME TO GLORIFY YOUR NAME.

JOHN ELDREDGE

You've been far more than forgiven. . . . You've been delivered of what held you back from what you were meant to be.

THE AFFAIR

In a popular romance novel, the night before her wedding, a bride is caught with her former boyfriend. She had left him and the pain he'd caused her, for the prospective groom, who loved and protected her. Her life had improved marvelously, yet despite her fiancé's love, she'd returned to her former sweetheart. His lies possessed her mind, telling her that he was the one she loved, that he was better for her than the groom. She ran back to her ex-boyfriend, even though he had made her feel betrayed and worthless. The readers turn the pages faster and faster, eager to discover if the girl will come to her senses and return to the one who truly loves her.

In like manner, we too often return to the very sins Jesus saved us from. Yet, even when we betray him, he takes us back in his arms, loves and forgives us, and enables us to be who he created us to be. Our relationship with Jesus is a love story that has a happy ending.

Read Romans 6:1–14.

LORD, KEEP ME FROM SIN. MOLD ME TO YOUR WILL.

MADAME GUYON

Turn to the Scripture. . . . Take in fully, gently, and carefully what you are reading. Taste it and digest it as you read.

TAKE AND EAT

At times God seems so mysterious, but he has revealed more of his thoughts to us than we may realize. He imagined the entire universe and crafted the creation to give evidence to his character. We see part of God's thoughts every day when we look out our window or in the mirror. More importantly, though, God has given us the ability to know his thoughts through his written Word, the Bible.

The Bible is an invaluable resource to us. It takes us beyond creation and science to the concept of who we are in relation to God. In the pages of Scripture, God has made himself an open book in which he tells us of his love, his desires for us, and his plans for the future. He loves revealing himself to us and is never happier than when we seek him.

Open the book. Read it with reverence and care. Taste it. Digest it. It is food for your soul.

Read Psalm 119:97–104.

LORD, SPEAK TO ME AS I READ YOUR PRECIOUS WORD TODAY.

OCTOBER

G. K. CHESTERTON

The Christian ideal has not been tried and found wanting; it has been found difficult, and left untried.

WHICH YOKE?

We like to do things our own way and often bristle at following the rules or being told what to do. The Israelites, too, resisted God's commands and often turned from the laws of the Lord. But instead of finding liberation, they merely exchanged one set of regulations for another. They ran from the boundaries of God and his love and became slaves to this world—a heavy yoke that leads only to sin and death.

Jesus tells us to take his yoke and find rest. Does that sound strange? Jesus knows what we might refuse to admit—a yoke is not a device of torture but an implement necessary to do a job effectively and efficiently. A yoke distributes force, enabling more work to come from less effort. A yoke joins a pair, unites a team, and keeps them together so the row is plowed straight. Jesus says to us, "Join my team. We have work to do, and if you stick with me, you will go faster, farther." His yoke is easy, and his burden is light. He leads us with ropes of kindness and love.

Which yoke will you choose?

Read Hosea 11:1–4.

TODAY I CHOOSE YOUR YOKE OVER THE
HEAVY BURDENS OF THIS WORLD.

OSWALD CHAMBERS

No sin is worse than the sin of self-pity, because it obliterates God and puts self-interest on the throne.

READING THE RIGHT JOURNAL

It's been a rough week. Your kids haven't cooperated, work projects have been frustrating, and friends haven't returned your phone calls. Curling up under a blanket to write in your journal about the week's events seems a perfect way to unwind and destress. However, with the penning of each line of your memoir, your sorrow increases instead of decreasing.

Take a different memoir off your memory shelf. In this one, God is the author and main character. Its chapters are filled with stories of God's mercy, grace, and forgiveness. Its pages chronicle his care, provision, and kindness during both joyful and challenging times. The words illuminate God instead of obliterating him.

The shelf may be a little dusty today, but don't let the cobwebs scare you away. Open up God's memoir—the Bible. You'll be glad you did. You're still part of the story, but in this one, God is on the throne—right where he should be.

Read Ephesians 4:17–25.

KEEP ME FOCUSED ON YOU TODAY, LORD, AND NOT MYSELF.

MIKE MASON

Where your wounds are most tender, joy finds a soft place to settle.

FINDING JOY

Sometimes pain is necessary in order to bring about health. Healing may require surgery to remove an ailment or to reset a broken bone. When we're in the operating room, our wounds are tender and we often cannot see anything good during our time of pain—but it is in those very wounds that joy can settle.

God wants the very best for us. He works in all of his people's lives to create beauty instead of ashes (Isaiah 61:3) and to restore us to spiritual health so that we might glorify him. He takes our pain and gives us joy.

Every little step of trust and faith that we take—even when we are wounded in life's battles, even when we're in pain—is a step that pushes back the darkness and confusion Satan uses to overwhelm us. Each step of faith says to God, "I hurt, but I trust you."

Then joy has a soft place to settle.

Read Hebrews 12:1–2.

IN THE MIDST OF LIFE'S WOUNDS, DEAR LORD, GIVE ME JOY!

AUGUSTINE OF HIPPO

I shall therefore also go beyond this power of my nature, ascending by degrees to Him who made me.

NOT WHO I USED TO BE

One of the most remarkable things about the Christian life is the progression we make from where we once were to where we are now. Just as our bodies mature physically, our faith also matures spiritually. The longer we know Christ, the more we become like him.

That doesn't mean we ever attain perfection while we are on earth, but as we continue our Christian journey, our lives should demonstrate a gradual progression of becoming more and more like the One who saved us. As we grow closer to him, Christ empowers us to resist temptation, to adopt his heart when it comes to caring for others, and to do countless things for his glory that we never could do in our own power.

Christ is changing us—even when we aren't aware of it or can't always see it—to become more like him. Rejoice that you no longer are who you once were.

Read 1 Thessalonians 5:23–24.

FATHER, THANK YOU FOR CHANGING ME TO
BECOME MORE LIKE YOUR SON.

Elisabeth Elliot

To forgive . . . is to give up one's right to self, which is precisely what Jesus requires of anyone who wants to be his disciple.

WHEN LIFE ISN'T FAIR

When we hear of such human atrocities as death camps at Auschwitz, the killing fields of Cambodia, or tribal cleansing in Rwanda, we see the fragility of human justice in an evil world. On a much smaller scale, perhaps someone takes your parking place, a colleague gets the accolades for your hard work, or your life savings are cut in half by a recession. Or maybe you've been devastated by a spouse's betrayal or physically injured by violent crime.

When we encounter circumstances like these, we cry, "It's not fair!" We feel that we have a right to be treated fairly, and we are often angered by the injustice in this world.

In some way, at some level, when we are treated unfairly we need to make the same decision as those who suffer human atrocities: either bitterness or forgiveness. It is not about getting our right to justice; that is God's job. It is about forgiving others as the Lord has forgiven you.

Read Matthew 18:21–35.

LORD, WHEN I AM TREATED UNFAIRLY TODAY, GIVE
GRACE TO FORGIVE AS YOU HAVE FORGIVEN ME.

TERTULLIAN

Christ Jesus has even made us kings for God, His Father.

UNLIKELY KINGS

The Bible provides two unlikely snapshots of royalty. One focuses on a thief dying on a wooden cross. While the crowd jeered, the thief dared to believe that the man next to him—Jesus—had a kingdom waiting for him and could take him to an eternal paradise (Luke 23;39–43). The second comes in the fourth chapter of Revelation where a group of believers in heaven cast their crowns before the throne of God. Because of Jesus, the unlikely are made kings in a place they would have no hope of gaining without him.

Through God's grace, you too will someday bear a crown that no one can take away. Salvation, the guarantee of your future inheritance, clothes you with royal authority like a kingly mantle. God chose you to rule with him.

On a day when you might feel helpless or powerless, remember that you're royalty—you're a child of the King!

Read Revelation 4:4–11.

LORD, I AM EXCITED FOR THE FUTURE
WHEN I WILL REIGN WITH YOU.

MAX LUCADO

[Jesus] was so moved by the people's hurts that he put his hurts on the back burner. Maybe that's why God brings hurting people into your world, too.

BEAR ONE ANOTHER'S BURDENS

Dick and Rick Hoyt love marathons. They run as a team, father and son. The 2009 Boston Marathon was their one-thousandth race. That isn't the only remarkable thing about them, though.

Dick Hoyt is almost seventy years old, and Rick Hoyt has had cerebral palsy since birth. Dick pushes his son's wheelchair every inch of every race. Rick depends on his father, but Dick gets a whole lot of encouragement from his son.

We need one another. People around us are hurting, and sometimes the pain can become overwhelming. At those times, we need to put our hurts on the back burner so that we can help others. Then, when the time comes, they will give us a place to lean as well.

And in front of us is the glory of the finish line.

Read 2 Corinthians 1:3–5.

GOD, HELP ME TO SUPPORT THOSE WHO NEED MY HELP TODAY.

GREGORY OF NYSSA

He brought us back to the place from which we strayed, becoming mere flesh and blood by sin.

PRONE TO WANDER

Sheep always need a shepherd. These defenseless animals require someone to guide them to water, to lead them to edible pastureland, and to help them avoid harm. When they stray—and some will—they need a firm hand to guide them back to the fold.

Does that behavior sound familiar? No wonder psalmists like David and prophets like Isaiah compared people to helpless sheep. While such a metaphor might cause us to feel sheepish, it is apt when we consider the times we've wandered away from God. Straying doesn't always mean a big step. Sometimes the little decisions we make—"God says to do *this,* but I want to do *this*"—can be a step that leads us in the wrong direction.

Jesus is our "good shepherd" (John 10:14 NKJV). He is an expert at caring for his flock. Because of his humanity, he understands our propensity to stray. Because of his deity, he was the perfect sacrifice for sin. When we stray, he gently guides us back to the fold.

Read Isaiah 53:4–9.

I'M GRATEFUL FOR YOUR SHEPHERDING CARE.

JONI EARECKSON TADA

Heartache forces us to embrace God out of desperate, urgent need. God is never closer than when your heart is aching.

PRAYERS OF AN ACHING HEART

Every Christian experiences pain, weakness, and tragedy. In those times we may find it difficult to pray. It's not that we don't want to pray; in times of distress, we know we need God more than ever! But when our heart is breaking, prayer sometimes seems impossible. We may turn toward God, but in our anguish we can't even form the words to express our sorrow.

God provided the Holy Spirit to be our comforter. In those times when our heart is aching and our vision clouded by confusion and grief, the Spirit comes close to us and wraps us in the soothing embrace of God's presence. When we are overwhelmed beyond words, the Spirit takes our unformed prayers to God on our behalf.

When your heart is breaking, remember that God is near to comfort you.

Read Romans 8:26–27.

HILARY OF POITIERS

The Creator of great things is supreme in greatness. Of every beautiful thing He is superior in beauty.

A BEAUTIFUL SIGHT

What's the most beautiful sight you've ever seen? Was it the ocean or the mountains, a cherished possession, or perhaps your spouse on your wedding day? People are clearly captivated by beauty and seem to enjoy making lists of people, places, and things considered "most beautiful," from *People* magazine's annual "Most Beautiful People" issue to the Internet rankings of most beautiful cities in the world.

God has equipped each of us with a desire for beauty. Yet beauty by society's definition is an ever-shifting commodity. What was beautiful thirty years ago may not be deemed beautiful today.

The most beautiful sight is one we haven't yet fully seen: God himself. Through the eyes of faith we can glimpse his presence in his creation and in his Word, but one day we will finally be able to gaze upon our Lord in all of his beauty and splendor. No matter what standard of beauty society imposes on its people, God will always be superior.

Craving beauty? Come and fill your gaze with the most beautiful sight in the universe.

Read Psalm 27:1–4.

MOVE ME TO TAKE TIME TO GAZE AT YOUR BEAUTY TODAY, LORD.

ROBERT H. SCHULLER

Anyone can count the seeds in an apple, but only God can count the number of apples in a seed.

UNLIMITED KNOWLEDGE

God is the only being to possess limitless knowledge. He knows all that ever occurred in the past. He knows everything that is happening at this moment. He knows what will happen in the future. He is prepared to meet our needs even before we know we are in need.

Because God knows the future, nothing can surprise him. He not only knows the circumstances we are facing, but he knows the way through them.

Why do we so often think we know better than God? So often we second-guess his plans for us. Sometimes we even go so far as to think he doesn't understand what we are going through. At times, we even think that God has forgotten about us.

But God loves us and wants to guide us into the future that only he knows. Let us sit at his feet, soaking up all he has to teach us.

Read Psalm 139:1–4.

TEACH ME, LORD. I WANT TO LEARN FROM YOU.

LEO THE GREAT

Believe the Son of God to be co-eternal with the Father by Whom all things were made and without Whom nothing was made.

BY HIS HANDS

Looking at the magnificence of the Grand Canyon or the wonder of Victoria Falls, perhaps you can easily picture a big God who created such breathtaking beauty. Gaze upon your own hands, whether thin fingered or work roughened. Could your hands create such wonders?

Jesus could. Though Jesus was a carpenter with calloused hands, the apostle John proclaimed him to be the one by whom all things were made. Jesus Christ was both man and God. By his word the beluga whale and the butterfly sprang into being. And during his incarnation, the power of creation was evident in his hands—the very hands of God—as he miraculously turned water into wine, calmed the raging sea, and turned one boy's meager lunch into a feast for well over five thousand people.

The next time you look at your hands, consider what Jesus, the eternal creator and sustainer of all things, can do with them.

Read John 1:1–5.

USE MY HANDS, LORD, TO DO WHAT NEEDS TO BE DONE.

JOSH McDOWELL

God can see the way through the moral maze so much better than we; and His commands are given to keep us from heading down dead ends.

NAVIGATING THE MORAL MAZE

Some cornfield mazes have a platform where a knowledgeable person can shout out directions to anyone who is lost: "Take two rights and then four lefts." To those who are not too proud to accept them, such directions can take the stress out of traversing a maze and make it feel like more of an adventure.

Oh, that we would not be too proud to listen to God, who is trying, through his Word, to offer us direction as we wander the moral maze of this life! We could save ourselves a lot of panic and confusion if only we would consistently open our hearts to his wisdom and guidance.

Thankfully, we don't have to guess when to go right and when to go left in this maze. We have a knowledgeable guide. And he is not shouting at us from above but rather walking through the maze with us at every twist and turn.

Read Proverbs 16:25.

THANK YOU, FATHER, FOR BEING MY COMPANION AND GUIDE IN THIS MAZE OF LIFE.

DIETRICH BONHOEFFER

Those who would learn to serve must first learn to think little of themselves . . . (Rom. 12:3).

ADJUSTING OUR VIEW OF SELF

How many times each day do you hear messages in advertisements and media that tell us that we are important, that our needs and desires are paramount, and that we should not let others stand in the way of our goals and happiness? We are inundated with these messages daily.

Yet that is not the radical approach to life that Christ modeled for us. His thinking goes against our modern times, but it also went against the messages conveyed throughout all of human history.

If we truly want to walk closer to Christ and follow his plan for our lives, we must be willing to humble ourselves and submit to him—and to others. This attitude of selflessness is certainly difficult and not of this world, but it's necessary if we are to serve him.

Scripture reminds us not to think too highly of ourselves and commands us to treat our neighbors as we want to be treated. This radical, biblical challenge is filled with wonderful possibilities.

Read Romans 12:3–8.

FATHER, DON'T LET ME THINK TOO HIGHLY OF MYSELF. MAKE ME WILLING TO SERVE.

CHARLES HADDON SPURGEON

What you keep to yourselves you shall lose, but what you give to Him you save and gain.

GIVING HIM OUR ALL

Perhaps one of the most difficult lessons of the Christian faith is that this life is temporary, yet what we do in it has eternal consequences. Jesus said, "For whoever desires to save his life will lose it, but whoever loses his life for My sake will find it" (Matthew 16:25 NKJV). Scripture is full of examples of this. The same principle holds true when it comes to how we treat others and what we give them spiritually.

We have been blessed with an eternal reward far outweighing what we deserve—our salvation in Christ. By giving away the love and care that Christ has given us, we know that our efforts will not only have consequences on this planet but also will have eternal results. Giving him our lives and our passions ensures that they will be used for greater gain.

Let's be eager to share what we have been given, knowing that Christ has greater plans for it than we could ever imagine.

Read Matthew 25:14–29.

HELP ME TO GIVE FREELY OF THE LOVE YOU HAVE GIVEN ME, JESUS.

C. S. LEWIS

[Jesus says,] I have not come to torment your natural self, but to kill it.

SELF-SURRENDER

Jesus wants every piece of us. He doesn't merely want our good deeds here or there. He wants more than our weekly church attendance and spotty prayer life. He wants every ounce of us—not only our outward actions but also our inner being with all of its desires, thoughts, and dreams.

The marathon runner decides every morning to get up, lace well-worn shoes, and open the door for yet another run. He puts aside his desire for another hour of sleep and stays focused on his goal. He receives a reward for those daily decisions when he crosses the finish line ahead of those who decided to take a day off and sleep in.

Giving up control of self requires a conscious decision each morning. We must choose to die to our natural self and to stay focused on our new life in Christ. As we give Christ control of our lives, he kills our natural self and replaces it with his life.

When that last piece of self is handed over in surrender to Christ, you will be living a new life, the best life ever.

Read Colossians 3:1–14.

LORD JESUS, I SURRENDER MYSELF TO YOU. FILL ME WITH YOU.

BROTHER LAWRENCE

We ought . . . to put our whole trust in God and make a total surrender of ourselves to Him, secure that He would not deceive us.

GOD WILL NOT DECEIVE US

Have you ever been betrayed? Many of us have experienced the disappointment of discovering that someone we trusted was not truthful with us. Others have suffered the crushing heartache of realizing that a close friend or loved one intentionally deceived or harmed them in some manner. Since we live in a fallen world, lies and deception are a lamentable reality.

Yet what a blessing to know that our Creator—the One who designed us and formed us in our mothers' wombs—will never deceive us. His promises to care for us, to love us unconditionally, to provide for us, never to abandon us, and to prepare an eternal home for us are true. These promises cannot and will not be broken.

So when we put our trust in God and daily surrender ourselves to his leadership of our lives, we can rest completely in the fact that his Word cannot be broken. His promises in Scripture are ironclad.

Read Psalm 9.

LORD, HELP ME TO SURRENDER MORE OF MYSELF TO YOU, KNOWING THAT YOU WILL NEVER DECEIVE ME.

LLOYD JOHN OGILVIE

What we criticize in others may be unresolved in us.

THE DIRTIER FACE

Catherine diligently worked on her chalk drawing for the entire hour of art class. She had blended colors, swirled sponges to darken or fade hues, and used a heavy piece of soft black coal to outline a border. Looking over at her friend Anna's smudged attempt to make a chalk drawing of a face, Catherine laughed. "That's one of the messiest faces I've ever seen," she said critically. Anna first looked offended, then amused. She reached into her purse, extracted a compact, and held the mirror in front of Catherine. "Not as messy as this face," Anna countered. To her surprise, Catherine saw her reflection, her sweaty cheeks smeared with chalk colors and hair filled with coal dust.

Too often we are quick to criticize the flaws of others without realizing our own flaws. It's easy to point out the failings of others instead of examining ourselves to discover that we may be the greater sinner. Yet acceptance and love do far more to help others than insults and ridicule. Instead of pointing out others' sins, let's confess our own sins to God. Then, cleansed by his forgiveness, we can reach out to others with kindness and love.

Read Matthew 7:1–5.

I LONG TO BE THE TYPE OF PERSON WHO FOCUSES ON FIXING MY OWN FAULTS INSTEAD OF OTHERS'. HELP ME, FATHER.

BILLY GRAHAM

The world can argue against Christianity as an institution, but there is no convincing argument against a person who has been made Christlike.

FOR THE BETTER

When we come face-to-face with Jesus, we change for the better. As we seek to follow in the footsteps of our Savior, we become more like him. The Holy Spirit comes into our lives and begins to grow his special fruit in our lives—love, joy, peace, patience, kindness, goodness, faithfulness, gentleness, and self-control (see Galatians 5:22–23). And face it, when our lives start to exhibit *those* characteristics, people can't help but notice the difference in us.

Peter wrote to scattered Christians and encouraged them to live good lives in front of their unbelieving neighbors. The advice is important for us today as well. People can deny the existence of a far-off God that they discuss only in theory, but the stark reality of a life that has been changed by Christ cannot be disputed. The world can argue doctrine and find fault with the traditions and rituals of Christianity, but when they meet Jesus in the life and heart of a transformed believer, all objections fall away.

Read 1 Peter 2:11–12.

JESUS, LET THE CHANGES IN MY LIFE POINT OTHERS TO YOU.

J. OSWALD SANDERS

Our God knows no unfinished task. He completes what He begins.

THE FINISH LINE

On October 20, 1968, the Mexico City Olympic Stadium was both the starting line and the finish line of the Olympic marathon. During the race, John Stephen Akhwari of Tanzania stumbled and seriously hurt his leg. Medics bandaged the man's bloody calf, and then Akhwari rose and began to hobble forward. Though in agonizing pain, Akhwari continued, mile after mile. As he finally entered the stadium, he completed the final lap, hobbling all the way. The crowd rose and cheered, but Akhwari simply finished the lap and left the stadium. Later, a sportswriter asked, "Why didn't you just quit?" Akhwari responded, "My country did not send me 7,000 miles to *start* the race. It sent me to *finish* the race."

Our God finishes what he starts. James tells us "perseverance must *finish* its work" (italics added) so that we can be mature in our righteousness. Let us also complete the good work we start.

Read James 1:2–8.

LORD, GIVE ME THE STRENGTH TO BE LIKE YOU—
SOMEONE WHO COMPLETES GOOD WORK.

PHILIP YANCEY

Many things remain hidden and unclear. [Jesus] says just enough to keep us on tiptoe, watching and hoping.

HIDE AND SEEK

Something makes us want to search for hidden treasures. We seek for birthday presents tucked away in closets or basements. We explore the recesses of couch cushions hoping to find some change. We shake the gifts piled under the Christmas tree, straining to hear a crinkle or jingle that might give away the contents.

Jesus knew our penchant for seeking hidden things. He spoke in parables and riddles, using word games to capture the attention of his audience. He hinted at things to come and a time when all would be made known. His whispers caused the listeners to lean in closer. He related stories of places unseen, of secrets soon to be unveiled, of heavenly riches for those who believe.

Like children, we wait eagerly, imagining all Jesus has planned for us, watching for a glimpse of the glory he's prepared for us. In the meantime, we can tell his secrets to others.

Read Matthew 10:24–27.

HELP ME INVITE OTHERS TO EXPERIENCE YOUR HIDDEN PROMISES FOR THEM.

DON WILLIAMS

Notice that the action of worship, the how, is based upon revelation, the why.

CAUSE AND EFFECT

Cause and effect is simple. Every junior-high science student understands that adding some substances to others creates a reaction—sometimes positive, sometimes negative. You might get a compound of beautiful color and scent; you might get an explosion.

How we worship is based on *why* we worship—cause and effect. Are we worshiping because it's the thing to do, because our friends do it, because it's a habit? If so, our worship will be stale, flat, without emotion. In fact, it might not be true worship at all.

However, if we are worshiping because of our love for this God who saves us, transforms us, and promises us eternity with him, then our worship will reach to heaven and bring us close to him. In order to worship God as he should be worshiped, we need to focus completely on who he is and what he has done. Cause and effect.

Read Psalm 29:1–2.

EMPTY ME OF MYSELF AND FILL ME WITH YOU, FATHER.

HANNAH HURNARD

Our Lord laid greater emphasis on the absolute necessity of willingness to forgive than on anything else.

PLEASE FORGIVE

I'msorrywillyoupleaseforgiveme?" mumbled the five-year-old to his big sister for the third time that day. He had accidentally stepped on her chalk drawing in the morning, spilled his drink all over her sandwich at lunch, and then broken her favorite toy while playing with it that afternoon. He was so remorseful that every time he asked, she willingly forgave.

The little boy was learning a valuable lesson. Each time he messed up, his sister had to start over—new drawing, new sandwich, fixed toy. Yet each time, she loved him enough to forgive. Because she was willing to forgive, he saw the importance of forgiving others.

Forgiveness doesn't come naturally. It isn't always easy. Forgiveness requires self-sacrifice and humility. It lets go of the need for revenge. It releases the past so that you can move forward.

Jesus is our example. Of his murderers he said, "Father, forgive them, for they do not know what they do" (Luke 23:34 NKJV).

Read Luke 23:32–34.

FORGIVER OF ALL, ALLOW ME GRACE TO EXTEND THE SAME.

DAVE VEERMAN

You're not alone. The Comforter is close, wrapping his arms around you and whispering words of love.

GOD'S EMBRACE

Concerts. Churches. Festivals. Football stadiums. What do they have in common? Huge crowds. Ironically, though, at any of these events, it's possible—easy, even—to feel alone. It's no secret that humans can feel lonely anywhere. Most of us will go to any length to make a connection. Some of us seek it through romance, others through popularity, and still others via social networks or online games. Connecting is one of our most desperate longings, and we'll strive for it wherever we can get it.

But there's a problem: no matter where we try to find it, true connection will elude us if we seek it in anything but God. For a time, these intimacy substitutes will satisfy, but inevitably they will leave us unfulfilled.

With God, however, we are never alone. As our Comforter, he is close to us, arms stretched out, ready to hold us. Embrace him. He won't let go.

Read Psalm 46:1–11.

FATHER, HOLD ME. I DO NOT WANT TO BE ALONE.

ROBERT COLEMAN

*It all started by Jesus calling a few men to follow Him. . . . His
concern was not with programs to reach the multitudes, but with
men whom the multitudes could follow.*

FOLLOW ME

"Follow me." Two simple words uttered by a passing Jewish
teacher called the fishermen, two brothers, a tax collector.
All who heard Jesus' command followed without question. Did
the disciples know who he was? Did they know where they
were going? Surely the disciples couldn't have predicted that
they would follow him to heal the sick. They couldn't have
known they would follow him as he fed the multitudes with a
little boy's lunch. They couldn't have guessed that the man they
followed would teach them a new covenant, wash their feet,
and take their place on a cross. Yet they followed anyway.

They healed people in his name. They fed generations
with the Bread of Life that they carried far and wide. They
recorded his teachings, spread the gospel of love, and remained
faithful even unto death.

All this the disciples learned by serving God, loving their
neighbor, and remaining faithful to Jesus' two-word invitation:
"Follow me." And he gives us the same invitation today.

Love God. Love others. Follow Jesus.

Read John 12:23–26.

GOD, HELP ME TO FOLLOW YOU TODAY AND EVERY DAY.

SAM STORMS

Thank God for the "but God's" of the Bible! "But God, who comforts the downcast, comforted us by the coming of Titus" (2 Cor. 7:6).

BUT GOD . . .

God is sometimes incorrectly labeled as unreasonable or cruel. Unbelievers think that like a callous judge, God thunders from heaven with anger, malice, or punishment for the slightest infraction. Some people argue that God is a celestial killjoy, taking away our pleasure with a list of "Thou shalts" and "Thou shalt nots."

Praise God that he is not like that! Instead of delighting in our downfall, the Bible tells us that God, in his goodness, is a God of second chances. He comes to the rescue of his children, even when their difficulties are of their own making. The Bible lists many instances of trials that changed to blessings simply because God intervened. *But God . . .* "is a mediator," "had mercy," "disciplines us for our good," "promised a legacy," "raised Jesus," "remembered the needy," "answered," "listened," "preserved," "testifies," "gave protection and warning."

Perhaps the loveliest "but God" in the page of Scripture is found in Romans 5:8: "*But God* demonstrates his own love for us in this: While we were still sinners, Christ died for us."

Read Romans 5:6–11.

LET ME RECOGNIZE EVERY "BUT GOD" BLESSING IN MY LIFE TODAY.

DWIGHT L. MOODY

It is. . .better to live a holy life than to talk about it. Light-houses do not ring bells to call attention to their shining—they just shine.

SHINE ON!

Moses stretched out his hand and darkness covered Egypt. Not a rosy dusk. Not a sapphire twilight. Not the inky velvet of a star-studded summer night. Darkness so deep you couldn't see an inch into the blackness. Agonizing, claustrophobic, crushing darkness.

"Yet all the Israelites had light in the place where they lived." In the midst of the plague of darkness, the light of the presence of the Lord shone on his chosen ones. God's light pierced the darkness, appearing even brighter in relation to the oppression surrounding it. Life-giving, liberating, sustaining light.

Darkness covers our world in the form of sin and evil. Many people are lost in darkness so deep that they can't see a way out. But when we shine the light and love of Christ, those around us can't help but notice. Our testimony is a valuable thing, but sometimes, more than our words, more than a choice verse of Scripture, people need to see the presence of the Lord reflected in our life, directing them to the Light of the world. Shine on!

Read Exodus 10:21–23.

MAY MY LIGHT SHINE TODAY, DRAWING OTHERS TO YOU.

SELWYN HUGHES

O Father, what You want for my life, I want too—for my will and Your will to coincide.

EAGER TO FILL

Jesus wept and laughed. He fed the multitudes and taught thousands. He grew angry at the moneychangers and welcomed the children with open arms. He expressed many emotions during his ministry on earth, but Jesus was the most gentle and tender toward those who came to him simply to worship him, soaking in his presence and power.

Mary of Bethany, who sat and listened at his feet, earned a place of honor. Jesus defended the woman who came to him and drenched his feet with her tears, saying she wanted only to be near him and to worship him.

Each of these believers came to Jesus to worship him—to pour out their longings, their fears, and their devotion to him. In return, Jesus eagerly filled them with his love, his healing, and his peace.

Spending time worshiping Jesus unites his heart with yours. When you draw near to him, he responds by eagerly filling you with his presence and love.

Read Psalm 16:9–11.

UNITE MY HEART WITH YOURS, LORD. FILL ME
WITH YOUR PRESENCE AND LOVE.

SUSANNAH WESLEY

There are two things to do about the gospel: believe it and behave it.

DO NOT MERELY LISTEN

Browse any Christian bookstore and you might get the feeling that following Jesus is a difficult and complex proposition. Thousands of books line the shelves in sections labeled "Christian Living," "Women's Interest," and "Study Materials." One book tells you to follow Jesus through a specific method, while another book outlines a different set of requirements. You might be overwhelmed by all the plans and steps and doctrines and programs that various authors have dictated as paths to following Christ.

But the gospel is simple: *declare with your mouth and believe with your heart that Jesus is the Son of God.* God doesn't make the faith walk a mystery with puzzles to solve or codes to break. He tells us in his Word all he desires of us and for us, and then he says, "Do what it says."

Jesus condensed the Bible to two directives: love God and love your neighbor as yourself. When we worship and revere God for his position as our Creator and Redeemer and when we treat others the way we would like to be treated, the gospel is winsome.

Read James 1:22–27.

HELP ME TODAY TO LIVE OUT THE PRECEPTS
FOUND IN YOUR WORD.

John Calvin

Christ pronounces those to be happy who, chastened and subdued by their problems, submit themselves wholly to God.

HAPPILY HUMBLED

The prodigal son envisioned a life of entertainment and pleasure outside the confines of his country home. He longed to broaden his horizons beyond his boring life and the watchful eye of his father. So he demanded his inheritance and struck out on his own. But he squandered his wealth, lived a wild existence, and returned home broken and humbled.

Before, the boundaries of his father's land had felt confining. Now the son longed for the security of home. Once, his father's wealth had given him all the food he needed to survive. But the inheritance he left home with only fed his folly. Previously, his father's arms made him struggle for liberty; now they offered protection.

The son learned the difficult lesson that freedom comes within the margins of lovingly set boundaries.

Our loving heavenly Father also gives us limits. His boundaries are not to keep his children in, but to keep danger and evil out. His rules are not to limit us, but to sustain us. Within his walls we find refuge, acceptance, and provision. In his arms, we find our home.

Read Hebrews 12:7–11.

FATHER, HELP ME TO SUBMIT WILLINGLY
TO YOUR LOVING BOUNDARIES.

CHARLES SWINDOLL

We are all faced with opportunities brilliantly disguised as impossible situations.

UNMASKING IMPOSSIBILITY

It's impossible," we say with a resigned sigh. We can't see a way out. All the choices lead to unpleasant results—if there are any choices at all. We may be tempted to give up in despair in the face of what appears to be an impossible situation. What a change of perspective, then, when we see that impossible situation as an opportunity from God that has merely been brilliantly disguised!

God wants us to look at our difficult situations as if we were attending a masquerade party—what we think is impossible and scary is merely an illusion. Like the moment of unmasking at a party, it's time to reveal the true identity of what has appeared to be an impossible situation—opportunity.

Take off opportunity's disguise today. As you unmask your impossible situation and reveal it as an opportunity from God, the greatness of God is just waiting to show itself in your life.

Read Jeremiah 32:17–19.

OPEN MY EYES TO SEE YOUR OPPORTUNITY
IN MY IMPOSSIBLE SITUATION, GOD.

NOVEMBER

TERESA OF AVILA

God appeals to us through. . .people, through sermons or through. . .good books. Sometimes He calls through our sicknesses and our trials as He bids us to pray.

PROMPTINGS TO PRAY

A refrain heard regularly from new Christians who are learning the practice of prayer is, "I don't know what to pray about." This is something we all struggle with periodically as we seek to draw closer to God in prayer throughout our Christian journeys.

Yet God allows many circumstances in our world and in our individual lives to serve as promptings to prayer. He speaks to us through our friends, relatives, and even those we might view as our enemies. He speaks to us through a pastor's sermon, radio message, or a book. He even speaks to us through our illnesses and our difficulties. He also speaks to us through things for which we should pray.

Ultimately, through our prayer, God wants us to spend more time with him, to draw closer to him, and to see and sense his heart. He uses things all around us to prompt us to pray, and he earnestly desires that our prayers lead us closer to him.

Read Luke 22:39–46.

GIVE ME A SENSE OF YOUR HEART, FATHER, SO THAT MY PRAYER LIFE DRAWS ME CLOSER TO YOU.

T. D. JAKES

Something inside of you has been locked up. God wants to unlock it. He knows what gifts and abilities and dreams He has put in you.

UNLOCKED POTENTIAL

Go into any local bookstore, and you'll find shelves lined with self-help books that tout the authors' ability to unlock the potential of a person. And in sold-out conference centers and arenas, motivational speakers assure us that if we would just follow these seven steps or buy this product, then we will notice a difference in our lives in a matter of days. Or so we are told.

Yet God alone is the ultimate locksmith of our hearts. He can unlock potential no one even dreamed of, because he designed it and put it there. He has given each of us specific gifts and abilities and dreams. He knows the full measure of our potential. Best of all, he doesn't assign an "expiration date" or an age limit for the realization of that potential. You can be all that God calls you to be whenever God wills.

Lay your heart before the One who knows it better than even you do. Let him unlock your potential.

Read 1 Corinthians 12:27–31.

LORD, GUIDE ME IN THE WAY THAT YOU WOULD HAVE ME GO.

AUGUSTINE OF HIPPO

My God, let me remember you with gratitude. . . . Let my bones be penetrated with your love and exclaim: "Lord, who is like unto you?"

NO ONE LIKE HIM

Who are we without God? What do we have that he has not granted us? Our hearts should be overwhelmed with gratitude every day for the blessings he has given. His mercy on us has been great and completely undeserved.

There is no God like our God. He is infinite, omnipotent, omniscient, real. He spoke all of creation into existence, yet dresses the wildflowers in beauty. He brought all of humanity to life, yet saw you in your mother's womb and knew every day of your life before it was written.

In all of heaven and earth, there is none like God, and no one can love us as he does. That awesome fact should penetrate into our very bones, making us cry out to him, "Lord, who is like unto you?"

Thank him today for his mercy and love.

Read Psalm 139.

GOD, YOU ARE WORTHY OF MY AWE, AND
I WILL WORSHIP YOU FOREVER.

JOHN MACARTHUR

Praying right does not mean letting God in our plans, but calling for God to fulfill His own.

THE EVENT COORDINATOR

When we have a jam-packed schedule, it's easy to fall into the trap of approaching the day like a busy event coordinator. Excited about our plans, our prayer—if we make time to offer one—becomes a passionate monologue telling God everything we're going to do that day. We approach God looking for his stamp of approval on our plans instead of asking for his direction.

But oh, the blessing that comes when we let God be the Event Coordinator and we humbly take our place as his assistant. When we give control of our daily schedule to God things may not turn out exactly as we would have planned, but isn't God the ultimate planner? He is omniscient, omnipotent, and omnipresent—attributes that make him the greatest Event Coordinator possible. No matter how capable we are, God is infinitely more capable.

Ask him to not only fulfill his plan for you, but to lead that plan. Do more than just include him in your plans—let him be in charge.

Read Matthew 6:9–13.

FULFILL YOUR PLANS FOR ME TODAY.

DONALD MILLER

I believe that the greatest trick of the devil is not to get us into some sort of evil but rather have us wasting time.

IDLE HANDS

I dle hands are the devil's workshop," our parents used to tell us when we were little and complaining of boredom. They encouraged us to find something to do or they would find something for us—which usually entailed some kind of chore. Keeping busy can be valuable, but what happens if even our busyness is no more than wasting time?

The world is filled with distractions that make us feel like our hands are anything but idle, yet we have little of value to show for it. If God didn't desire for us to relax, he would have never committed an entire day to it. However, there is also a reason that he didn't commit every day to rest. We must continually remind ourselves that the time we have in this world is limited. Of course we can rest and have fun, but we must beware of wasting too much of that precious resource that God has granted us.

Read Ephesians 5:15–17.

LORD, BUSY MY HANDS WITH YOUR WORK.

ORIGEN

The true Light, endowed with life, knows who to reveal His full splendor to and to whom His light.

TRUE LIGHT

Ever worry about how to share your faith? Perhaps you worry not only about who you'll talk to but what you'll say and how you'll say it. The good news is that God does the bulk of the work in spreading the good news. As you share your faith with others, he not only reminds you of the truth but he also shines his light through you.

The apostle John wrote of Jesus as the Light who revealed himself to a people trapped in darkness. While some preferred the darkness, others gravitated toward the light of his truth. The more they sought the light, the more they saw how splendid it was and how desperately they needed it. After his resurrection, Jesus sent the Holy Spirit to help bear witness of his truth to them and to you.

Ask God to show you someone you can talk with about your faith. The Holy Spirit will help you be a light in a dark world.

Read John 1:9–18.

HERE I AM, LORD. PLEASE SEND ME TO
SHARE YOUR LIGHT WITH OTHERS.

SARAH YOUNG

I believe that God yearns for these quiet moments with us even more than we do.

COME WITH ME

Jesus was a busy man. Healing the sick, casting out demons, teaching, traveling, and communing with his Father kept him busy from dawn until the evening hours. But Jesus frequently pulled away from the crowds to find quiet and rest. He was fully God yet fully man—and as a human being, he needed time to physically rest and recharge.

Sometimes he invited his friends to come along with him into the quiet places. He used these times of solitude with his disciples to explain, to mentor, and to train. Away from the crowds, Jesus taught them the meanings of his parables and shared secrets that they couldn't yet understand. His followers used these times to ask questions, to seek answers, and to share their deepest thoughts with their Teacher.

Jesus still longs for quiet time with us today, so he can teach us and train us. It is in these times of quiet and rest that he answers our questions and the deepest stirrings of our hearts.

Read Mark 6:30–32.

BLESS MY TIME OF QUIET WITH YOU TODAY. I WANT TO HEAR YOU.

OSWALD CHAMBERS

Nothing is so important as to keep right spiritually. The great solution is the simple one— "Come unto Me."

ONE DAY AT A TIME

How can we possibly stay on track spiritually in all of life's ups and downs? How can we know that we'll be able to stay faithful to God tomorrow when we have no idea what tomorrow will bring—much less next month, next year?

A Chinese proverb says that the journey of a thousand miles begins with a single step. So it is with life. We do not know what the future holds, but we trust God and walk into it one step at a time. If we are faithful in this moment, and then faithful in the next moment, and so on and so on, then this will build up to a life of spiritual faithfulness.

And what does that faithfulness look like? It is simply coming unto Jesus, staying close to him, seeking to honor him in all we do—in the strength he himself gives.

All of those obedient steps will add up to a life of obedience.

Read Matthew 11:25–30.

TODAY I COME TO YOU, JESUS. TEACH ME TO DO SO EVERY MOMENT.

JIM CYMBALA

Never in the Gospels was Jesus astounded by anybody's righteousness. Never was he impressed with anyone's education. But he was amazed by one thing: people's faith.

AMAZED BY FAITH

What could possibly cause Jesus to be amazed? Present at the creation of the world, Jesus experienced breathtaking splendor. When he left the majesty of heaven to enter our world, Jesus was familiar with the miraculous: bringing sight to the blind, feeding the multitudes with a young boy's lunch, and even raising the dead. During his ministry on earth, Jesus encountered the rich and the righteous, the proud and the poor, the official and the outcast. Yet he stood amazed only in the face of one thing—unwavering faith.

The Roman centurion knew the protocol of authority. He knew the hierarchy of power. He obeyed his superiors and demanded complete submission from those under his leadership. He also believed in the authority of Jesus. The man knew Jesus commanded everything seen and unseen with just a word, so he told Jesus that he believed his servant would be healed if Jesus would simply give the command.

And Jesus stood *amazed* at this type of faith.

Read Matthew 8:5–10.

I BELIEVE YOU HOLD ALL POWER AND
AUTHORITY FOR ALL MY NEEDS, LORD.

CHRYSOSTOM

We shouldn't think of anything as our own. For even faith itself isn't our own, but more God's than ours.

MINE!

One of the first words a young child learns to say is, "Mine!" At an early age, we greedily hold on to toys and treasures that we want to keep all to ourselves. And we never outgrow our desire to claim what's ours. We jealously guard our family time or our leisure time. We keep a tight grip on our possessions. We hold our wallets close when churches and charities make appeals.

This tendency to mark what's ours sometimes extends to faith. We talk about owning *our* faith. But faith is a gift from God just as life itself is. As the apostle Paul explains, our faith comes through hearing the word of the Lord.

Romans 10:17 and Ephesians 2:8 remind us that salvation is a gift offered to us from God. Through the acceptance of this gift, God looks at you and says, "Mine."

When you belong to God, everything you have is his: your possessions, your time, yourself. Why not offer all to God today?

Read Romans 10:14–17.

LORD, ALL THAT I HAVE AND ALL THAT I AM IS YOURS.

A. B. SIMPSON

The Holy Spirit's life is manifested in His indwelling in human hearts, His making our bodies His temples, and His infinite . . . care in our spiritual life and training.

THE HOLY SPIRIT'S CARE FOR US

All of us experience periods of difficulty and pain in our lives—times when we wonder what God has in store for us. These times can also feel particularly lonely, as we seem to struggle by ourselves to determine the path God has prepared for us.

Yet in these painful times, as well as during periods of comfort and satisfaction, we must never forget that the Holy Spirit continues to indwell our hearts. He lives in us as One who cares deeply about everything in our lives.

His indwelling serves an eternal purpose, as well. For at all times in our lives, the infinite Holy Spirit is guiding us, caring for us, and ultimately deepening our connection to him as our physical bodies become his holy temples.

Don't underestimate the refining and care the Holy Spirit is undertaking in your daily life. Know that his ceaseless love is unmatched, and he will never leave his people.

Read Romans 8:11–17.

PLEASE REFINE MY LIFE TO MAKE ME MORE LIKE YOU, LORD.

RANDY ALCORN

Paradoxically, our home is a place we've never been. But it's the place we were made for, the place made for us.

HOME

Home. Often the word invokes images of smiles and warmth, of acceptance and love. Home is where we come after a long day in the work world. Home is where students come after a long day at school. We still may have a home to return to even after we've grown up and moved away and made our own homes in other places. Home is where we are able to be who we are and know that we will be loved anyway.

As wonderful as our home is, as believers we look forward to something better—heaven itself, our eternal home. We haven't yet been there, and we can't even really imagine what it will be like. But something deep inside tells us that heaven will be perfect because our God who loves us is preparing a place for us there. He invites us to join him in this eternal home so that we can be with him always—accepted, loved, and perfect.

Read Hebrews 11:13–16.

I LOOK FORWARD TO MY ETERNAL HOME WITH YOU, DEAR JESUS.

MOTHER TERESA

God does not demand that I be successful. God demands that I be faithful.

FAITHFUL

What comes to mind when you think of *success*? Business suits, multimillion-dollar budgets, and a wall full of trophies? Or maybe healthy children, surplus income for travel and leisure, and a thriving ministry? The real secret to success is faith-driven obedience.

Paul knew the gritty reality of obedience. This giant of the faith listed quite a résumé of suffering in 2 Corinthians 11. He knew hunger and thirst. He fought against rivers, bandits, sleeplessness, and cold. Paul was imprisoned, flogged, stoned, and shipwrecked. He was stripped of his clothing and faced death on several occasions. And he struggled against a thorn in his flesh. Yet Paul boasted in his hardships.

Paul knew that God measures success by a faithful heart. A life committed to God, living his commands, loving his people, and spreading his Word results in the only bottom line that matters—souls saved and the body edified. In God's economy, that's the secret of success.

Read Philippians 1:18–21.

I LONG TO REMAIN FAITHFUL NO MATTER WHAT COMES MY WAY, GOD. SUSTAIN ME.

CYPRIAN

Don't look to things behind us that the devil calls us back to. Instead look to things ahead of us that Christ calls us to.

DON'T LOOK BACK

Lot's wife will be forever remembered as the one who looked back to her detriment (Genesis 19:17, 26). With one last anxious peek at the city she left behind, she turned into a pillar of salt. Her longing for the past ended up destroying her.

Like Lot's wife, how many times have we anxiously glanced back at the "glory days" that we think will never come again? Or maybe our backward gaze is at a past mistake that haunts us.

While the enemy whispers, "Keep looking back," in order to discourage us or push us toward discontentment, the Lord Jesus urges us to look ahead and focus on him. The apostle Paul reminds us to forget the past and look toward the prize that awaits us: eternal life with the Savior. His blood covers our sins and provides us the hope of glory. We can choose to dwell on that hope now or be destroyed by clinging to the hopelessness of the past.

Which will you choose?

Read Philippians 3:12–16.

FATHER GOD, GRANT ME THE COURAGE TO
KEEP LOOKING FORWARD, NOT BACK.

BILLY GRAHAM

Patience is the transcendent radiance of a loving and tender heart which, in its dealings with those around it, looks kindly and graciously upon them.

PATIENCE

As Christians, when we think about the consequences of our sin, we are quickly—and thankfully—reminded of the saving work of Christ in our lives and how we won't have to pay this penalty. Through his saving grace, Christ demonstrated an incredible love for us.

Christ is also incredibly patient toward us. Some of us spent years running away from him, some of us regularly stumble into sin, and others of us struggle with faith. Nevertheless, Christ continues to patiently wait for us, helping us overcome our hurdles and drawing us closer to himself.

With Christ's patience demonstrated in our lives, should we not also be stirred to demonstrate patience toward those around us? How can we who have received such loving patience not look kindly and graciously toward those who have offended us?

Our Christ-infused heart should stir within us a deep and abiding love for others.

Read Romans 15:1–5.

FATHER, HELP ME TO DEMONSTRATE THE SAME PATIENCE TOWARD OTHERS THAT YOU HAVE DEMONSTRATED TOWARD ME.

CHARLES HADDON SPURGEON

He who does not desire the salvation of those who are his own kith and kin, "how dwelleth the love of God in him?"

PRAYING FOR THE SALVATION OF FAMILY MEMBERS

Very few of us come from families where every family member knows Jesus. If you do, know that you are extremely blessed. The rest of us come from families in which lives that have been transformed through salvation in Jesus are present only sporadically—among a brother or a sister, a parent or an uncle. Regardless of how many of our family members know Jesus, we should earnestly pray for and desire that each one come to saving faith in Christ.

When we accepted the gift of salvation through Jesus Christ, the love of Christ filled our hearts, causing us to desire what he desires. Paramount among the desires of Christ now implanted in us is the desire to see lost people find their eternal home in Christ. What better place to start than with the Christ-infused compulsion to pray for and witness to those closest to us—our own family members?

Read John 3:16–17.

GIVE ME A CHRIST-INFUSED DESIRE TO PRAY FOR
THE SALVATION OF MY FAMILY MEMBERS.

JOHN ORTBERG

The truth is that the term spiritual life is simply a way of refer-ring to one's life—every moment and facet of it—from God's perspective.

A LIFE OF PURPOSE

As a teenager, you decide you want to go to college. So in high school, you get a part-time job in a fast-food restaurant and make the best grades you can to help you get into and pay for your college tuition. When you are accepted into college, you study hard to achieve the best university grades and take every opportunity to add to your résumé so that you can be hired for your dream job. Finally in your desired career, you work up the ladder to better positions and more pay to put away for retirement. You work your whole life so you can eventually stop working and end your days in relaxation.

If this is life, what's the point?

With God, life has purpose. You are on an adventure and a mission. Looking through the lenses of your spiritual life, you have the privilege of being able to see your life the way God does and discovering how he makes everything in your life work together for his purpose.

Read Ecclesiastes 3:1–11.

DEAR FATHER, OPEN MY EYES TO YOUR PURPOSE FOR ME.

ROBERT McGEE

Our natural strengths will always fight against our dependence on God.

ONLY IN WEAKNESS

Gideon farmed. Moses led sheep. Martha bustled and served. The disciples fished.

Then God came calling.

God used Gideon to grow an army. God told Moses to lead his people. Jesus told Martha to sit and learn. The disciples left their nets and fished for men.

God removed each of them—and many others—from their comfortable, ordinary existence and propelled them into a ministry opportunity that stretched them beyond their natural talents. They learned new skills. They went new places. At times while they served God out of their weakness, they stumbled and he caught them. God put them into circumstances that forced them to depend on him.

Security and aptitude often breed autonomy. But God knows that dependence and uncertainty foster reliance, and reliance fosters relationship. So he often calls us out of our comfort zones to learn that it is only through *his* strength that we are made strong and only through *his* provision that we accomplish great deeds.

Read Judges 7.

I SURRENDER MY TALENTS, GOD, KNOWING YOU WILL EQUIP ME FOR EVERY GOOD WORK.

SØREN KIERKEGAARD

Prayer does not change God, but it changes him who prays.

WHY WE PRAY

What benefit is there in presenting requests to a God who already knows the future? If he knows all things and can do all things, doesn't he have an answer before the words even leave our lips?

We pray not because prayer changes our circumstances, but because it changes our plea. As we plead with the Judge, the relationship becomes personal. He works out our circumstances in other matters and we draw closer to him, thankful for his wisdom and provision. As we pray and seek him, the Judge becomes our Friend.

The fires of waiting refine our prayers even further. We pour out our hearts to God and he encourages us, comforts us, and teaches us. Our friendship with him deepens and strengthens. We begin to understand him so well that we know his desires in general—and for us, specifically.

The more we pray, the more our prayer requests change. Once we wanted what *we* wanted, now we want what *God* wants for us. Our childish desires now echo the will of our Father in heaven.

Read Psalm 37:3–7.

GOD, I ASK THAT YOU REFINE MY REQUESTS UNTIL
MY DESIRES ARE YOUR DESIRES FOR ME.

A. W. TOZER

The heart that is constantly overflowing with gratitude will be safe from those attacks of resentfulness and gloom that bother so many.

A PROTECTED HEART

How difficult it is to be grateful in our daily lives. We are constantly making comparisons. We compare children, hoping ours are the smartest and the strongest. We compare our talents with those of others—and our possessions. But watch out: comparison is a dangerous game. Sadly, we often come up on the short end—the losing side—and it breeds resentment and gloom.

God never intended for us to compare our lives or our stuff with others. Instead, he commanded us to look to him— the giver of life, hope, peace, love, security. Understanding his gifts causes our hearts to well up with gratitude. He gives so much; we deserve so little. Only in acknowledging the Giver, appreciating his unwarranted, incomparable, and unmerited gifts, will our hearts be safe from bitterness and depression.

Read Hebrews 12:28.

LORD, MY HEART WELLS UP WITH GRATITUDE
FOR ALL THAT YOU HAVE GIVEN TO ME.

JOSEPH STOWELL

If you love Jesus you will prove it by actively caring for people.

ON THE WINGS OF LOVE

Slaves, obey your masters." We read that verse in the Bible and our eyes skim over it. *That doesn't apply to me; I'm not a slave,* you might think. Let's not miss the wisdom and the truth found in this verse. While we may not be slaves, many of us still have people in our lives whom we can, and should, work to please.

Do you report to a demanding superior? Respect his place of authority over you and submit willingly. Do you have an unbelieving spouse? Serve him wholeheartedly, as if you were serving the Lord. Do you volunteer on committees or ministries under challenging leaders? Work with diligence and integrity whether they are watching or not.

Our love for Jesus should be more than a private experience, held tightly to our breast. Let your love for Jesus take flight on the wings of respect and honor, service and love, sincerity and integrity toward all those who are in authority over you. Through your actions, they may see the light of Christ in you and come to know Jesus, the one who has all authority in heaven and earth.

Read Ephesians 6:5–8.

LORD, LET MY RESPECT FOR PEOPLE IN
AUTHORITY POINT THEM TO YOU.

SERITA JAKES

Thousands upon thousands of women can give testimony to the provision of the Lord, but please experience His love for yourself.

WHAT ABOUT YOU?

One day as Jesus and his disciples walked along the road, he posed a question. "Who do people say the Son of Man is?" Did Jesus ask that question because he didn't know what people were saying? Had he been warned that some mistook him for John the Baptist, Elijah, or Jeremiah? Had he heard the whispered debates of his followers?

It's likely that Jesus used the question as an opening to the real question he wanted his disciples to answer—"Who do you say I am?" Peter answered for himself, but did all the disciples agree? Could they have each answered according to who they thought he was? Savior. Teacher. Messiah. Rabbi. Brother.

Who do *you* say Jesus is? Can you answer for yourself, or must you rely on the answers of your parents, your spouse, or your church leaders?

One day every knee will bow and every tongue confess the name of Jesus Christ our Lord. What about you? Who do you say he is?

Read Matthew 16:13–17.

JESUS, I WANT TO EXPERIENCE YOUR LOVE
AND YOUR POWER IN MY LIFE.

JOHN MURRAY

The rich mercy of grace is certified by the veracity and faithful-ness of God.

THE MERCY OF GRACE

Grace is unmerited divine assistance. It has been called "amazing" for good reason.

Grace took root in the Garden of Eden, sprouting hope amid the thorns of first sin. Grace followed the Israelites in and out of captivity, to foreign lands, and through the wilderness. Grace took the form of a wooden ark, a scarlet thread, and a kinsman redeemer.

Grace came to the world clothed in the flesh of a helpless infant. Grace took the form of a carpenter's son. Grace walked the earth, touched hurting souls, and healed the sick. Grace gave one life as a ransom for many and secured our salvation.

Grace provides a way out. Grace gives a second chance . . . and a third. Grace restores what the locust has eaten. Grace secures the salvation of the one who would believe. Grace turns a sinner into a saint.

Grace is the embodiment of God's enduring faithfulness and love. That's what is so amazing about grace!

Read Titus 2:11–14.

TODAY MAY YOUR GRACE FLOW OVER ME, AROUND ME, AND THROUGH ME.

MAX LUCADO

Jesus had a place for misfits. In his book the last became first, and even the loser had value.

THE VALUE OF BEING AVAILABLE

The Bible shows us over and over that God favors the unfavorable. He guided a nation to freedom through a stuttering shepherd. He placed the king's crown on the head of a gangly teenager. He delivered his people through an orphan girl turned unlikely queen. Through their stories, he is still celebrated today.

Jesus desired the undesirable. He broke bread with tax collectors and prostitutes. He touched the unclean and infirm. He conversed with foreigners and children. He used ordinary people to spread the good news of his message. Through the lives of these misfits-turned-missionaries, he is known today.

Jesus doesn't require his followers to be *able*, just to be *available*. When Jesus enters the lives of those who are foolish, weak, lowly, or despised and changes them, people notice. When he accomplishes his will in spite of someone's natural weakness, he can't help but receive the glory. All throughout history God has used weak or broken vessels to accomplish great things for his glory. And he still does today.

Read 1 Corinthians 1:26–31.

I KNOW THAT IF I MAKE MYSELF AVAILABLE TO YOUR PLANS, GOD, YOU WILL MAKE ME ABLE.

MIKE MASON

Far from originating joy, humans are meant to be like an echo, reverberating with God's joy and sending it back to Him.

ECHOES OF JOY

"Thank you." These two small words are among the first in a child's vocabulary. They roll easily off our tongues to convey common courtesy—to the grocery clerk, the waitress, or the stranger who holds the door.

Yet sometimes those two little syllables seem very inadequate. How can the same two words convey the tidal wave of emotion we want to express to the organ donor, the birth mother, or the friend who listens without judgment?

How can we express our gratitude for all God has given us? How can we tell him how grateful we are for all he's forgiven us? Our words of deep gratitude would fill a book, if we were to write them down. Our sacrifices of thanksgiving would reach to heaven, if we were to pile them up. Yet all God requires is our life, lived for his glory, returning to him all the goodness he has freely and graciously bestowed upon us.

Read Psalm 50:14–15.

LORD, MAY MY LIFE BE A SONG OF PRAISE,
BRINGING YOU JOY TODAY.

JOHN WESLEY

The right and true Christian faith is . . . to have a sure trust and confidence to be saved from everlasting damnation by Christ.

CONFIDENCE IN THE FUTURE

How often do we walk timidly into the future, unsure of each day's challenges or dangers? We can become frightened and anxious when we think about the uncertain future in our fallen world.

Yet as Christians, we have no reason to fear. If we truly believe our salvation spares us from the wrath of God's judgment and ensures us an eternal home with the Savior, then we are able to embrace each new day with confidence, knowing that the God who saved us will also protect us and work out his plan for our lives.

That confidence in the future should also provide us with the willingness to follow Christ's commands, knowing that it is through his love for us that he is guiding us. Our future is already secure in his hands. Instead of worrying about what tomorrow holds, let's commit to walking boldly into the future that God has planned for us, following his commands each day until we enter our eternal home with him.

Read 1 Peter 1:3–11.

GIVE ME THE CONFIDENCE IN MY FUTURE TO EARNESTLY FOLLOW YOUR DESIRES AND COMMANDS.

FREDERICK BUECHNER

There is perhaps no better proof for the existence of God than that. . .the whole God enterprise survives despite the way the professionally godly promote it.

KNOWING HE IS REAL

Why do you believe in God, anyway?" If you have been a Christian for any length of time, you have likely been asked a question like this about your Christian faith. Maybe the question comes after an embarrassing news story about the fall of a television evangelist or maybe someone challenges you that Christians act no different than non-Christians—and he has specific examples. When the question comes from an honest seeker, it deserves a compelling answer.

We may point to the beauty of creation, or the miraculous healing from disease of a friend, or the incredible life change of someone who used to be far away from God but who now lives a life completely reliant on him. Or we can show them the proof in history—our resurrected Lord.

While our answers may vary, they all point to a timeless, transcendent, convincing reason for the faith we profess. No human argument can erase that.

Read Hebrews 11:1–3.

MAY I EVER HAVE FAITH IN YOU, EVEN WHEN IT IS DIFFICULT.

BOOKER T. WASHINGTON

Holding a grudge doesn't hurt the person against whom the grudge is held, it hurts the one who holds it.

LETTING GO OF THE GRUDGE

You spent hours painstakingly painting those stripes in the kitchen. In your eyes, the wall looked perfect—even stripes, straight lines, and subtle color changes. However, your spouse and others in the family didn't agree. When our efforts are rejected by others—whether in something minor like painting a wall or something much more significant—disappointment and frustration well up within us. It's easy to feel misunderstood, inconvenienced, or insulted.

Holding on to those feelings sets the table for a "grudge soup" in our soul as heavy as the soup's hot iron pot. And the longer we let the soup simmer, the heavier and hotter that pot gets.

We don't have to hold on, though. Give your grudges to God today. He can handle the weight and the heat. And then let him pour soothing balm over those tired hands. Let him fill your heart with a new, savory meal of grace and forgiveness that nourishes you and others.

Read Leviticus 19:18.

HEAL MY HEART TODAY, GOD. I'M READY TO GIVE YOU MY GRUDGES.

JIM ELLIOT

He is no fool who gives what he cannot keep to gain that which he cannot lose.

LOSS AND GAIN

Everything we have will one day be left behind. As the saying goes, you will never see a hearse pulling a U-Haul. This may be a rather morbid and depressing thought, but the reality is that no matter how hard we work and how successful we are during our years on earth, we can't take our stuff with us when we die. The only thing that will go with us into eternity is the soul we have entrusted to our God.

It is important to remember this perspective when we consider our belongings and ambitions. Everything we possess is only on loan from God, entrusted to us on a temporary basis. He wants us to be good managers of his resources, using what he has given us to increase his kingdom.

Are we willing to give what we cannot keep (our material goods, wealth, even our very lives) in order to gain what we cannot lose (our souls and eternal life in heaven)?

Read Philippians 3:7–11.

WHATEVER YOU ASK OF ME, LORD, HELP ME TO COMPLETE IT.

J. I. PACKER

God's revelation is called his Word because it is reasoned verbal discourse which has God as its subject and source.

THE WORD

The Bible is often called the Word of God because it is God's words to us. So often people cast about wishing that God would tell them what to do, looking for a sign in the sky, wanting God to speak to them, complaining that God is so unknown and unknowable. All the while, however, they have access to everything God wanted to say to us, neatly packaged in his Word.

The Bible is God's full revelation to us, telling us everything we need to know to live this life and to have access to heaven in the next. God's Word tells us what the problem is (sin) and how God dealt with it (sending his Son). It tells us how to respond to God's gift of salvation and how to live in ways that will please and honor him.

When we read the Word of God, we hear his words to us. It's really just that simple—and that astounding!

Read Hebrews 4:12–13.

THANK YOU FOR YOUR WORD THAT TELLS ME ALL I NEED TO KNOW.

DECEMBER

JOHN MACARTHUR

We should be so consumed with God's glory that we hurt when He is dishonored.

ACHE JOYOUSLY FOR GOD'S GLORY

After a first winter snow, when the earth is blanketed with a fresh, white quilt, life seems serene. Muffled sounds travel farther, and people whisper so as not to disturb the quiet. Such a winter scene can mesmerize us, encouraging us to stop, to be still, and to think deeply.

Then it happens. In the freshly laid snow, the first set of car tracks, a stranger's careless footsteps, or even worse, the city's snowplow rips down the street with no regard, even contempt, for our winter scene. We sigh from regret at the loss of the pristine.

God sighs too when he sees the glory of his creation corrupted by our sin and evil. Can he fix things? Certainly, but he has chosen not to do so completely until the end of time. Until the Day arrives, we look upon our sin-stained world and ache for God's glory to be fully displayed.

Read Romans 8:18–25.

GOD, MAY I ACHE JOYOUSLY TO DISPLAY YOUR GLORY TODAY.

DIETRICH BONHOEFFER

Thus every word, every work, every labor of the Christian becomes a prayer . . . in a real breaking through the hard "it" to the gracious Thou.

OUR LIFE'S WORK BECOMES A PRAYER

How many times do we feel like our efforts are in vain? We work so hard at something, yet the result we desire or the outcome we endeavor to bring about just doesn't appear. Our lives are full of moments such as these—either personally, in our jobs, or in some other aspect of our lives.

For those who claim faith in Christ, we can rest assured that when we commit our actions to him, the results will be fruitful. Maybe success doesn't automatically appear each time we commit something to Christ, but the effort we apply— done in cooperation with him—becomes Christ-infused.

When we commit our lives to serving Christ, our work no longer centers just on us, but it becomes part of something larger, more significant . . . something eternal. When we commit our life to God and focus on him as we complete our tasks, every effort becomes a prayer. By cooperating with Christ's will, our life's work is no longer in vain.

Read Philippians 2:5–13.

FATHER, SHOW ME HOW TO COOPERATE
WITH YOUR WILL IN MY LIFE.

BRENNAN MANNING

Abba. The overtones of this small word will always escape us. Yet in it we sense the intense intimacy of Jesus with his Father.

OUR ABBA FATHER

We are part of a family. Not just the physical family we were born into, but also our spiritual family. When we invited Christ into our lives, God adopted us as his own children and welcomed us into his family. When we look to God to take care of us as a father would, we look to the God who has a Son of his own. When we read the Bible and see the faithfulness Jesus showed to God's plan and the trust he placed in his heavenly Father, we can begin to understand how magnificent this intimate, familial relationship with God can be.

The word *Abba,* the Hebrew word for "father," is a term of affection much like "daddy" spoken by a child. It describes more than just the intimacy between Jesus and God. It describes closeness, familiarity, and a trusting love that is bigger and deeper than we can imagine.

And *Abba* is what we, his children, are invited to call our heavenly Father.

Read Romans 8:12–17.

THANK YOU, DEAR ABBA, FOR LOVING ME.

JULIAN OF NORWICH

No created being can ever know how much and how sweetly and tenderly God loves them.

SWEET AND TENDER LOVE

How do we know that God loves us—really? At times we may wonder. We look around at a suffering world and question if God really cares. We face moments of frustration and doubt if God really loves us. When we deal with times of intense grief, we wonder if God notices. But when the days are light and happy we think, *Ah yes! Now I know God loves me.*

God loves us as deeply in the times of hurt and pain and suffering as he does in the good days. He is always present, never changing, always constant. As mere human beings, we have a limited perspective and cannot begin to understand the sweet and tender love that God has for us.

Whether we feel it or not, God loves us. Whether we understand it or not, God loves us. Whether we return it or not, God loves us.

Today feel it, sense it, know it—God's sweet and tender love for you.

Read Psalm 36:5–9.

LET ME SENSE YOUR LOVE FOR ME AS I GO ABOUT THIS DAY.

C. S. LEWIS

We have all been taught...to...offer [our suffering]...to God as our little, little share of Christ's sufferings—but it is so hard to do.

OUR OFFERING OF SUFFERING

Most of the time, it feels like we're at the mercy of an unmerciful world. How else can we begin to understand the pain and suffering we see all around us?

We may live in an unmerciful world, but we do not have an unmerciful God. He promises to love us and to be with us every moment of our life's journey. Trusting in God doesn't necessarily keep bad things from happening, however. God's Son experienced suffering, so how can we expect any less? When we experience suffering, we are in his company. He truly understands how we feel.

When we face great suffering, God gives us the precious gift of his Son to walk with us through it. Instead of blinding ourselves with questions about why this had to happen, we can take our sufferings and offer them to Christ as our little share in his sufferings. It's not easy, but it's vital. For when we give our heavy burdens to Christ, he takes them, wraps his arm around us, and guides us through the darkness into the light of his presence.

Read John 16:33.

JESUS, TAKE MY BURDEN AND WALK WITH ME THROUGH THE DARKNESS.

BROTHER LAWRENCE

We ought not to be weary of doing little things for. . .God, who regards not the greatness of the work, but the love with which it is performed.

SMALL ACTS

We can certainly express our love for someone by doing big things for our beloved, but faithfulness in doing the small things quickly adds up. The loyal husband of many years who still leaves love notes on his wife's pillow and comes home every evening to help her with the kids and household chores is as valued and appreciated as the one who dazzles his bride with expensive jewelry and presents.

This is especially true in our interactions with God. Not every Christian can do something stupendous for the Lord. There are very few people like Billy Graham or Mother Teresa, recognized for their huge contributions to the faith. But plenty of us live for Jesus every day doing our little, unnoticed pieces of obedience. We can honor Jesus in what we do, no matter how insignificant it may seem, by doing it with all of our heart.

God regards not the greatness of the work, but the love for him with which we do even the smallest act.

Read 1 Corinthians 10:24.

MY GOAL IS TO DO EVERYTHING IN LOVE FOR YOU AND OTHERS. HELP ME STAY THE COURSE.

LEO THE GREAT

Christ makes people reconciled instead of enemies, adopted children instead of strangers, righteous instead of ungodly.

RADICAL LOVE

If you've made up with a friend or family member after a heated argument, you know the blessing of reconciliation. But consider the challenge of being reconciled to an enemy. Getting over the hump of hatred or misunderstanding would take a radical love—the kind of love only God has. While we were still his enemies, he took upon himself the impossible burden of reconciling us to himself through Jesus' death. Not content to merely leave us his "non-enemies," God also adopted us as his children.

There's always room for one more child in God's family. All he asks is that we open our hearts to allow for an outpouring of his radical love. His is the kind of radical love that doesn't play favorites and never denies admission to anyone—even to those who hurt him.

When you were most in need of love, God offered it. Are you willing to do the same for someone else today?

Read Matthew 5:43–48.

FILL ME WITH YOUR RADICAL LOVE TODAY, DEAR JESUS.

CHARLES SWINDOLL

Persevering becomes essential to living—the only key that unlocks the door of hope.

KEEP GOING

Your full key ring clinks and clatters as you struggle with your bags and try to find the right key to open the door. When the first key doesn't work, you try another. And another, and another, and another, and another. Just when you are ready to give up, you finally hear a clicking sound as the key turns in the lock. Perseverance has given you victory and hope.

When circumstances last longer than we expect, are harder than we thought they would be, or just plain don't go as planned, persevering is often the last thing we want to do. But God calls us to endure so that we can discover the hope that is unlocked by perseverance.

What challenges are you facing today? Perseverance may be the key you need not only to survive, but to thrive. With that key you can open the door victoriously because God has strengthened your character, built your trust in him, and given you hope.

Put perseverance in the lock today, and watch what God does.

Read Romans 5:1–5.

GIVE ME STRENGTH TO PERSEVERE TODAY, LORD.

C. T. Studd

If Jesus Christ be God and died for me, then no sacrifice can be too great for me to make for Him.

NO SACRIFICE TOO GREAT

He didn't have to do it. When sin entered the world, God could have turned away and left humanity to fend for itself. Instead, out of his great love for us, he sent his one and only Son to give up the glories of heaven to take on a human body. Christ lived among us, felt the physical pangs of hunger and thirst, and experienced the pure exhaustion after a long day in the heat. He experienced sorrow at people's unbelief; he wept at what death does to us.

Then he gave the ultimate sacrifice on the cross, for only his death could bridge the gap of sin between us and God. Only his death could cover our sin. Instead of *us* dying, Jesus Christ—the sinless Son of God—died *for* us.

When we contemplate what he did for us, is any sacrifice too much for us to make for him?

Read 1 John 4:7–11.

LORD, I WILL GLADLY SACRIFICE ANYTHING
THAT KEEPS ME FROM YOU.

EUGENE PETERSON

But the way of faith itself is in tune with what God has done and is doing.

STAYING IN TUNE

The composer and the conductor—both are indispensable to an orchestra. As the musicians follow both the notes that have been written and how they are being directed, a beautiful piece of music results.

God is our Composer and Conductor; our faith is the orchestra. As he creates the beautiful tune of his grace in our lives, we must keep our eyes on him. Let outside pressures fade away into the background as you keep your eyes on God and what he is doing. Ignore the audience's rustling programs, hacking coughs, and cell phones that haven't been silenced. Take captive any doubt, fear, or anxieties that try to discourage you as you play. Be confident in a Conductor who knows what he's doing because he has composed the music.

And if you experience a day, or even a season, when your notes sound off-key or you can't seem to keep the beat, retune your instrument. Remember God's faithfulness in the past and pick up where you left off. There's another recital tomorrow.

Read Judges 5:3.

GOD, HELP ME TO KEEP FAITH WITH YOU TODAY.

FRANCIS SCHAEFFER

Christ is the Lord of our whole life, and the Christian life should produce not only truth . . . but also beauty.

THE DIFFERENCE MAKERS

Creativity fuels every aspect of our lives. Whether in the food we eat, the houses we live in, or simply our everyday wanderings, the spark of invention thrives within all of us. This area of our creativity is where God's work flourishes in us. Whether we are changing the world or changing ourselves, the ideas and designs that help us achieve these goals come through God's natural gifts to us. In using those gifts we reveal God to the world.

Intelligence is a tool that God gives us to make our world function, and talent is the brush he gives us to make it beautiful. With everything we create, we represent our Creator. This great gift endows us with unimaginable responsibility but also enables each of us to make a difference in the world. We are all important because God is acting within each of us. When he is within us we become the best possible version of ourselves.

What will you do to make a difference today?

Read Ecclesiastes 3:10–15.

CONTINUE TO WORK THROUGH ME, THAT I
MAY FEEL YOUR GREATNESS, GOD.

GREGORY OF NYSSA

God has placed older believers as a lighthouse for those of us who live around them.

BE A LIGHTHOUSE

In the eighteenth and nineteenth centuries, lighthouses were widely used to warn ships of hazardous coastlines and shoals. In dark and treacherous weather, the constant beam from the lighthouse helped guide ships into safe harbors and kept them from wrecking. The development of the Fresnel lens in 1822 made the beams of lighthouses shine over greater distances, making them even more effective.

Older believers should be like lighthouses to those around them. No matter how long you have been a Christian, you can be a lighthouse for a younger believer. Like a lighthouse, you can shine as a constant example of God's light and can warn those around you of spiritual dangers that will wreck their lives.

The Holy Spirit is the light source that makes you effective and sure. Trusting in the Lord turns on the light switch. Go on and shine that light. Let the Holy Spirit use it to guide others safely to the Rock that is Jesus.

Read Titus 2:1–5.

I CHOOSE TO SHINE MY LIGHT FOR YOU, GOD.

LLOYD JOHN OGILVIE

The Lord does not ridicule our fears; He comes to walk through them with us.

THE ULTIMATE WALKING PARTNER

You were expecting to receive empathy and comfort, but instead you heard laughter. Now you want to run and hide. It seemed like a safe moment to share your fears. You thought others could relate and even offer support. Instead, your heart was trampled by ridicule and embarrassment reddened your face.

Turn to the Lord. Without laughing or smirking, he always listens as you tell him your deepest fears. He knows what you are going through. He has experienced it all—dusty roads stung his eyes, those closest to him rejected him, and spasms of pain shook his body. In his humanity he relates to what we're going through, and in his divinity he offers us the ultimate comfort.

When uneven terrain makes us wobbly, he steadies us. Against relentless winds, he helps us stand firm. And in the face of a steep path that looks insurmountable, he gives expert guidance. Take your fears to God today. Invite him to help you find a way through them. He's ready to walk with you.

Read Psalm 34:1–10.

THANK YOU FOR NOT RIDICULING MY FEARS,
LORD. WALK WITH ME TODAY.

JEROME

The Saviour of the world . . . in His virtues and His mode of life has left us an example to follow.

BIG SHOES TO FILL

When you were little, did you ever try to walk in your dad's shoes? Your small feet felt dwarfed in your father's shoes. The size of the shoes affected your ability to walk. But when your dad slipped his feet into those shoes and balanced your feet on top, you could walk just fine.

Following Jesus' perfect example can seem like slipping on a pair of shoes that are too big for us to handle—or so we think. But through the Holy Spirit, Jesus' feet are still in the shoes. His feet are underneath ours, guiding our steps and equipping us to do what he has called us to do. We can follow his example gladly, because he goes with us. And as we walk with Christ, others may be inspired to follow along behind us.

Feeling like you have big shoes to fill? Relax. His feet are under yours, guiding you each step of the way.

Read John 13:12–17.

GUIDE ME AND GO WITH ME, LORD, AS I FOLLOW YOU.

RAY STEDMAN

So, put on the whole armor of God—all that Christ is! Then pray! Then, having done all, stand your ground!

CONQUERING SNOWDRIFTS

If we tried to battle four-foot snowdrifts in our driveway without the right equipment, we wouldn't be very effective. Wearing shorts and flip-flops in the bitter cold, we'd soon start sniffling, shivering, and shaking. And without the right tools for the job—shovels and maybe even a powerful snow blower—we'd never make any headway. The snowdrift would defeat us no matter how hard we tried. The key to success is being prepared.

We may chuckle at the idea of fighting snowdrifts in flip-flops, but how many times have we tried to tackle life's spiritual battles without the right armor? We forget to put on the shield of faith to protect our hearts, or the helmet of salvation to protect our minds, or the sword of the Spirit—God's Word—to show us the truth.

Whether you're heading out to shovel snow or simply going out your door to face the day ahead, be prepared. Then, no matter what happens, you'll be able to stand your ground.

Read Ephesians 6:10–17.

FATHER, HELP ME TO STAND STRONG IN YOU TODAY.

JONI EARECKSON TADA

Feel small and insignificant if you must, but know this: You are not small in His eyes.

EYE OF THE BEHOLDER

Flying high above the clouds in a passenger jet makes it possible to see mountain ranges, large cities, and a patchwork quilt of countryside farmlands. From thirty-five thousand feet we can barely make out the colors of the landscape, much less the details of individual people. And if that's the view through a tiny airplane window, imagine what God's view of the entire earth must be like!

Kind of a simplistic view of God, isn't it? We have a picture in our mind's eye of God looking down on humanity from lofty heights. But the reality is that God is always in our midst. Unlike the limited perspective from the windows of a 747, God's view of each one of us is unobstructed, clear, and deeply personal.

To God, we are not insignificant dots in a faraway landscape. We are his sons and daughters. Take the time today to thank him for his personal involvement in your life.

Read Luke 12:6–7.

THANK YOU, LORD, FOR CARING ABOUT ME AS AN INDIVIDUAL.

BLAISE PASCAL

It is the heart which experiences God, not the reason.

EXPERIENCE HIM

In today's world, logic is the standard we most often use. We tend to measure the validity of something by how logical it is. We think logically about our choices. We solve dilemmas by using logic. We readily toss aside choices because they just "make no sense."

Too often people do this with God. After all, a lot about God simply isn't logical; it doesn't seem to make sense. But God's ways don't always follow our human rules of logic. It isn't that we have to set aside all logic in order to believe in God; instead, we have to be willing to realize that as finite human beings, we can never completely understand an infinite God. He is beyond and outside of our reasoning abilities.

We should understand what we can logically, but we should also let ourselves *experience* God, for only then will we understand more than we ever can with our minds. We experience the reality of true love, of peace, of having a life with purpose and meaning.

With our hearts, we know him. Our minds will follow.

Read Ephesians 1:15–23.

THANK YOU FOR PROVING YOURSELF TO ME, EVEN WHEN I CANNOT UNDERSTAND WHAT YOU ARE DOING.

PHILIP YANCEY

It's hard to be full of grace when you're full of fear.

RELAX INTO GRACE

Relax, relax, relax," chant the explorers as they lean into the freezing arctic wind on the way to their destination. Their mantra reminds them to resist the urge to tense up because doing so only causes the body to lapse into shivers. Staying calm will help them stay warm.

Tensing up in fear makes it difficult for grace to enter in. If we believe that we need to rely solely on our abilities, we will experience fear, for we know that most of our problems go beyond our ability to understand or solve.

Like oil and water, fear and grace do not mix. Fear involves taking back control over circumstances that God promised to handle. Grace allows humbly accepting that there is nothing in us able to provide the solution. Once we understand his grace, God can pour more of it into the places left empty by fear, and then through his power we can have the confidence to move forward.

So relax. And let his grace fill you.

Read Hebrews 4:14–16.

DRAIN AWAY MY FEAR, I PRAY, AND FILL ME WITH FRESH GRACE.

BERNARD OF CLAIRVAUX

The Word of God is living and effective. His voice is a voice of magnificence and power.

A MAGNIFICENT ARTIST

A snow-capped mountain in the distance. Majestic. Powerful. Steep.

Come. Step closer. Magnificent details abound in this painting. Nestled in the brushstrokes are beautiful plants, trees, and rivers. Hikers, snowboarders, and skiers crisscross the mountainside. Smoke wafts out of chimneys. It's a mountain scene both majestic and alive. And the more you study it, the more you are drawn into its splendor.

You feel like you're hiking the mountain yourself. Snow sprays your jacket as skiers swoosh past you down the mountain. Steam rises off the frozen river. Your boots crunch the snow in steady rhythm as you walk.

God's Word is like that painting. Come, step closer—the museum's protective rope is down. It's a painting you can touch, feel, and experience. And the artist is giving autographs. He'll engrave his very name upon your heart.

Read Hebrews 4:12.

AUTOGRAPH MY LIFE TODAY WITH YOUR MAGNIFICENCE, O GOD.

PHILIP YANCEY AND PAUL BRAND

The analogy of skin—soft, warm, and touchable—conveys the message of a God who is eager to relate in love to His creations.

MIGHTY TENDERNESS

God with skin on. God in the flesh—with beating heart, healthy mind, and blood coursing through his veins. God come to earth in the skin of our humanity in order to bring the message that he is eager to relate to us, know us, understand us, intercede for us.

This is Jesus.

Jesus—who walked along the dusty roads of Judea, reached out to heal the lepers, cast out demons, calmed the sea, held children on his lap. Jesus—who lived, laughed, wept, died, and rose again.

This is Jesus.

So in love with you that he not only cares enough to know you completely but loves you intimately, unconditionally, without wavering.

This is Jesus.

Read Philippians 2:5–11.

LORD, EMBRACE ME TODAY IN YOUR MIGHTY, TENDER LOVE.

WAYNE GRUDEM

That . . . infinite God became one person with finite man will remain for eternity the most profound miracle and the most profound mystery in all the universe.

THE MOST PROFOUND MYSTERY

A newborn evokes deep awe and great delight from adults. We exclaim, "Just look at the little fingers and toes. Listen to those cute baby sounds. What an adorable button nose."

Imagine the wonder Mary and Joseph must have experienced as they saw their firstborn baby wrapped in swaddling clothes and lying in a manger. As they exclaimed in delight over his little fingers and toes, endearing baby noises, and his tiny nose, they no doubt recalled Gabriel's words to them—this baby was conceived by the Holy Spirit.

Did they grasp the fullness of that miracle? Their newborn son, who seemed so finite and powerless, was the One who created the stars on that night, the donkey that carried Mary to Bethlehem, and the angels from the heavens who heralded to shepherds their baby's birth. Mary and Joseph must have looked in awe upon the most profound mystery—their tiny, helpless infant was the Son of God, the maker of heaven and earth!

Read Luke 2:8–20.

GOD, MAY I TREASURE UP IN MY HEART THIS PROFOUND MYSTERY THAT A SAVIOR WAS BORN FOR ME.

J. I. PACKER

God is immutable and can never cease to be what he is.

PERFECTION NEEDS NO ALTERATIONS

One of the themes we revisit every Christmas season is an individual's capability of changing from bad to good character. Ebenezer Scrooge goes from being a rude, miserly skinflint to a generous, loving old man. Even the Grinch finds his heart growing in kindness to the point that he returns all the stolen gifts to the citizens of Whoville. The reasons these stories resonate with us is that we all recognize the depravity of mankind, and we yearn for a universal peace that too often eludes us.

Christ, however, has no need for change. He was and continues to be perfect. Hebrews 13:8 promises us, "Jesus Christ is the same yesterday and today and forever." The Jesus who made the blind see, the lame walk, the leper clean, and the unrighteous pure is the same Jesus who today comforts our souls, hears our prayers, and meets our needs. He is timeless, flawless, and immutable. Hallelujah!

Read Hebrews 13:1–8.

LORD, I AM CONTENT AND SECURE BECAUSE I
KNOW YOU ARE PERFECT IN ALL YOU DO.

FREDERICK BUECHNER

The extraordinary thing that is about to happen is matched only by the extraordinary moment just before it happens. Advent is the name of that moment.

ADVENT

Life is filled with moments. Ordinary. Routine. Everyday. Mundane. Like the ticking of the mantel clock, the minutes come one after another. *Tick. Tock.* But then, out of the ordinary comes the extraordinary. A graduation. A promotion. A marriage proposal. The birth of a child. A heroic act.

Sometimes the extraordinary happening is preceded by an extraordinary moment: matriculation leads to graduation, diligence yields a promotion, courtship consummates in holy matrimony, conception produces a child, courage begets heroism.

The universe once surrendered its motion for divinity to step into human affairs. God is present, invading and occupying the moments. He awakens us to the new and the real. He comes into our midst, reminding us of his plan and his role.

Advent. The extraordinary is dawning.

Read Matthew 1:23.

LORD, HELP ME TO SEE YOU IN THE MOMENTS.

BILLY GRAHAM

When we come to Jesus Christ, the unknown becomes known;
we experience God Himself.

KNOW THE UNKNOWN

The Greeks addressed their unexplainable questions of origin through intricately woven stories of gods and goddesses. Thousands of years and technological light-years later, scientists break down the smallest pieces of life and travel to planets beyond our own in the continued pursuit of discovering answers to the unknown. Every mystery cries out for an explanation.

Humans find it hard to allow a question to remain unanswered. God summarized the answer to all of life's unknown questions when Jesus entered the world as a baby; though at first glance, a virgin birthing a child raises more questions than it answers.

Today, allow yourself to move past the mysteries of the manger and enter into deeper intimacy with Jesus. Sit quietly. Talk to him. Search for evidences of him in even the smallest details.

Experience his presence and discover the answers to your most desperate questions.

Read Acts 17:22–28.

LORD JESUS, HONOR MY SEARCHING QUESTIONS
WITH EXPERIENCES OF YOU.

OSWALD CHAMBERS

Love is not premeditated, it is spontaneous, i.e., it bursts up in extraordinary ways.

SPONTANEOUS LOVE

We all enjoy receiving gifts from friends and loved ones. We look forward to birthday gifts, Christmas gifts, and presents we receive on anniversaries and other special occasions. But especially treasured are those "just because" gifts that come on ordinary days, simply to show that a loved one is thinking of us. Spontaneous gifts represent the love of the sender—someone demonstrating his or her love by giving something away.

A heart filled with Christ's love is eager to show that love in any number of ways. As we experience more and more of Christ's love, our hearts are filled and we are eager to pour out that love to others at the first awareness of a need.

This love has no limits, as Christ demonstrated to the world when he died on the cross. His love, now living and moving in us, should daily overflow our hearts to comfort and restore a broken world. While this demonstration of love is often planned, many times it bursts forth spontaneously because our hearts are so full of Christ that his love simply spills over into others' lives.

Read John 15:9–17.

FATHER, SO FILL MY HEART WITH YOUR LOVE THAT IT
OVERFLOWS TO HELP REPAIR A BROKEN WORLD.

DONALD BARNHOUSE

Love that goes upward is worship; love that goes outward is affection; love that stoops is grace.

THE STOOP OF GRACE

In the birth of Jesus, God burst upon our sin-darkened world and the whole drama of God's redemptive plan for the human race was personified. The One who created the world came into the world as a humble baby. The incomprehensible became comprehensible. God stooped. Divinity became humanity.

That moment rocked the planet—and the world has never gotten over it. It separated the human calendar, distinguishing B.C. from A.D.

British royalty is known for its sophisticated aloofness. But on occasion, a member of the royal family will stop and reach out to a commoner. That is grace.

Our nature does not deserve our King's blessing; our actions do not earn his approval. But lovingly God came to us, touched us, blessed us, redeemed us. God stooped.

That action should humbly compel us to respond to him with worship, affection, and love.

Read Titus 2:11–14.

LORD, THANK YOU FOR YOUR TOUCH.

JOHN BUNYAN

Without your heart in it, prayer is like a sound without a life. And a heart will never pray to God unless it is lifted up by the Holy Spirit.

PRAYER POWER

It's not exactly the superpower we would have asked for as kids. In fact, as children we may have thought prayer was just the appetizer to a meal or the precursor to bedtime. So how do we allow prayer to grow in our lives into what can only be described as a "superpower" from the Holy Spirit? It can't be how original our words are, for the Lord's Prayer, given to us by Jesus himself, has great power even though we all pray the same words.

So how do our prayers have power? It begins first of all with the power of the Holy Spirit within us. Then, we get prayer power by putting our hearts into our prayers—by being genuine, by praying honestly about our desires, and by meaning what we say as we communicate with our Father.

The Holy Spirit will take your genuine words and infuse them with great power and wonderful results.

Read James 5:13–18.

REMIND US, O LORD, TO PRAY WITH A GENUINE HEART.

JOHN CALVIN

Let us therefore not seek our own, but that which pleases the Lord and is helpful to the promotion of his glory.

FOR HIS GLORY

The latest computer, the most upgraded cell phone, the newest reading device, the latest car, the largest screen TV . . . often, this obsession with possessing something new gets in the way of what is most important in life—pleasing the Lord and seeking to glorify him. We can end up more focused on buying the latest technology than we do in becoming more like Christ.

It's not that we can't or shouldn't enjoy the latest computer or cell phone or other gadget, but we must always keep a biblical perspective on our possessions. Are we buying these things and considering them "our own," or are we carefully using them so that they are pleasing to the Lord and helpful in promoting his glory? As Christians, we are to seek the things that please God.

Don't settle for bells and whistles. Instead, invest in the treasure that lasts: the eternal rewards of our infinitely generous Creator.

Read Matthew 6:19–21.

MAY I HOLD DEAR ONLY WHAT MATTERS, LORD.

THOMAS MERTON

For His Cross is the source of all our life, and without it prayer dries up and everything goes dead.

THE OLD RUGGED CROSS

It seems unusual, doesn't it? That an instrument of death is considered to be a source of life? Yet that is exactly what the cross of Jesus is to us. The cross, cruelly created as a form of torturous execution and used often by the Roman Empire to keep its subjects in line, was the place where our Lord gave his life for us. Because of that death—and only because of that death—we are given new life. His sacrifice paid the price for our sins and brought us into a relationship with the holy God.

And now we have access to God. We can "come boldly to the throne of grace, that we may obtain mercy and find grace to help in time of need" (Hebrews 4:16 NKJV). Our prayers are alive and welcomed in God's throne room because of what Jesus did for us. Without the cross, we would have no recourse, no prayer, no one to hear and help.

Thank God for the cross—the source of all our life.

Read Hebrews 4:14–16.

JESUS, THANK YOU FOR WHAT YOU DID FOR ME ON THAT CROSS.

E. M. BOUNDS

How all-inclusive Jesus Christ makes prayer! It has no limitations in extent or things!

NO LIMITS

On a clear day, there's no limit to what we can see. On a clear night, countless shimmery stars light up the galaxy. Whether big or small, each star is part of the night's beauty. And as you gaze into the night sky, you gain a sense of being part of something bigger than yourself.

As we pour out our thoughts, fears, dreams, and hopes to God in prayer, we realize that we are part of something bigger than ourselves. What do you need to talk to Jesus about today? Your prayer is not a limited conversation. Just like no star is too big or small to take its place in our solar system, nothing we face is too big or small to take its place in our prayers.

We don't have to wait until the sky is clear to begin. Start the conversation now. There are no taboo subjects. There are no time limits. No matter what you need to talk to God about in prayer, he's listening.

Read Psalm 19.

THANK YOU, GOD, FOR THE GIFT OF PRAYER.

PETER MARSHALL

God knows each one of you, and He has a plan for you. God made one you—and only one.

YOU'RE A WONDER

They are called the seven natural wonders of the world: Aurora Borealis, Grand Canyon, Paricutin, Victoria Falls, Mount Everest, Great Barrier Reef, Harbor of Rio de Janeiro. When you see them they evoke a response of wonder and awe. They're one of a kind.

Go ahead and add yourself to that list. You are a wonder. You're one of a kind. God made just one of you—only one person with your exact looks, your exact set of abilities and interests and background and experiences.

And while those seven wonders of the world are there for us to simply look at and enjoy, *you* are created for a reason. You have a job to do on this planet in this particular span of years that only you can accomplish.

The new year will dawn tomorrow. A new year of hopes and possibilities. They're all yours for the taking. They're all yours for the doing.

Are you ready?

Read Psalm 103.

LORD, HELP ME SEE HOW I MAY PRAISE YOU AND
KNOW THE FULLNESS OF MY JOY IN YOU TODAY.

January

1. Chambers, Oswald. *My Utmost for His Highest* (Westwood, NJ: Barbour and Company, 1935, 1963), 111.

2. Merton, Thomas. "Only One Unhappiness" in *A Year with Thomas Merton: Daily Meditations from His Journals* (New York: HarperCollins, 2004), 123.

3. Bernard of Clairvaux. "On Loving God" in *Bernard of Clairvaux: Selected Works* (New York: HarperCollins, 2005). Original translation by Paulist Press, 997 Macarthur Blvd., Mahwah, NJ 07430.

4. Graham, Billy. *The Secret of Happiness* (Nashville: Thomas Nelson, 1955, 1985, 2002), 136–37.

5. Whitney, Donald S. *Spiritual Disciplines for the Christian Life* (Colorado Springs: NavPress, 1991), 191.

6. Hendricks, Howard. *Heaven Help the Home* (Wheaton, IL: Victor Books, 1976), 60.

7. Tutu, Archbishop Desmond. *No Future Without Forgiveness* (New York: Image/Doubleday, 2000), 82.

8. Teresa of Avila. Chapter 1 of "The Second Dwelling Places," in *Teresa of Avila: Selections from "The Interior Castle"* (New York: HarperCollins, 2004). Original translation published by Paulist Press, 997 Macarthur Blvd., Mahwah, NJ 07430. Copyright © 1979 by the Washington Province of Discalced Carmelites, Inc.

9. Ogilvie, Lloyd John. *God's Best for My Life* (Eugene, OR: Harvest House, 1997), 139.

10. John of the Cross. Chapter 5 of "The Dark Night" in *John of the Cross: Selections from "The Dark Night" and Other Writings* (New York: HarperCollins, 2004). Original translation published by Paulist Press, 997 Macarthur Blvd., Mahwah, NJ 07430.

11. Alexander, Archibald. Sermon based on Colossians 1:27, quoted by W. Andrew Hoffecker in *Piety and the Princeton Theologians* (Phillipsburg NJ: Presbyterian and Reformed Publishing, 1981).

12. Lewis, C. S. *Surprised by Joy* (Barnes & Noble Classics, 2002), 227. First published in 1955.

13. Edman, V. Raymond. *The Disciplines of Life* (Colorado Springs: Victor Books, 2003), 34, 36.

14. Hurnard, Hannah. *Mountains of Spice* (Wheaton: IL: Tyndale House, 1977), 243.

15. King, Martin Luther, Jr. Address to sanitation workers, Memphis, TN, April 3, 1968, quoted in *New York Times*, April 5, 1968, 24. http://www.bartleby.com/73/572.html

16. Augustine of Hippo. Chapter 15, book 14, "On the Trinity" in *Augustine of Hippo: Selected Works* (New York: HarperCollins, 2006). Original translation by Paulist Press, 997 Macarthur Blvd., Mahwah, NJ 07430. Copyright © 1984 by Mary T. Clark.

17. McDowell, Josh, and Bob Hostetler. *Right from Wrong* (Dallas: Word, 1994), 85.

18. Keller, W. Phillip. *A Layman Looks at the Lord's Prayer* (Chicago: Moody Press, 1976), 69.

19. Water, Mark, ed. *The New Encyclopedia of Christian Quotations* (Grand Rapids: Baker Books, 2000), 1073.

20. Buechner, Frederick. *Beyond Words* (New York: HarperCollins, 2004), 38.

21. Chesterton, G. K. *Orthodoxy* (Charlotte, NC: Saint Benedict Press/Baronius Press, 2006), 150.

22. Engstrom, Ted. *The Making of a Christian Leader* (Grand Rapids: Zondervan, 1976), 6.

23. Foster, Richard. *Celebration of Discipline* (New York: Harper & Row, 1978), 81.

24. Packer, J. I. *Knowing God* (Downers Grove, IL: InterVarsity Press, 1973), 91.

25. Murphey, Cecil. *Invading the Privacy of God* (Ann Arbor: Vine Books, 1997), 106.

26. Marshall, Catherine. *Adventures in Prayer* (Westwood, NJ: Fleming H. Revell, 1975), 59.

27. Kesler, Jay. *Grandparenting: The Agony & the Ecstasy* (Ann Arbor: Servant Publications, 1993), 112.

28. Sproul, R. C. *Surprised by Suffering* (Wheaton, IL: Tyndale House, 1988), 77.

29. Bunyan, John. *Pilgrim's Prayer Book: A Month of Meditations on Prayer by the Author of "Pilgrim's Progress,"* ed. Louis Gifford Parkhurst, Jr. (Wheaton: IL: Tyndale House, 1986), 73.

30. Edwards, Jonathan. "A Divine and Supernatural Light, Immediately Imparted to the Soul by the Spirit of God, Shown to Be Both Scriptural and Rational Doctrine," a sermon preached at Northampton, and published at the desire of some of the hearers, 1734. Quoted on http://www.ccel.org/ccel/edwards/sermons.supernatural_light.html

31. Merton, Thomas. *Seeds of Contemplation* (New York: Dell, 1949), 23.

February

1. Graham, Billy. *The Holy Spirit* (Waco, TX: Word, 1978), 108.

2. Hybels, Bill. *Who You Are When No One's Looking* (Downers Grove, IL: InterVarsity Press, 1987), 10.

3. Blackaby, Henry T., and Richard Blackaby. *Experiencing God Day-by-Day Devotional* (Nashville: B&H Publishing Group, 2006), 71.

4. Chambers, Oswald. *My Utmost for His Highest* (Westwood, NJ: Barbour and Company, 1935, 1963), 86.

5. Clare of Assisi. "The Second Letter to Blessed Agnes of Prague" in *Francis & Clare of Assisi: Selected Works* (New York: HarperCollins, 2005). Original translation by Paulist Press, 997 Macarthur Blvd., Mahwah, NJ 07430.

6. White, John. *The Fight* (Downers Grove, IL: InterVarsity Press, 1979), 158.

7. Saint Thérèse of Lisieux. *The Story of a Soul: The Autobiography of Saint Thérèse of Lisieux* (Charlotte, NC: Saint Benedict Press/Baronius Press, 2006), 184.

8. Swindoll, Charles. *Great Days with the Great Lives* (Nashville: W Publishing Group/Thomas Nelson, 2005), 307.

9. Seamands, David A. *Healing for Damaged Emotions* (Wheaton, IL: Victor Books, 1981), 22.

10. Francis of Assisi. "The Later Rule" in *Francis & Clare of Assisi: Selected Works* (New York: HarperCollins, 2005). Original translation by Paulist Press, 997 Macarthur Blvd., Mahwah, NJ 1982.

11. Lewis, C. S. *Mere Christianity* (New York: HarperCollins, 1952), 50.

12. Lucado, Max. *Grace for the Moment*, Vol. II (Nashville: Thomas Nelson, 2006), 19.

13. Bonhoeffer, Dietrich. "Listen," from *Life Together* quoted in *A Year with Dietrich Bonhoeffer: Daily Meditations from His Letters, Writings, and Sermons*, Carla Barnhill, ed. (New York: HarperCollins, 2005), 98.

14. Bernard of Clairvaux. "On Loving God" in *Bernard of Clairvaux: Selected Works* (New York: HarperCollins, 2005). Original translation by Paulist Press, 997 Macarthur Blvd., Mahwah, NJ 07430.

15. Augustine, Saint Aurelius. "The Confessions of St. Augustine," Great Literature Online, 1997–2011. http://augustine.classicauthors.net/ConfessionsOfStAugustineThe/ConfessionsOfStAugustine TCo2.html

16. Stott, John R. W. *Basic Christianity* (Grand Rapids: Wm. B. Eerdmans, 1978), 15.

17. Mason, Mike. *Champagne for the Soul* (Colorado Springs: WaterBrook Press, 2003), 25.

18. Rice, John R. *All About Christian Giving* (Murfreesboro, TN: Sword of the Lord Publications, 1954), 58.

19. Packer, J. I. *Knowing God* (Downers Grove, IL: InterVarsity Press, 1973, 1993), 196.

20. John of the Cross. Commentary on stanza 1 of "The Living Flame of Love" in *John of the Cross: Selections from "The Dark Night" and Other Writings* (New York: HarperCollins, 2004). Original translation published by Paulist Press, 997 Macarthur Blvd., Mahwah, NJ 07430.

21. Teresa of Avila. Chapter 1 of "The Second Dwelling Places," in *Teresa of Avila: Selections from "The Interior Castle"* (New York: HarperCollins, 2004). Original translation published by Paulist Press, 997 Macarthur Blvd., Mahwah, NJ 07430. Copyright © 1979 by the Washington Province of Discalced Carmelites, Inc.

22. Ortberg, John. *Love Beyond Reason* (Grand Rapids: Zondervan, 1998), 16.

23. Ogilvie, Lloyd John. *God's Best for My Life* (Eugene, OR: Harvest House, 1997), 57.

24. Phillips, J. B. *God Our Contemporary* (New York: Macmillan, 1960), 137.

25. Bayly, Joseph. *Heaven* (Elgin, IL: David C. Cook, 1977), 64.

26. Thomas, W. Ian. *The Saving Life of Christ* (Grand Rapids: Zondervan, 1961), 81.

27. Spurgeon, Charles Haddon. Quoted on Spurgeon.US, "Quotes," http://www.spurgeon.us/mind_and_heart/quotes/b.htm#beauty

28. Wilkerson, David. *I'm Not Mad at God* (Minneapolis: Bethany House, 1967), 51.

MARCH

1. Crosby, Fanny. Quoted on Christianity.com. http://www.christianity.com/Christian%20Foundations/The%20Essentials/11528733/

2. Taylor, Hudson. Quoted in J. C. Pollock, *Hudson Taylor and Maria: Pioneers in China* (Grand Rapids: Zondervan, 1962), 109.

3. Stowell, Joseph M. *Simply Jesus* (Sisters, OR: Multnomah, 2002), 47.

4. MacArthur, John. *Truth for Today* (Nashville: J. Countryman/Thomas Nelson, 2001), 17.

5. Fénelon, Francis. "A Will No Longer Divided" in *Devotional Classics: Selected Readings for Individuals and Groups* (New York: HarperCollins, 1990, 1991, 1993), 47.

6. Boice, James Montgomery. *The Parables of Jesus* (Chicago: Moody Press, 1983), 61.

7. Muggeridge, Malcolm. Quoted in *The Westminster Collection of Christian Quotations,* comp. Martin H. Manser (Louisville, KY: Westminster John Knox, 2001), 263.

8. Alcorn, Randy. *The Treasure Principle* (Sisters, OR: Multnomah 2001), 94.

9. Elliot, Elisabeth. *Trusting God in a Twisted World* (Old Tappan, NJ: Fleming H. Revell, 1989), 149.

10. Lewis, C. S. *The Problem of Pain* (New York: HarperOne, 2001), 91.

11. Graham, Billy. *Hope for the Troubled Heart* (Nashville: Thomas Nelson, 1991), 85.

12. Colson, Charles W. *Born Again* (Old Tappan, NJ: Fleming H. Revell, 1976), 340.

13. Donne, John. "Holy Sonnet XIV" in *John Donne's Poetry,* selected and edited by A. L. Clements (New York: W. W. Norton & Company, 1966), 86.

14. Piper, John. *Desiring God* (Sisters, OR: Multnomah, 1986), 139.

15. Augustine of Hippo. "The Happy Life" in *Augustine of Hippo: Selected Works* (New York: HarperCollins, 2006). Original translation by Paulist Press, 997 Macarthur Blvd., Mahwah, NJ, 07430. Copyright © 1984 by Mary T. Clark.

16. Bunyan, John. *Pilgrim's Prayer Book: A Month of Meditations on Prayer by the Author of "Pilgrim's Progress,"* ed. Louis Gifford Parkhurst, Jr. (Wheaton: IL: Tyndale House, 1986), 13.

17. St. Patrick. Quoted on ThinkExist.com, "Saint Patrick Quotes." http://thinkexist.com/quotes/saint_patrick/

18. Wiersbe, Warren W. *Real Worship* (Grand Rapids: Baker Books, 2000), 43.

19. Lucado, Max. *3:16, The Numbers of Hope* (Nashville: Thomas Nelson, 2007), 110.

20. Ogilvie, Lloyd J. *Congratulations—God Believes in You* (Waco, TX: Word Books, 1980), 82.

21. Swindoll, Charles. "Perfect Trust," quoted in *A Daybook of Prayer* (Nashville: Thomas Nelson, 2006), 9.

22. Briscoe, D. Stuart. *The Fullness of Christ* (Grand Rapids: Zondervan, 1965), 139.

23. Herbert, George. "Love III" in *George Herbert and the Seventeenth-Century Religious Poets,* ed. Mario A. Di Cesare (New York: W. W. Norton & Company, 1978), 69.

24. Guinness, Os. *The Call* (Nashville: Word, 1998), 4.

25. Graham, Ruth Bell. "I Think It Harder, Lord" in *Prodigals and Those Who Love Them* (Grand Rapids: Zondervan, 1991), 136.

26. Luther, Martin. *By Faith Alone: Martin Luther,* ed. James Galvin (Grand Rapids: World Publishing, 1998), February 5.

27. Schaeffer, Francis. Quoted in *The Westminster Collection of Christian Quotations,* comp. Martin H. Manser (Louisville, KY: Westminster John Knox, 2001), 235.

28. Bounds, E. M. Quoted in *The Westminster Collection of Christian Quotations,* comp. Martin H. Manser (Louisville, KY: Westminster John Knox, 2001), 226.

29. Yancey, Philip, and Paul Brand. *In His Image* (Grand Rapids: Zondervan, 1984), 157.

30. Peterson, Eugene. *Christ Plays in Ten Thousand Places* (Grand Rapids: William B. Eerdmans, 2005), 337.

31. Packer, J. I. *Knowing God* (Downers Grove, IL: InterVarsity Press, 1973), 30.

APRIL

1. Hurnard, Hannah. *God's Transmitters* (Wheaton, IL: Tyndale House, 1978), 23.

2. Chambers, Oswald. *My Utmost for His Highest* (Westwood, NJ: Barbour and Company, 1935, 1963), 187.

3. Hybels, Bill. *Too Busy Not to Pray* (Downers Grove, IL: InterVarsity Press, 1988), 95.

4. Catherine of Siena. *The Dialogue of St. Catherine of Siena* (Charlotte, NC: Saint Benedict Press/ Baronius Press, 2006), 40.

5. Miller, Calvin. *Once Upon a Tree* (Grand Rapids: Baker Book House, 1967), 76.

6. Jones, E. Stanley. *A Song of Ascents* (Nashville: Abingdon, 1968), 150.

7. Stott, John R. W. *Basic Christianity* (Grand Rapids, MI: Wm. B. Eerdmans, 1958, 1971), 43–44.

8. Bonhoeffer, Dietrich. "God's Love for Our Enemies," from *A Testament to Freedom* (p. 285) quoted in *A Year with Dietrich Bonhoeffer: Daily Meditations from His Letters, Writings, and Sermons*, ed. Carla Barnhill (New York: HarperCollins, 2005).

9. Augustine of Hippo. Book 10 of "Confessions" in *Augustine of Hippo: Selected Works* (New York: HarperCollins, 2006). Original translation by Paulist Press, 997 Macarthur Blvd., Mahwah, NJ, 07430. Copyright © 1984 by Mary T. Clark.

10. Bernard of Clairvaux. "On Conversion" in *Bernard of Clairvaux: Selected Works* (New York: HarperCollins, 2005). Original translation by Paulist Press, 997 Macarthur Blvd., Mahwah, NJ 07430.

11. Tozer, A. W. *The Pursuit of God* (Wheaton, IL: Tyndale House, 1982), 34.

12. Meyer, Joyce. *Me and My Big Mouth!* (New York: Warner Faith, 1997), 136.

13. Merton, Thomas. "Perplexities and New Birth" in *A Year with Thomas Merton: Daily Meditations from His Journals* (New York: HarperCollins, 2004), 139.

14. Sproul, R. C. *Surprised by Suffering* (Wheaton, IL: Tyndale House, 1989), 137.

15. Lucado, Max. *God Came Near*, Vol. II (Portland, OR: Multnomah, 1987), 104.

16. Saint Thérèse of Lisieux. *The Soul of a Story: The Autobiography of Saint Thérèse of Lisieux* (Charlotte, NC: Saint Benedict Press/Baronius Press, 2006), 162.

17. Seamands, David A. *Freedom from the Performance Trap* (Wheaton, IL: Victor Books, 1988), 115.

18. John of the Cross. "Purifying the Soul" in *Devotional Classics: Selected Readings for Individuals and Groups* (New York: HarperCollins, 1990, 1991, 1993), 35.

19. Marshall, Catherine. *Adventures in Prayer* (Old Tappan, NJ: Fleming H. Revell, 1975), 10.

20. Zacharias, Ravi. *Recapture the Wonder* (Nashville: Integrity Publishers, 2003), 163.

21. Ortberg, John. *The Life You've Always Wanted* (Grand Rapids: Zondervan, 1997, 2002), 181.

22. Teresa of Avila. Chapter II in "The Fifth Mansion," *Interior Castles*, Christian Classics Ethereal Library, http://www.ccel.org/ccel/teresa/castle2.ix.ii.html

23. Arterburn, Stephen. *Healing Is a Choice* (Nashville: J. Countryman/Thomas Nelson, 2005), 89.

24. Spurgeon, Charles Haddon. *The Limitless Love of Christ* (New Kensington, PA: Whitaker, 1996), 36.

25. Maxwell, John. *Partners in Prayer* (Nashville: Thomas Nelson, 1996), 63.

26. Trueblood, Elton. *A Place to Stand* (New York: Harper & Row, 1969), 128.

27. Stedman, Ray C. *Spiritual Warfare: Winning the Daily Battle with Satan* (Grand Rapids: Discovery House, 1999), 76.

28. Newbigin, Lesslie. Quoted in Alan Sell, *The Spirit of Our Life* (New York: Ragged Edge Press, 2000), 39.

29. Bunyan, John. *Pilgrim's Prayer Book: A Month of Meditations on Prayer by the Author of "Pilgrim's Progress,"* ed. Louis Gifford Parkhurst, Jr. (Wheaton, IL: Tyndale House, 1986), 98.

30. Packer J. I. *Knowing God* (Downers Grove, IL: InterVarsity Press, 1973, 1993), 47.

MAY

1. Smith, Hannah Whitall. *The Christian's Secret of a Happy Life* (Old Tappan, NJ: Fleming H. Revell, 1942, 1970), 36.

2. Luther, Martin. *By Faith Alone: Martin Luther*, ed. James Galvin (Grand Rapids, MI: World Publishing, 1998), October 17.

3. Swindoll, Charles R. *Three Steps Forward, Two Steps Back* (Nashville: Thomas Nelson, 1980), 49.

4. Underhill, Evelyn. *Concerning the Inner Life* (Oxford, England: Oneworld Publications, 1995), 33.

5. White, John. *The Fight* (Downers Grove, IL: InterVarsity Press, 1976), 111.

6. Yancey, Philip. *What's So Amazing about Grace?* (Grand Rapids, MI: Zondervan, 1997), 42.

7. Fernando, Ajith. *The Supremacy of Christ* (Wheaton, IL: Crossway Books, 1995), 183.

8. Stanley, Charles. *Finding Peace* (Nashville: Thomas Nelson, 2003), 23.

9. Whitefield, George. Quoted in *The Westminster Collection of Christian Quotations*, comp. Martin H. Manser (Louisville, KY: Westminster John Knox, 2001), 381.

10. Evans, Tony. *Time to Get Serious* (Wheaton, IL: Crossway Books, 1995), 149.

11. Miller, Donald. *Blue Like Jazz* (Nashville: Thomas Nelson, 2003), 86.

12. Brother Lawrence of the Resurrection, *The Practice of the Presence of God* (Brewster, MA: Paraclete Press, 2010 edition), 32.

13. Lewis, C. S. *The Weight of Glory* (San Francisco: HarperCollins, 1949), 111.

14. Laurie, Greg. *Why Believe? Exploring the Honest Questions of Seekers* (Wheaton, IL: Tyndale House, 1995), 135.

15. Nouwen, Henri J. M. *Adam: God's Beloved* (Maryknoll, NY: Orbis Books, 1997), 117.

16. Gire, Ken. *Intimate Moments with the Savior* (Grand Rapids, MI: Zondervan, 1989), 5.

17. Ogilvie, Lloyd John. *God's Best for My Life* (Eugene, OR: Harvest House, 1997), 179.

18. Kierkegaard, Søren. *Training in Christianity* (New York: Random House, 2004), 6.

19. ten Boom, Corrie. Quoted on Cobblestone Road Ministries site, "Famous Christian Quotes," http://www.cobblestoneroadministry.org/2005_CRM/Famous_ChristianQuotes.html

20. Alcorn, Randy. *The Treasure Principle* (Sisters, OR: Multnomah, 2001), 81.

21. Mason, Mike. *Champagne for the Soul* (Colorado Springs: WaterBrook Press, 2003), 11.

22. Tada, Joni Eareckson. *Diamonds in the Dust: 366 Sparkling Devotions* (Grand Rapids: Zondervan, 1993), Nov. 5.

23. L'Engle, Madeleine. *Bright Evening Star: Mystery of the Incarnation* (Wheaton, IL: Harold Shaw, 1997), 113.

24. Moody, Dwight L. Quoted on BrainyQuote.com, http://brainyquote.com/quotes/authors/d/dwight_l_moody.html

25. Peterson, Eugene. *The Contemplative Pastor* (Grand Rapids, MI: Eerdmans, 1993), 17.

26. Pippert, Rebecca Manley. *Out of the Salt Shaker* (Downers Grove, IL: InterVarsity Press, 1979, 1999), 28.

27. Teresa of Avila, chapter 1 of "The First Dwelling Places," in *Teresa of Avila: Selections from "The Interior Castle"* (New York: HarperCollins, 2004). Original translation published by Paulist Press, 997 Macarthur Blvd., Mahwah, NJ 07430. Copyright © 1979 by the Washington Province of Discalced Carmelites, Inc.

28. Augustine of Hippo. Quoted on FamousQuotes.com, http://www.1-famous-quotes.com/cgi-bin/viewquotes.cgi?action=search&Category=CHRISTIAN

29. Saint Thérèse of Lisieux, *The Soul of a Story: The Autobiography of Saint Thérèse of Lisieux* (Charlotte, NC: Saint Benedict Press/Baronius Press, 2006), 141.

30. Graham, Ruth, Jerry Sittser, and Joni Eareckson Tada. *When Your Rope Breaks* (Grand Rapids: Zondervan, 2009), 6.

31. Ortberg, John. *Love Beyond Reason* (Grand Rapids, MI: Zondervan, 2001), 209.

JUNE

1. Stanley, Charles. *How to Listen to God* (Nashville: Thomas Nelson, 1985), 48.

2. Lucado, Max. *When God Whispers Your Name* (Dallas: Word, 1994), 43.

3. Dyson, Freeman. Quoted on FamousQuotes.com, http://www.1-famous-quotes.com/ cgi-bin/db.cgi?db=db&uid=default&Author_First_Name=Freeman&Author_Last_ Name=Dyson&mh=10&sb=---&so=ASC&ww=on&view_records=View+Records

4. Dillard, Annie. Quoted by Philip Yancey in *Open Doors* (Westchester, IL: Crossway Books, 1982), 143.

5. Catherine of Siena. Quoted in *Devotional Classics, Selected Readings for Individuals & Groups*, eds. Richard J. Foster and James Bryan Smith (New York: HarperCollins, 1993), 288.

6. Chapman, Mary Beth, with Ellen Vaughn. *Choosing to SEE* (Grand Rapids: Revell, 2010), 25.

7. à Kempis, Thomas. *The Imitation of Christ*, Book II, chap. ix (Mineola, NY: Dover Publications, 2003), n.p.

8. Mueller, George. Quoted on FamousQuotes.com, http://www.1-famous-quotes.com/ cgi-bin/db.cgi?db=db&uid=default&Author_First_Name=George&Author_Last_ Name=Mueller&mh=10&sb=---&so=ASC&ww=on&view_records=View+Records

9. Bonhoeffer, Dietrich. *Dietrich Bonhoeffer Works, Vol. 4* (Minneapolis: Augsburg Fortress, 2001), 53.

10. Chambers, Oswald. *My Utmost for His Highest* (Grand Rapids, MI: Discovery House, 1992), November 1.

11. Colson, Charles, with Nancy R. Pearcey. *A Dangerous Grace* (Dallas: Word, 1994), 47.

12. Meyer, Joyce. *Secrets to Exceptional Living* (New York: Warner Faith, 2002), 19.

13. Spurgeon, Charles Haddon. *Morning and Evening*, July 15, morning.

14. Graham, Billy. Quoted on BrainyQuote.com, http://brainyquote.com/quotes/authors/b/billy_ graham.htmlbrainyquote.com

15. Lotz, Anne Graham. *God's Story* (Nashville: Thomas Nelson, 1999), 273.

16. Merton, Thomas. "History and the Passion of Christ" in *A Year with Thomas Merton: Daily Meditations from His Journals* (New York: HarperCollins, 2004), May 4.

17. Briscoe, Jill, ed. *Daily Study Bible for Women* (Wheaton, IL: Tyndale House, 1999), 1365.

18. Barth, Karl. Quoted on FamousQuotes.com, http://www.1-famous-quotes.com/cgi-bin/ db.cgi?db=db&uid=default&Author_First_Name=Karl&Author_Last_Name=Barth&mh=10&sb=-- -&so=ASC&ww=on&view_records=View+Records

19. Elliot, Elisabeth. Quoted in *The Westminster Collection of Christian Quotations*, comp. Martin H. Manser (Louisville, KY: Westminster John Knox, 2001), 301.

20. Arterburn, Stephen. *Healing Is a Choice Devotional* (Nashville: J. Countryman/Thomas Nelson, 2005), 59.

21. Bunyan, John. *Pilgrim's Prayer Book: A Month of Meditations on Prayer by the Author of "Pilgrim's Progress,"* ed. Louis Gifford Parkhurst, Jr. (Wheaton, IL: Tyndale House, 1986), 8.

22. St. Teresa of Avila. Quoted in *The Cloister Walk* by Kathleen Norris (New York: Riverhead Books, 1996), 328.

23. Tada, Joni Eareckson. *Heaven: Your Real Home* (Grand Rapids: Zondervan, 1995), 121.

24. Swindoll, Charles. *So, You Want to Be Like Christ?* (Nashville: W Publishing Group/Thomas Nelson, 2005), 9.

25. Stanley, Charles. *How to Listen to God* (Nashville: Thomas Nelson, 1985, 2002), 74.

26. Lewis, C. S. *The Screwtape Letters* (New York: HarperCollins, 2001 ed.), 40.

27. Moody, Dwight L. Quoted on FamousQuotes.com, http://www.1-famous-quotes.com/ cgi-bin/db.cgi?db=db&uid=default&Author_First_Name=Dwight+L.&Author_Last_ Name=Moody&mh=10&sb=---&so=ASC&ww=on&view_records=View+Records

28. Yancey, Philip. *The Jesus I Never Knew* (Grand Rapids: Zondervan, 1995), 261.

29. Smith, Hannah Whitall. *The God of All Comfort* (Chicago: Moody Press, 1956), 253.

30. Ogilvie, Lloyd John. *God's Best for My Life* (Eugene, OR: Harvest House, 1997), 93.

JULY

1. Ortberg, John. *The Life You've Always Wanted* (Grand Rapids: Zondervan, 1997), 213.
2. Ambrose. From "The Grape Cluster," in *Day by Day with the Early Church Fathers*, compiled and edited by Christopher D. Hudson, J. Alan Sharrer, and Lindsay Vanker (Peabody, MA: Hendrickson Publishers, 1999), 265.
3. Packer, J. I. *Evangelism and the Sovereignty of God* (Downers Grove, IL: InterVarsity Press, 1961, 1971), 11.
4. Jerome. From "The Best Offering," in *Day by Day with the Early Church Fathers*, eds. Christopher D. Hudson, J. Alan Sharrer, and Lindsay Vanker (Peabody, MA: Hendrickson Publishers, 1999), 225.
5. Chan, Francis. *Crazy Love* (Colorado Springs, CO: David C. Cook, 2008), 138.
6. Bernard of Clairvaux. "On Conversion" in *Bernard of Clairvaux: Selected Works* (New York: HarperCollins, 2005). Original translation by Paulist Press, 997 Macarthur Blvd., Mahwah, NJ 07430.
7. Keller, Helen. Quoted in *The Westminster Collection of Christian Quotations*, comp. Martin H. Manswer (Louisville, KY: Westminster John Knox, 2001), 366.
8. Cyprian. From "Save the Wounded," in *Day by Day with the Early Church Fathers*, eds. Christopher D. Hudson, J. Alan Sharrer, and Lindsay Vanker (Peabody, MA: Hendrickson Publishers, 1999), 209.
9. Sanders, J. Oswald. *Spiritual Discipleship* (Chicago: Moody Press, 1990, 1994), 31.
10. Father Jonathan Morris, *The Promise* (New York: HarperOne, 2008), 147.
11. Washington, Booker T. Quoted on The Quotation Page, http://www.quotationspage.com/quotes/Booker_T._Washington/
12. Mason, Mike. *Champagne for the Soul* (Colorado Springs: WaterBrook Press, 2003), 8.
13. Tozer, A. W. *The Knowledge of the Holy* (New York: Harper and Brothers, 1961), 51.
14. Spurgeon, Charles Haddon. Quoted on The Quotations Page, http://www.quotationspage.com/quotes/Charles_Haddon_Spurgeon/
15. Stott, John. *Focus on Christ* (Cleveland: Collins Publishers, 1979), 141.
16. Orr, J. Edwin. *Full Surrender* (London: Marshall, Morgan & Scott, 1951), 22.
17. John of the Cross. Commentary on stanza 4 of "The Living Flame of Love" in *John of the Cross: Selections from "The Dark Night" and Other Writings* (New York: HarperCollins, 2004). Original translation published by Paulist Press, 997 Macarthur Blvd., Mahwah, NJ 07430.
18. Piper, John. *Seeing and Savoring Jesus Christ* (Wheaton, IL: Crossway, 2001), 41.
19. Graham, Billy. Quoted on BrainyQuote.com, http://brainyquote.com/quotes/authors/b/billy_graham.html
20. Lloyd-Jones, Martyn. *Spiritual Depression: Its Cause and Cure* (Grand Rapids: Eerdmans, 2001), 291.
21. Chesterton, G. K. *Orthodoxy* (Charlotte, NC: Saint Benedict Press/Baronius Press, 2006), 62.
22. Lucado, Max. *A Gentle Thunder* (Nashville: W Publishing Group/Thomas Nelson, 1995), 75.
23. Swindoll, Charles. *Three Steps Forward, Two Steps Back* (Nashville: Thomas Nelson, 1980), 73.
24. Lewis, C.S. Quoted on FamousQuotes.com, http://www.1-famous-quotes.com/cgi-bin/db.cgi?db=db&uid=default&Author_First_Name=C.S.&Author_Last_Name=Lewis&mh=10&sb=--&so=ASC&ww=on&view_records=View+Records&nh=1
25. Blackaby, Henry T. *Created to Be God's Friend* (Nashville: Thomas Nelson, 1999), 7.
26. à Kempis, Thomas. *The Imitation of Christ*, trans. Aloysius Croft and Harold Bolton (Milwaukee: The Bruce Publishing Company, 1940), book 2, chapter 12, on Christian Classics Ethereal Library, http://www.ccel.org/ccel/kempis/imitation.html.
27. L'Engle, Madeleine. *Walking on Water: Reflections on Faith & Art* (Wheaton, IL: Harold Shaw, 1980), 59.
28. Bonhoeffer, Dietrich. Quoted on Kjos Ministries Web site in "Excerpts from The Cost of Discipleship," "Discipleship and the Cross," http://www.crossroad.to/Persecution/Bonhoffer.html
29. Augustine of Hippo. "The Happy Life" in *Augustine of Hippo: Selected Works* (New York: HarperCollins, 2006). Original translation by Paulist Press, 997 Macarthur Blvd., Mahwah, NJ, 07430. Copyright © 1984 by Mary T. Clark.
30. Moody, Dwight L. Quoted on BrainyQuote.com, http://www.brainyquote.com/quotes/authors/d/dwight_l_moody.html
31. Tada, Joni Eareckson. *The God I Love* (Grand Rapids: Zondervan, 2003), 357.

August

1. Curtis, Brent and John Eldredge. *The Sacred Romance: Drawing Closer to the Heart of God* (Nashville: Thomas Nelson, 1997), 137.

2. Chrysostom. From "Shelter," in *Day by Day with the Early Church Fathers*, eds. Christopher D. Hudson, J. Alan Sharrer, and Lindsay Vanker (Peabody, MA: Hendrickson Publishers, 1999), 357.

3. Jakes, T. D., ed. *Holy Bible: Woman Thou Art Loosed!* edition (Nashville: Thomas Nelson, 1998), 1086.

4. Luther, Martin. Quoted on FamousQuotes.com, http://www.1-famous-quotes.com/cgi-bin/db.cgi?db=db&uid=default&Author_First_Name=Martin&Author_Last_Name=Luther&mh=10&sb=---&so=ASC&ww=on&view_records=View+Records&nh=7

5. Peterson, Eugene H. *A Long Obedience in the Same Direction*, 2nd ed. (Downers Grove, IL: InterVarsity, 2009), 100.

6. Jerome. From "Test of Will," in *Day by Day with the Early Church Fathers*, eds. Christopher D. Hudson, J. Alan Sharrer, and Lindsay Vanker (Peabody, MA: Hendrickson Publishers, 1999), 334.

7. Manning, Brennan. *Ruthless Trust* (New York: HarperCollins, 2000), 48.

8. Tozer, A. W. *A Treasury of A. W. Tozer: A Collection of Tozer Favorites* (Grand Rapids, MI: Baker, 1980), 19.

9. Mason, Mike. *Champagne for the Soul* (Colorado Springs: WaterBrook Press, 2003), 24.

10. Stowe, Harriet Beecher. Quoted on FamousQuotesandAuthors.com, http://famousquotesandauthors.com/authors/harriet_beecher_stowe_quotes.html

11. Brown, Steve. *Approaching God* (New York: Howard Books, 2008), 33.

12. John of Damascus. From "God's Providence," in *Day by Day with the Early Church Fathers*, compiled and edited by Christopher D. Hudson, J. Alan Sharrer, and Lindsay Vanker (Peabody, MA: Hendrickson Publishers, 1999), 268.

13. Mother Teresa. *Mother Teresa: In My Own Words* (New York: Gramercy Books, 1996), 23.

14. Cloud, Henry and John Townsend. *God Will Make a Way* (Nashville: Integrity Publishers, 2002), 6.

15. Hemas. From "Despise Doubt," in *Day by Day with the Early Church Fathers*, eds. Christopher D. Hudson, J. Alan Sharrer, and Lindsay Vanker (Peabody, MA: Hendrickson Publishers, 1999), 102.

16. Willard, Dallas. Quoted in *Devotional Classics*, eds. Richard J. Foster and James Bryan Smith (San Francisco: HarperSanFrancisco, 1993), 14.

17. Anderson, Hans Christian. Quoted on FamousQuotes.com, http://www.1-famous-quotes.com/cgi-bin/db.cgi?db=db&uid=default&Author_First_Name=Hans+Christian&Author_Last_Name=Anderson&mh=10&sb=---&so=ASC&ww=on&view_records=View+Records

18. Buechner, Frederick. *The Hungering Dark* (New York: HarperOne, 1985), 72.

19. Kinlaw, Dennis F. *Let's Start With Jesus: A New Way of Doing Theology* (Grand Rapids, MI: Zondervan, 2005), 146.

20. Stanley, Charles. *How to Listen to God* (Nashville: Thomas Nelson, 1985), 94.

21. Lutzer, Erwin W. *The Da Vinci Deception* (Wheaton, IL: Tyndale House, 2004), 109–10.

22. Elliot, Elisabeth. *These Strange Ashes* (New York, Harper & Row: 1975), 129.

23. Newton, Isaac. Quoted on FamousQuotes.com, http://www.1-famous-quotes.com/cgi-bin/db.cgi?db=db&uid=default&Author_First_Name=Isaac&Author_Last_Name=Newton&mh=10&sb=---&so=ASC&ww=on&view_records=View+Records

24. Warren, Rick. *The Purpose Driven Life: What on Earth Am I Here For?* (Grand Rapids: Zondervan, 2002), 71.

25. Gregory of Nyssa. From "The Right Path," in *Day by Day with the Early Church Fathers*, eds. Christopher D. Hudson, J. Alan Sharrer, and Lindsay Vanker (Peabody, MA: Hendrickson Publishers, 1999), 226.

26. Lewis, C. S. *Letters to Malcolm, Chiefly on Prayer* (New York: Harcourt, Brace & World, 1964), 93.

27. Graham, Billy. "The Reverend Billy Graham, After the Oklahoma City Bombing, Offers a Sermon on the 'Mystery of Evil,'" quoted in *In Our Own Words: Extraordinary Speeches of the American Century* (New York: Kodanska International, 1999), 415.

28. Lucado, Max. *When God Whispers Your Name* (Dallas: Word, 1994), 42.

29. Ogilvie, Lloyd John. *God's Best for My Life* (Eugene, OR: Harvest House, 1997), 353.

30. Chambers, Oswald. *My Utmost for His Highest* (Grand Rapids, MI: Discovery House, 1992), June 13.

31. Augustine. *On Christian Doctrine* (Indianapolis: Bobbs-Merrill Educational Publishing, 1983), 9.

September

1. Bonhoeffer, Dietrich. "Peace in Suffering," from *A Testament to Freedom* quoted in *A Year with Dietrich Bonhoeffer: Daily Meditations from His Letters, Writings, and Sermons*, ed. Carla Barnhill (New York: HarperCollins, 2005), 291.

2. Tada, Joni Eareckson. *When God Weeps* (Grand Rapids: Zondervan, 1997), 171.

3. Yancey, Philip. *What's So Amazing About Grace?* (Grand Rapids, MI: Zondervan, 1997), 71.

4. Clement of Rome. From "Our Whole Strength," in *Day by Day with the Early Church Fathers*, eds. Christopher D. Hudson, J. Alan Sharrer, and Lindsay Vanker (Peabody, MA: Hendrickson Publishers, 1999), 250.

5. Brown, Steve. *Approaching God: Accepting the Invitation to Stand in the Presence of God* (New York: Howard Books, 2008), 188.

6. Athanasius. "Letter X, Easter, 338," section 4. *Athanasius: Select Works and Letters. Nicene and Post-Nicene Fathers,* 2nd series, vol. 4, eds. Philip Schaff and Henry Wace (Peabody, MA: Hendrickson Publishers, 1994), 531.

7. MacArthur, John, Jr. *Jesus' Pattern of Prayer* (Chicago: Moody Press, 1981), 20.

8. Lactantius. From "The Worship of God," in *Day by Day with the Early Church Fathers*, eds. Christopher D. Hudson, J. Alan Sharrer, and Lindsay Vanker (Peabody, MA: Hendrickson Publishers, 1999), 256.

9. Merton, Thomas. "Solitude and Gentleness" in *A Year with Thomas Merton: Daily Meditations from His Journals* (New York: HarperCollins, 2004), 8.

10. Origen. From "Partakers of God," in *Day by Day with the Early Church Fathers*, eds. Christopher D. Hudson, J. Alan Sharrer, and Lindsay Vanker (Peabody, MA: Hendrickson Publishers, 1999), 212.

11. Miller, Donald. *Blue Like Jazz* (Nashville: Thomas Nelson, 2003), 203.

12. Chrysostom. "Homily XLIX," section 4. *Chrysostom: Homilies on the Gospel of Saint Matthew. Nicene and Post-Nicene Fathers,* 1st series, vol. 10, eds. Philip Schaff and Henry Wace (Peabody, MA: Hendrickson Publishers, 1994), 306.

13. Little, Paul E. *Know Why You Believe* (Downers Grove, IL: InterVarsity Press, 1968, 1988, 2000), 35.

14. Spurgeon, Charles Haddon. Quoted in *The Power of Christ's Prayer Life*, ed. Lance C. Wubbels, (Lynnwood, WA: Emerald Books, 1995), 60.

15. Saint Augustine. *Confessions* (New York: Penguin Books, 1961), 207.

16. Bernard of Clairvaux, *The Love of God*, ed. James M. Houston (Portland, OR: Multnomah Press, 1983), 208.

17. Ortberg, John. *The Life You've Always Wanted* (Grand Rapids: Zondervan, 1997), 70.

18. John of the Cross. Stanza 11 of "The Spiritual Canticle" in *John of the Cross: Selections from "The Dark Night" and Other Writings* (New York: HarperCollins, 2004). Original translation published by Paulist Press, 997 Macarthur Blvd., Mahwah, NJ 07430.

19. Ogilvie, Lloyd John. *God's Best for My Life* (Eugene, OR: Harvest House, 1997), 123.

20. Graham, Billy. *The Holy Spirit* (Nashville: Thomas Nelson, 1978, 1988), 55.

21. Tozer, A. W. *The Knowledge of the Holy* (New York: Harper and Brothers, 1961), 52.

22. Lewis, C. S. *Surprised by Joy: The Shape of My Early Life* (New York: Harcourt Brace, 1955), 231–32.

23. Swindoll, Charles. *So, You Want to Be Like Christ?* (Nashville: Thomas Nelson, 2005), 142.

24. Sproul, R. C. *The Mystery of the Holy Spirit* (Wheaton, IL: Tyndale House, 1990), 168.

25. Newton, John. Quoted in *The Spirit Our Life*, Alan Sell (New York: Ragged Edge Press, 2000), 47.

26. Snyder, James L. *In Pursuit of God: The Life of A.W. Tozer* (Camp Hill, PA: Christian Publications, 2009), 14–15.

27. Nouwen, Henri J. M. *Here and Now: Living in the Spirit* (New York: Crossroad, 1999), 18.

28. Powell, Eleanor. Quoted on ThinkExist.com, http://thinkexist.com/quotations/god/

29. Eldredge, John. *Waking the Dead* (Nashville: Thomas Nelson, 2003), 63.

30. Madame Guyon. Quoted in *Devotional Classics*, eds. Richard J. Foster and James Bryan Smith (San Francisco: HarperSanFrancisco, 1993), 320.

OCTOBER

1. Chesterton, G. K. *What's Wrong with the World* (London: Cassell, 1910), 39.

2. Chambers, Oswald. *My Utmost for His Highest* (Westwood, NJ: Barbour and Company, 1935, 1963), 99.

3. Mason, Mike. *Champagne for the Soul* (Colorado Springs: WaterBrook Press, 2003), 6.

4. Augustine of Hippo. Book 10 of "Confessions" in *Augustine of Hippo: Selected Works* (New York: HarperCollins, 2006). Original translation by Paulist Press, 997 Macarthur Blvd., Mahwah, NJ, 07430. Copyright © 1984 by Mary T. Clark.

5. Elliot, Elisabeth. *Love Has a Price Tag* (Ann Arbor, MI: Servant Books, 1979), 47.

6. Tertullian. From "Heavenly Crowns," in *Day by Day with the Early Church Fathers*, eds. Christopher D. Hudson, J. Alan Sharrer, and Lindsay Vanker (Peabody, MA: Hendrickson Publishers, 1999), 190.

7. Lucado, Max. *In the Eye of the Storm* (Dallas: Word, 1991), 54.

8. Gregory of Nyssa. From "Our Father," in *Day by Day with the Early Church Fathers*, eds. Christopher D. Hudson, J. Alan Sharrer, and Lindsay Vanker (Peabody, MA: Hendrickson Publishers, 1999), 275.

9. Tada, Joni Eareckson. Quoted on GoodReads.com, http://www.goodreads.com/author/quotes/3715.Joni_Eareckson_Tada

10. Hilary of Poitiers. From "God's Beauty," in *Day by Day with the Early Church Fathers*, eds. Christopher D. Hudson, J. Alan Sharrer, and Lindsay Vanker (Peabody, MA: Hendrickson Publishers, 1999), 310.

11. Schuller, Robert H. Quoted on BrainyQuote.com, http://www.brainyquote.com/quotes/authors/r/robert_h_schuller.html

12. Leo the Great. "Sermon XLVL, On Lent, VIII," section III. *Leo the Great, Gregory the Great. Nicene and Post-Nicene Fathers*, 2nd series, vol. 12, eds. Philip Schaff and Henry Wace (Peabody, MA: Hendrickson Publishers, 1994), 159.

13. McDowell, Josh, and Bob Hostetler. *Right from Wrong* (Dallas: Word, 1994), 106.

14. Bonhoeffer, Dietrich. "The Wisdom of Humility," from *Life Together* (p. 96) quoted in *A Year with Dietrich Bonhoeffer: Daily Meditations from His Letters, Writings, and Sermons*, ed. Carla Barnhill (New York: HarperCollins, 2005).

15. Spurgeon, Charles H. *Evangelistic Sermons* (London: Marshall, Morgan & Scott, 1959), 213.

16. Lewis, C. S. *Mere Christianity* (New York: HarperCollins, 1952, 1980, 2001), 196.

17. Brother Lawrence. Quoted in *A Daybook of Prayer* (entry for May 26). (Nashville: Thomas Nelson, 2006), 152.

18. Ogilvie, Lloyd John. *God's Best for My Life* (Eugene, OR: Harvest House, 1997), 247.

19. Graham, Billy. *Day by Day with Billy Graham* (Minneapolis, MN: World Wide Publications, 1976), 10.

20. Sanders, J. Oswald. *Spiritual Maturity* (Chicago: Moody Press, 1962, 1994), 25.

21. Yancey, Philip. *Finding God in Unexpected Places* (Nashville: Moorings, 1995), 240.

22. Williams, Don. Quoted in *The Heart of Worship Files*, ed. Matt Redman (Ventura, CA: Regal, 2003), 161.

23. Hurnard, Hannah. *God's Transmitters* (Wheaton: IL: Tyndale House, 1978), 61.

24. Veerman, Dave. *Beside Still Waters* (Wheaton, IL: Tyndale House, 1986), Day 68.

25. Coleman, Robert E. *The Master Plan of Evangelism* (Westwood, NJ: Fleming H. Revell, 1963, 1964), 21.

26. Storms, Sam. *A Sincere and Pure Devotion to Christ: 100 Daily Meditations on 2 Corinthians* (Wheaton, IL: Crossway Books, 2010), 21.

27. Moody, D. L. Quoted in *All-American Quote Book*, eds. Michael Reagan and Bob Phillips (Eugene, OR: Harvest House, 1995), 195.

28. Hughes, Selwyn. *Every Day with Jesus* (Nashville: Broadman & Holman, 2003), 53.

29. Wesley, Susannah. Quoted in *The Last Word: A Treasury of Women's Quotes*, ed. Carolyn Warner (Englewood Cliffs, NJ: Prentice Hall, 1992), 247.

30. Calvin, John. Quoted in *Day by Day with John Calvin*, eds. Mark Fackler, Philip Christman, Donald Dumbacher, and Paul Stob (Peabody, MA: Hendrickson Publishers, 2002), 83.

31. Swindoll, Charles R. *Three Steps Forward, Two Steps Back* (Nashville: Thomas Nelson, 1980), 74.

NOVEMBER

1. Teresa of Avila. Quoted in *Devotional Classics: Selected Readings for Individuals and Groups*, eds. Richard J. Foster and James Bryan Smith (San Francisco: HarperSanFrancisco, 1990, 1991), 197.

2. Jakes, T. D., ed. *Holy Bible: Woman Thou Art Loosed!* edition (Nashville: Thomas Nelson Publishers, 1998), 1282.

3. Augustine of Hippo. Book 8 of "Confessions" in *Augustine of Hippo: Selected Works* (New York: HarperCollins, 2006). Original translation by Paulist Press, 997 Macarthur Blvd., Mahwah, NJ, 07430. Copyright © 1984 by Mary T. Clark.

4. MacArthur, John, Jr. *Jesus' Pattern of Prayer* (Chicago: Moody Press, 1981), 52.

5. Miller, Donald. *Blue Like Jazz* (Nashville: Thomas Nelson, 2003), 13.

6. Origen. From "Drawing Near," in *Day by Day with the Early Church Fathers*, eds. Christopher D. Hudson, J. Alan Sharrer, and Lindsay Vanker (Peabody, MA: Hendrickson Publishers, 1999), 359.

7. Young, Sarah. *Jesus Calling* (Nashville: Thomas Nelson, 2004), xii.

8. Chambers, Oswald. *My Utmost for His Highest* (Westwood, NJ: Barbour and Company, 1935, 1963), 170.

9. Cymbala, Jim. *Fresh Faith* (Grand Rapids, MI: Zondervan, 1999), 40.

10. Chrysostom. From "Noticed by God," in *Day by Day with the Early Church Fathers*, eds. Christopher D. Hudson, J. Alan Sharrer, and Lindsay Vanker (Peabody, MA: Hendrickson Publishers, 1999), 103.

11. Simpson, A. B. *When the Comforter Came* (Camp Hill, PA: Christian Publications, Inc., 1911), np.

12. Alcorn, Randy. *The Treasure Principle* (Sisters, OR: Multnomah, 2001), 48.

13. Mother Teresa. *Mother Teresa: In My Own Words* (New York: Gramercy Books, 1996), 40.

14. Cyprian. From "Look Ahead," in *Day by Day with the Early Church Fathers*, eds. Christopher D. Hudson, J. Alan Sharrer, and Lindsay Vanker (Peabody, MA: Hendrickson Publishers, 1999), 119.

15. Graham, Billy. Quoted in *The Faithful Christian: An Anthology of Billy Graham* Griffin, eds. William and Ruth Graham Dienart (New York: McCracken Press, 1994), 24.

16. Spurgeon, Charles H. *Sermons on Soul-Winning* (London: Marshall, Morgan & Scott, 1961), 181.

17. Ortberg, John. *The Life You've Always Wanted* (Grand Rapids, MI: Zondervan, 1997, 2002), 15.

18. McGee, Robert S. *The Search for Significance* (Nashville: W. Publishing Group/Thomas Nelson, 1998), 47.

19. Kierkegaard, Soren. Quoted in *All-American Quote Book*, eds. Michael Reagan and Bob Phillips (Eugene, OR: Harvest House, 1995), 246.

20. Tozer, A. W. *The Root of the Righteous* © 1955, 1986, by Lowell Tozer. Used by permission of WingSpread Publishers, a division of Zur Ltd., 800.884.4571, 140.

21. Stowell, Joseph M. *The Final Question of Jesus* (Sisters, OR: Multnomah, 2004), 55.

22. Jakes, Serita. *The Princess Within* (Bloomington, MN: Bethany House, 1999, 2010), 165.

23. Murray, John. *Redemption Accomplished and Applied* (Grand Rapids, MI: Wm B. Eerdmans, 1955), 110.

24. Lucado, Max. *Shaped by God* (Wheaton, IL: Tyndale House, 1985), 20.

25. Mason, Mike. *Champagne for the Soul* (Colorado Springs: WaterBrook Press, 2003), 8.

26. Wesley, John. Quoted in *John Wesley*, ed. Albert Outler (Oxford: Oxford University Press, 1964), 128.

27. Buechner, Frederick. *Beyond Words* (New York: HarperCollins, 2004), 16.

28. Washington, Booker T. http://www.billionquotes.com/index.php/Booker_T._Washington

29. Elliot, Jim. Diary entry for October 28, 1949, quoted in Elisabeth Elliot, *Shadow of the Almighty* (New York: Harper and Row, 1958), 108.

30. Packer, J. I. *In God's Presence: Daily Devotions with J. I. Packer*, ed. Jean Watson (Wheaton, IL: Harold Shaw, 1986, 1998), August 12.

DECEMBER

1. MacArthur, John. *Truth for Today* (Nashville: J. Countryman/Thomas Nelson, 2001), 51.

2. Bonhoeffer, Dietrich. *Life Together* (New York: Harper & Row, 1954), 71.

3. Manning, Brennan. *The Signature of Jesus* (Sisters, OR: Multnomah, 1988, 1992, 1996), 159.

4. Julian of Norwich. Quoted in *Devotional Classics*, eds. Richard J. Foster and James Bryan Smith (San Francisco: HarperSanFrancisco, 1993), 71.

5. Lewis, C. S. *Letters to an American Lady* (Grand Rapids: Wm. B. Eerdmans, 1967, 1971, 2000), 55.

6. Brother Lawrence. Quoted on OChristian.com, http://christian-quotes.ochristian.com/Brother-Lawrence-Quotes/

7. Leo the Great. From "Grafted In," in *Day by Day with the Early Church Fathers*, eds. Christopher D. Hudson, J. Alan Sharrer, and Lindsay Vanker (Peabody, MA: Hendrickson Publishers, 1999), 143.

8. Swindoll, Charles. *Three Steps Forward, Two Steps Back* (Nashville: Thomas Nelson, 1980), 186.

9. Studd, C.T. Quoted on Famous Quotes website, http://www.1-famous-quotes.com/cgi-bin/db.cgi?db=default&uid=default&Author_First_Name=C.+T.&Author_Last_Name=Studd&mh=10&sb=---&so=ASC&ww=on&view_records=View+Records

10. Peterson, Eugene H. *A Long Obedience in the Same Direction*, 2nd ed. (Downers Grove, IL: InterVarsity, 2009), 119.

11. Schaeffer, Francis A. *The Complete Works of Francis A. Schaeffer, Vol. 2* (Westchester, IL: Crossway Books, 1982), 391.

12. Gregory of Nyssa. From "Older Christians," in *Day by Day with the Early Church Fathers*, eds. Christopher D. Hudson, J. Alan Sharrer, and Lindsay Vanker (Peabody, MA: Hendrickson Publishers, 1999), 353.

13. Ogilvie, Lloyd John. *God's Best for My Life* (Eugene, OR: Harvest House, 1997), 12.

14. Jerome. "Letter CXXX," section III. *Jerome: Letters and Select Works. Nicene and Post-Nicene Fathers*, 2nd series, vol. 6, eds. Philip Schaff and Henry Wace (Peabody, MA: Hendrickson Publishers, 1994), 266.

15. Stedman, Ray C. *Spiritual Warfare: Winning the Daily Battle with Satan* (Grand Rapids: Discovery House, 1999), 196.

16. Tada, Joni Eareckson. *Seeking God* (Brentwood, TN: Wolgemuth & Hyatt, 1991), 17.

17. Pascal, Blaise. Quoted on ThinkExist.com, http://thinkexist.com/quotes/blaise_pascal/4.html

18. Yancey, Phillip. *Reaching for the Invisible God* (Grand Rapids, MI: Zondervan, 2000), 17.

19. Bernard of Clairvaux. "On Conversion," in *Bernard of Clairvaux: Selected Works* (New York: HarperCollins, 2005). Original translation by Paulist Press, 997 Macarthur Blvd., Mahwah, NJ 07430.

20. Yancey, Philip and Dr. Paul Brand. *Fearfully and Wonderfully Made* (Grand Rapids: Zondervan, 1980), 120.

21. Grudem, Wayne. *Bible Doctrine* (Grand Rapids: Zondervan, 1999), 246.

22. Packer, J. I. *Knowing God* (Downers Grove, IL: InterVarsity Press, 1973, 1993), 77.

23. Buechner, Frederick. *Beyond Words* (New York: HarperCollins, 2004), 141.

24. Graham, Billy. *How to Be Born Again* (Nashville: Thomas Nelson, 1977, 1989), 43.

25. Chambers, Oswald. *My Utmost for His Highest* (Westwood, NJ: Barbour and Company, 1935, 1963), 87.

26. Barnhouse, Donald. *Romans, Man's Ruin, Vol. 1* (Grand Rapids: Wm. B. Eerdmans, 1952), 72.

27. Bunyan, John. *Pilgrim's Prayer Book: A Month of Meditations on Prayer by the Author of "Pilgrim's Progress,"* ed. Louis Gifford Parkhurst, Jr. (Wheaton: IL: Tyndale House, 1986), 69.

28. Calvin, John. Quoted in *Devotional Classics*, eds. Richard J. Foster and James Bryan Smith (San Francisco: HarperSanFrancisco, 1993), 167.

29. Merton, Thomas. "Deepening the Present" in *A Year with Thomas Merton: Daily Meditations from His Journals* (New York: HarperCollins, 2004), 9.

30. Bounds, E. M. Quoted in *The Best of E. M. Bounds*, comp. Zylstra Cornelius (Grand Rapids: Baker, 1981), 179.
31. Marshall, Peter. Quoted in *Twenty Centuries of Great Preaching, Vol 12,* eds. Clyde E. Fant, Jr. and William M. Pinson, Jr. (Waco, TX: Word Books, 1971), 38.